"Your book changed my life. I used what I learned to change my routine, and it paid off immediately. I had thought that all my technology overuse had permanently damaged my ability to think and be productive, but now I'm seeing myself reversing the effects of that damage."

Emily Singer *is a user experience research director at AnswerLab*

"A team lead's understanding of the humanizing factors discussed in this book is critical to managing team cohesion, job satisfaction, and personal well-being. This is a highly recommended read for people in charge."

Mose O'Griffin *is the President of Advanced Prototype Engineering*

"This book is a must-read if you're spending a lot of your day on Zoom but still looking to establish and maintain meaningful relationships. Amy and Diane use their diverse backgrounds to explore where there's room for being human in virtual connections."

Harper Spero *is a business coach*

Humanizing the Remote Experience through Leadership and Coaching

This book responds to the growing need for understanding how we can foster wellness, raise engagement, and strengthen connections in professional contexts as human interactions become increasingly remote.

Through research and case studies, the authors outline a paradox: the digital technology we use to connect with others can leave us feeling less connected. To understand what is missing from remote interactions, the authors examine the use of space, sensory cues, group dynamics, and challenges people encounter when the innate need for human connection is unmet. They provide practical advice to improve remote experiences, including ways to manage stress, avoid cognitive overload, and prevent burnout. Ultimately, the book highlights what is possible when we focus not only on the quantity and efficiency of our interactions, but also on the quality and depth of our human connections.

The contemporary relevance of this topic makes the book essential for leaders, coaches, consultants, and other professionals working remotely, as well as students and interested individuals seeking to improve their personal and professional remote experiences.

Diane Lennard is a Professor of Management Communication at NYU Stern School of Business. Professor Lennard has taught courses on team communication, engaging audiences, and strategic communication to undergraduates, full-time and part-time MBA students, PhD students, and Executive MBA students. She has served as the Director of Langone Education for the Part-Time MBA program and a faculty development consultant for Stern's Center for Innovation in Teaching and Learning. She received the 2017 Distinguished Teaching Award in Recognition of Excellence in Teaching Innovation. Diane is the author of *Coaching Models: A Cultural Perspective* (Routledge, 2010) and *Strategic Communication at Work: The Impact Paradigm* (Routledge, 2018). She founded Lennard & Company, a firm that provides communication coaching services to educational institutions, corporations, and individuals who want to expand their communication skills and abilities for functioning in diverse work settings. She received her PhD in Education and Performance

Studies from Union Institute & University, her MS in Education from Bank Street College of Education, and her BA in Communication from Bard College.

Amy Mednick is a psychiatrist working in her own private practice. She utilizes psychotherapy, psychopharmacology, and a cutting-edge technology called transcranial magnetic stimulation to help adults experiencing anxiety, depression, and a range of psychiatric illnesses. Amy has a special interest in the overlap between the humanities and neuroscience, which is reflected in her interdisciplinary work, treatment, and exploratory style in practice. She leads lecture series for psychiatric residents in training, as well as social work and psychology trainees. She also utilizes writing to further explore these overlaps and enhance dialogue between different disciplines, and between patient and doctor. Her articles have been published in *Clinical Psychiatry News*. Amy's passions for teaching and science earned her a chief residency in Psychiatry at Mount Sinai Beth Israel Hospital in New York. She received her MD with Distinction in Research from Albert Einstein College of Medicine, and Bachelor of Science in Brain & Cognitive Sciences with a concentration in Creative Writing from MIT. She has been involved in both brain research and linguistic research.

Humanizing the Remote Experience through Leadership and Coaching

Strategies for Better Virtual Connections

Diane Lennard and Amy Mednick

NEW YORK AND LONDON

Cover image: TBC

First published 2023
by Routledge
605 Third Avenue, New York, NY 10158

and by Routledge
4 Park Square, Milton Park, Abingdon, Oxon OX14 4RN

Routledge is an imprint of the Taylor & Francis Group, an informa business

© 2023 Diane Lennard and Amy Mednick

The right of Diane Lennard and Amy Mednick to be identified as authors of this work has been asserted in accordance with sections 77 and 78 of the Copyright, Designs and Patents Act 1988.

All rights reserved. No part of this book may be reprinted or reproduced or utilized in any form or by any electronic, mechanical, or other means, now known or hereafter invented, including photocopying and recording, or in any information storage or retrieval system, without permission in writing from the publishers.

Trademark notice: Product or corporate names may be trademarks or registered trademarks, and are used only for identification and explanation without intent to infringe.

Library of Congress Cataloging-in-Publication Data
Names: Lennard, Diane, 1953- author. | Mednick, Amy, author.
Title: Humanizing the remote experience through leadership and coaching : strategies for better virtual connections / Diane Lennard PhD and Amy Mednick MD,
Description: 1 Edition. | New York, NY : Routledge, 2022. | Includes bibliographical references and index.
Identifiers: LCCN 2022007131 (print) | LCCN 2022007132 (ebook) | ISBN 9780367772574 (paperback) | ISBN 9780367758721 (hardback) | ISBN 9781003170488 (ebook)
Subjects: LCSH: Social interaction--Technological innovations. | Shared virtual environments. | Interpersonal communication--Psychological spects. | Leadership--Psychological aspects. | Executive coaching. | Employees--Coaching of.
Classification: LCC HM1111 .L46 2022 (print) | LCC HM1111 (ebook) | DDC 302--dc23/eng/20220323
LC record available at https://lccn.loc.gov/2022007131
LC ebook record available at https://lccn.loc.gov/2022007132

ISBN: 9780367758721 (hbk)
ISBN: 9780367772574 (pbk)
ISBN: 9781003170488 (ebk)

DOI: 10.4324/9781003170488

Typeset in Times New Roman
by Taylor & Francis Books

Contents

List of figures	viii
Preface	ix
Acknowledgments	xii

Introduction: The Paradox We Created	1

PART ONE
Doing More Together, Feeling Less Connected   23

1	Confined to the Digital Window	25
2	Missing the Signals	46
3	Lost in the Group	65

PART TWO
Connecting and Thriving   85

4	Wellness Matters	87
5	Energy to Engage	110
6	Social Creatures	131
7	Together Miles Apart	151
	Afterword	170

Appendix: Where to Find Additional Mental Health Support	171
References	173
Index	186

Figure

0.1 The paradox 1

Preface

This book comes from a teacher without her classroom and a psychiatrist without her couch.

We were midway through a global pandemic and several months into a total lockdown when we decided to write this book. Diane, a communication coach and university professor, was coaching clients remotely and teaching graduate students online. Amy, a psychiatrist, was treating her patients by telemedicine and teaching psychiatric trainees remotely.

Our remote work experiences required a significant shift in how we engaged with other people. We were curious about this shift and wanted to make sense of an intriguing paradox that was playing out all around us in real time: the technology people created and use to connect with others was leaving us feeling less connected. We were interacting with people online more than we ever had before. Birthdays, holidays, gatherings with family members and friends we hadn't seen in years, and social hours were all happening over Zoom. Although we were connecting more than ever, we felt less connected.

Amy was reshaping her private practice around an online model and trying to figure out how to keep her patients feeling connected when she could no longer pass them a box of tissues for comfort. After years of declining online coaching assignments and avoiding teaching online courses, Diane was doing all her work remotely and managing the extra cognitive load that came with it. We were starting to turn down invitations to Zoom social events because they felt exhausting. Both of us were finding it took too much effort to engage in remote group interactions.

Although we couldn't go anywhere, we could set out on a journey in our minds to better understand the human side of the remote experience. It seemed essential to approach this through a framework of human needs, including safety and comfort, understanding others, and belonging to a group. That led us to explore the workings of the human brain most affected when these needs were not met during remote interactions, such as attention, engagement, and human connection.

Co-writing *Humanizing the Remote Experience* was a remote experience in itself. During our remote work sessions, we discussed a wide range of relevant research studies and examined our own remote experiences. We also interviewed many of our colleagues, clients, students, patients, friends, and family members to learn about their challenges of working, learning, and socializing remotely. Then, we gathered information on strategies for adjusting to the remote experience that were supported by scientific research. Our fascination with the data from research studies and first-person lived experiences motivated us to dig deeper in our search for a more human-centered approach to the remote experience.

Together, we explored the remote experience from many angles, including neurobiological, educational, psychological, organizational, and philosophical. After considering the digital and human sides of the paradox, our starting point for writing Chapter 1 was the scientific exploration of attention processes. From her work as a psychiatrist, Amy knew that focused attention is vital to optimal functioning. Effective communication and group dynamics were important to Diane as an educator and communication coach whose work centers around establishing mutual engagement, expressing clear messages, and strengthening social connections. Both of us continually questioned aspects of the remote experience and explored perspectives from different disciplines to fill in the gaps during the year-long writing process.

In *Humanizing the Remote Experience*, we examine the key challenges people encounter in their remote experiences when the innate human need to connect with others is not met. We also offer perspectives on how leadership and coaching can be used to raise engagement, strengthen connections, and foster a sense of well-being in our increasingly remote lives. Excerpts from our interviews are woven throughout the book and a case study about an executive who worked with both of us at different times is included as well. Through her story, we illustrate both the challenges and the strategies she implemented to improve and humanize her remote experiences.

Part One of *Humanizing the Remote Experience* introduces the paradox that the technology we use to connect with others can leave us feeling less connected. It provides readers with a general understanding of how technology serves our efficiency needs but doesn't necessarily take our well-being or innate need for social connection into account. The Introduction begins with an overview of how our brains are wired for social connection so that we can better understand the human side of the paradox. It then explores the benefits of technology on the digital side of the paradox. Three chapters follow. Chapter 1 looks at how restricted movement in a flat, two-dimensional virtual space challenges our ability to fully express ourselves. Chapter 2 examines how significant parts of messages get lost or distorted in virtual settings, moving people away from having satisfying, meaningful social connections. Chapter 3 addresses how people feel in a virtual group, and the challenges of participating fully, feeling understood, and being in touch with the emotional state of others.

Part Two of *Humanizing the Remote Experience* demystifies the human need to connect and focuses on what we can do to improve our remote experiences. Chapter 4 explains the critical importance of intercepting the stress response early and taking control of it to protect your health and wellness in different facets of life. Chapter 5 describes ways to manage your energy to promote engagement during remote interactions, and suggests strategies for avoiding cognitive overload and preventing burnout. Chapter 6 discusses prioritizing people, communicating to connect, and cultivating a sense of purpose and meaning. Chapter 7 encourages readers to make choices and take actions that will result in a human-centered approach to the remote experience that mitigates the challenges of interacting through digital technology. This part of the book highlights what is possible when people focus not only on the quantity and efficiency of our interactions, but also the quality and depth of our human connections.

Acknowledgments

We would like to give special thanks to the many people who made this book possible:

- Emily Singer, Ellen Fisher, Shana Carroll, Davina Lennard, Jessy Hsieh, Anna Buchanan, Stephanie Stolberg, and Aron Mednick who read drafts, provided valuable feedback, and offered support along the way.
- Dianne Nersesian McGuire, Robert Anderson, Greg Alongi, Yu Shi, Beth Briggs, Chaffee Duckers, Joseph Mensah, Emily Drake, Jenn Wynn, Shelley London, Jennifer Hershey, Pat Ryan Lampl, Harper Spero, Maria Arnone, Steve Stumpf, Sean Diaz, Shay Seligman, Bailey Eisen, and Ellen Mednick who provided valuable input.
- Our clients, students, patients, and colleagues who contributed to the development of the ideas in this book.
- Our families—Aron, Cecylia, Claire, Dan, Davina, Ellen, Ellen, Ellen, Emily, Jen, Josh, Klieo, Mose, Naya, Niko, Ozzy, Pat, Paul, Pogo, Rafi, Sam, Shawo, Tom, Will, Zia, Ziva, and Z.—who support us through all of our remote experiences and inspire us every day.

Introduction
The Paradox We Created

People are working, learning, and engaging in social activities remotely now more than ever. Digital technology makes this possible. This technology has enabled people all around the globe to accomplish more with others at a rapid pace. Yet it often fails to satisfy the need for social connection and to fully capture the complexity of our human interactions. This brings up vital questions:

- How is it possible for us to do more together and yet feel less connected?
- How can we minimize misunderstanding and genuinely connect with others when space and movement are restricted to two dimensions?
- What can we do to avoid feeling lost in virtual groups?
- Why do we experience fatigue after prolonged virtual experiences?
- How can we improve our overall wellness when more and more of our interactions are remote?

These are some of the questions raised by the paradox we now face: the technology we use to connect with others often leaves us feeling less connected.

Created by humans to solve human problems, digital technology is having a major effect on our daily lives. While we have gained efficiency, access, and convenience, there is a significant human cost. Technology has

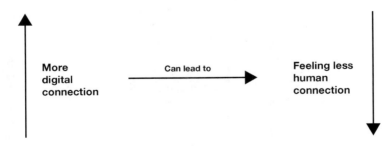

Figure 0.1 The paradox

DOI: 10.4324/9781003170488-1

changed how humans interact, fundamentally altering dimensions of human connection that are essential to overall wellness. The need for understanding what happens to human connection when we increasingly rely on digital technology to engage with others has never been greater.

This introduction will first provide an essential overview of how our brains are wired for social connection, specifically for safety and comfort, understanding, and belonging. It will explain the human side of the paradox: why we feel less connected at times. We will see the challenges people encounter in their remote experiences when the innate human need to connect with others is not met. Next, it will focus on the digital side of the paradox: how constant connectedness has solved some human problems with more efficiency, access, and convenience. These are the technological solutions to make our lives easier and faster that have created human problems for us socially, emotionally, and cognitively.

Human Brains Are Wired for Social Connection

Humans are social beings by nature. We are wired to feel safest around other humans. We have built-in capacities to enable us to understand each other and to be accepted and belong. The fact that our brains are designed to connect with others is evidence of how vital human connection is.

To understand social connection as a basic human need, we will look through the lenses of evolutionary psychology, neuroscience, developmental psychology, and social psychology. Examining the ways that the human brain is designed to ensure and enable connection will also reveal where this need is not fully satisfied in virtual interactions.

Wired to Connect: Feeling Safe and Comfortable

Connection Is Essential for Human Existence

Human connection is as basic and essential to survival as food. This is an age-old human need that has been in existence since the beginning of human evolution. To ensure survival, our brains are wired to make us feel safe and comfortable when we're around other humans.

Our early ancestors often faced predators with great physical prowess and speed. To successfully survive in a dangerous environment, humans had to rely on other humans. They could sleep safely through the night only if there were others to keep watch. They could go out to hunt only if there were others to look after their vulnerable young.

The humans who lived near other humans were better able to adapt to the environment than those who were isolated from others. They were more likely to survive and pass on helpful genes to their offspring. Natural selection, the process by which the most advantageous adaptations of a population to their environment are promoted over time, favored more socialized humans. We still feel most secure when we are connected with other people because that is the original setting in which our brains evolved.

Humans Are Hard-Wired to Seek Safety and Comfort

From the very beginning of an individual's life, the brain is wired to equate being in the presence of other people with a sense of safety and comfort. Many other animals can walk quickly after birth and become independent. For example, giraffes walk within 30–60 minutes of being born. Human infants, however, are completely helpless and dependent on caretakers for survival. Most important for human infants is having their caretakers nearby, engaged and invested in keeping them safe, warm, and happy. The presence of others is essential from day one, so our brains come hard-wired with a distress system to alert us to loss of human connection.

The distress system that was active in infanthood is still present in later life. In an adult, the distress system no longer needs to be as active as it was in the infant who could not walk, talk, or find food on its own. But the distress system does get activated when adults experience stress. Just as in childhood, it is quieted by the natural brain chemicals that circulate when the individual feels safe and comfortable. The distress system uses a brain pathway that is very similar to the one that conveys physical pain. This means that pain from social separation can feel as real as physical pain.

Social Thinking Is the Human Brain's Default

To ensure connection, our brains are wired for social thinking. One part of the brain is devoted to all social thoughts, such as: thinking about other people and their thoughts, feelings, or intentions; thinking about the past spent with people; planning for a future with people; or thinking about the self in relation to others. Social thinking is mostly accomplished in areas located near the midline of the brain.

Another part of the brain is active when we engage in non-social thinking, such as math, recalling facts, or reading. Non-social thinking tends to occur closer to the outer surface of the brain.

Matthew Lieberman, a social cognitive neuroscientist, found that the social parts of the brain become active the moment any non-social thinking stops. He describes this phenomenon as a "neural see-saw." In his book *Social: Why Our Brains Are Wired to Connect*, Lieberman explains how this see-saw tends to tip towards social thinking at any spare moment as a reflex. Even when we are zoned out or the mind is wandering, the social brain is active. Lieberman suggests that this automatic tendency implies that "evolution has made a major bet on the value of our becoming social experts, and in our being prepared in any given moment to think and behave socially."[1]

Human connection is such a necessity for survival that our brains are instinctually wired to think socially. As Lieberman states, social "is the brain's preferred state of being, one that it returns to literally the second it has a chance."[2]

Humanizing the Remote Experience: Attending to Our Safety and Comfort

When we come to a remote environment, as to any new environment, the brain's first requirement is to seek safety and comfort. Prominent trauma researcher Bessel A. Van der Kolk writes, "Being able to feel safe with other people is probably the single most important aspect of mental health; safe connections are fundamental to meaningful and satisfying lives."[3] Fulfilling human connection will not proceed as easily if this basic need to feel safe is not satisfied. For most of human existence, this need was easily met by being around other people. However, it is not always easy to meet our need for safety and comfort when we are virtually together while physically apart.

In the first chapter of this book, we will examine some of the challenges to finding a sense of safety and comfort in the remote environment. Even though we are with other people on screen, it doesn't always feel like we are connecting with them in a meaningful way. This is the human side of the paradox: we are together and yet can feel further apart. Identifying what we are missing in the remote experience helps to pinpoint what needs to be addressed to humanize our experiences.

Wired to Connect: Understanding

Humans Learn from Imitation

In addition to safety and comfort, we have a need to understand one another. Our brains are hard-wired to enable us to accomplish this. From birth on, humans are natural imitators. By five months of age, babies are mostly copying and preferring the specific sounds of their language over others. In childhood, we spend most of our time learning from others, often by imitation.

The brain is equipped with cells that mimic the behavior of someone performing a task, as if the observer were performing the exact same task. These brain cells help humans to learn from other humans and to be able to understand each other's actions. For example, when you play tennis, a certain part of your movement-controlling brain is active. When you're not playing but you're watching someone play, or even hearing the sounds of someone playing nearby, that same part of your movement-controlling brain will activate. It is as if your brain is practicing or preparing for the actions that those near to you are engaged in.

People also imitate behaviors that express feelings. It is very common to take on the facial expressions and body language of others. This usually occurs unconsciously, and tends to establish rapport, trust, or empathy between people when they interact.

The Brain Is a Predictor

There is so much stimulation in the environment that the brain has to take shortcuts to process it all. The brain uses past experiences to jump to the most logical conclusion. Rather than figuring everything out from scratch in each new experience, our brains are built to fill in the blanks based on what we already know.

Our brains serve as predictors to help us understand the world. Because human interactions are complex, our brains use predictions to interpret what others are doing. For example, imagine you are having an engaging phone conversation with a friend and the call ends suddenly. You may be more likely to predict there was a phone reception issue than that your friend got bored and suddenly hung up on you without notice. Your brain predicts what is most likely to have happened based on all the information that you already have about the world and how things usually work.

Neuroscience studies have shown prediction at work in the human brain. Patterns of activity that represent different mental states can be decoded and then compared using magnetic resonance imaging (MRI) scans. This has enabled researchers to actually see and confirm that predictions occur in the brain. They have shown how humans understand each other not only by observing current actions, but also simultaneously thinking about possible future actions. It has also been demonstrated that when expectations about future actions are not met, the brain gets highly activated. This shows that missed predictions are seen as a problem that needs to be fixed for this complicated process to run smoothly.[4] The brain is an extremely skilled predictor.

The Social Brain Interprets the State of Mind of Others

Imitation and prediction are two strategies that the brain uses to make sense of the complexity of human interaction. Humans also have the ability to understand the inner mental states of others. The ability to understand that another person has their own unique mind is called Theory of Mind, and is accomplished by a network of brain areas working in concert. It is this brain network that enables us to understand that another person has a subjective experience, and to make sense of what may be going on in their mind.

For example, you might intuit that a friend feels sad even though she is insisting that "everything is fine." This is not an easy task. In fact, it requires advanced calculations. First, you must understand that your friend has her own feelings separate from your own. Most humans gain this understanding by the age of three. Then, your brain has to take in information about what it sees, hears, and knows from memory about your friend. In a split second, your brain processes and resolves the conflicting information between what your friend says and what you have concluded. It decides what you think your friend really feels, and then provides what you consider to be the appropriate reaction and support.

Interpreting the state of mind of others is a lot of mental work that happens automatically. Our brains are wired to understand not just what people say, but also what they likely mean to say.

Humanizing the Remote Experience: Enhancing Understanding

The human brain is designed to make sense of the world. One of its main goals is to understand other people, and it has many tools to help it accomplish this. Although our brains are wired with the capacity to understand each other, our skills are learned through repetition and experience interacting in person. Not all of these skills translate easily into interactions that occur virtually.

In the second chapter of this book, we will explore the challenges of navigating complex human interactions. In remote experiences, missed and distorted signals can create confusion and miscommunication. This is the human side of the paradox: how we feel less connected when our need to understand one another is not met.

Wired to Connect: Belonging

Rejection Is Perceived as Pain

The human brain is wired to seek out others for safety and comfort, to understand other people, and to belong to a community. Humans have a biological imperative to be accepted by the group and to be contributing members of the group.

One way to prove that we are wired for belonging is to look at what happens when we do not have a sense of belonging. Being rejected from a group is perceived by the brain as so unwanted that we are wired to feel rejection the same way we feel pain.

Pain is the body's way of letting you know that something is wrong. If you touch a hot surface, you instantly withdraw your hand before you even have time to consciously register what has happened. The same part of your brain that sends a pain signal in the hot stove situation also sends one when you have been rejected. Naomi Eisenberger and Matthew Lieberman describe this overlap between rejection and pain in their research, localizing the pain signals from both physical and social pain to a specific brain region. Their study showed that this area was activated when participants were excluded from a game. Interestingly, the same brain activation was observed whether the study participants were unintentionally excluded (attributed to "technical difficulties") or intentionally excluded.[5]

Rejection is processed by the body as a painful event. And the so-called "social pain" of being rejected causes a visceral experience of pain. It hurts just as much when the exclusion is intentional as when it is accidental.

Humans Put Others First to Ensure Acceptance in the Group

Once individuals have become accepted members of a group, they make an effort to stay there. By putting others first, their position in the group can be secured. Humans are capable of holding back their own needs, impulses, or desires for the sake of others. This helps us to maintain membership in a group, instead of operating with an individualistic mindset.

One way of putting others first is by simply being able to inhibit thoughts. If you said the first thing that came into your mind all the time, you might not last long in your social group. Fortunately, there is a part of your brain responsible for self-control. It allows a person to hold back when necessary or socially appropriate.

In addition to holding back thoughts, humans are able to suppress immediate needs. Humans have the capacity to help others in their group even at the expense of their own needs. This capacity is evident when humans exhibit altruism, defined as "caring about the needs and happiness of other people and being willing to do things to help them, even if it brings no advantage to yourself."[6] Altruism is a complicated task for our brains. It involves thinking about others, reflecting on their needs and mental states, and making calculations about benefits and risks to the self. Although altruism is complex, our wiring promotes it by making people feel happier and experience better health outcomes over time. This has been shown in studies of people performing acts of kindness and volunteerism.[7] Altruism can even have direct pain-relieving effects.[8]

The Brain Responds to Social Influence

According to Christopher Cascio and colleagues at the University of Pennsylvania, "Social influence is omnipresent, occurring through implicit observation of cultural norms, face-to-face and mediated interpersonal communication, as well as mass mediated communication. Even though individuals are often unaware of the power of social influence, research shows its effects on behavior in a wide variety of circumstances."[9]

Our brain wiring enables us to belong securely within a group by being open to the influence of others. Cascio goes on to say that "Social psychologists have suggested that one core function of compliance and conformity is to maintain group harmony."[10] Social influence can motivate us to change our behavior and attitude to align with a group. Gaining acceptance satisfies the need for belonging.

Because you are wired to be open to the influence of others, your self-concept is partly shaped by how others see you. This is a positive adaptation that helps foster belonging. Others' opinions influence the thoughts you have about yourself. You are able to recognize the parts of yourself as reflected back to you through the eyes of others. Your socially influenced self can integrate their thoughts about you. Neuroscience research has confirmed that this process occurs in the brain.

Social cognitive neuroscientist Matthew Lieberman has conducted some of these studies examining the properties of the "self" parts of the brain when confronted with the ideas of others. Lieberman explains what he has seen happening in the brain in his book *Social: Why Our Brains Are Wired to Connect:* "It is not enough for us to recognize what the group believes and values. We have to adopt the beliefs and values as our own if they are to guide our behavior."[11]

Your sense of self has permeable boundaries. These boundaries permit thoughts from others to enter into your own concept of self. This allows you to deeply consider the thoughts, ideas, beliefs, and opinions of others, and even accept some as your own. Social influence promotes development of a shared value system with others, which enables belonging.

Humanizing the Remote Experience: Preserving Belonging

Humans require a sense of belonging, and it brings meaning to life. An unsettled or discontent feeling can arise from the absence of an established place within a group or a community. In virtual interactions, we can sometimes feel lost in a group, unheard or unseen.

We encounter challenges in remote experiences when the innate human need to connect with others is not met.

In the third chapter of this book, we will take a closer look at virtual group and team dynamics. This is the human side of the paradox: how we can sometimes feel disconnected even though we are more connected than ever by technology. It is essential that we establish and maintain meaningful connections within groups and teams even when we are physically apart.

The Digital Side of the Paradox

The role of digital technology in our lives is growing. We use this technology in business, education, and social activities. Our digital lives have become more efficient. With an internet connection, digital technology provides instant access to a vast array of useful resources, tools, services, and people around the world. Digital life is also extremely convenient.

Along with the benefits of increased efficiency, access, and convenience come human costs. In Pew Research Center's report *The Future of Well-Being in a Tech-Saturated World*, Janna Anderson and Lee Rainie write,

> People are using digital tools to solve problems, enhance their lives and improve their productivity. More advances are expected to emerge in the future that are likely to help people lead even better lives. However, there is increasing commentary and research about the effects digital technologies have on individuals' well-being, their level of stress, their ability to perform well at work and in social settings, their capability to focus their attention, their capacity to modulate their level of connectivity and their general happiness.[12]

We do not want to sacrifice the benefits, but we want to also make sure to recognize the human costs. Then we can let them guide us toward ways of thinking and acting that will strengthen social connections and improve the remote experience.

Efficiency

The use of technology allows us to do many things faster and more efficiently than before. We can increase our productivity while maximizing use of time and resources. For example, researcher Jacob Dankasa shares how technology made his work more efficient:

> Technology has connected me to achieve today what I couldn't imagine in the past. When I was doing my doctoral dissertation, I was supposed to travel to Nigeria from the US to conduct interviews with my research participants. Unfortunately, the Ebola epidemic blew up in Africa and I was unable to go. Fortunately, software existed that allowed me to interview the participants and automatically record the sessions as I interviewed them. The price was reasonable. It saved me money and time and avoided health hazards.[13]

Remote work and online learning are enabled by constant connectedness for those with a broadband connection. Not only can we link to people anywhere in the world at any time, we can engage in activities instantly

10 Doing More Together, Feeling Less Connected

from any location. We can also use free or low-cost digital tools, resources, and services in real time to get more done while saving time and energy.

Virtual Is the New Reality

The future of work and education will likely involve a hybrid model, with some days in the office or in the classroom and some days working or learning remotely.

McKinsey Global Institute did an extensive study on the potential for remote work in a range of different jobs. They found that three quarters of the time spent on tasks and activities in the finance and insurance sectors could be done remotely without a loss of productivity. In management, business services, and information technology, McKinsey estimates that more than half of employee time is spent on activities that could effectively be done remotely.[14]

Constant connectedness enables people to work and learn from their own homes or another convenient but remote location, as well as from a traditional office. Remote workers and online learners can use digital tools to communicate and collaborate remotely, anytime from anywhere. As a result, time spent on long commutes can be eliminated on the days when work is done remotely or classes are online. Productivity can increase, as can the flexibility of the individual's schedule. With more flexibility, they can more easily arrange their schedules to engage in professional development or career development through remote coaching and training programs.

New Approaches to Remote Work

Remote work can increase productivity and optimize the use of time and resources. However, when focus turns to making processes highly efficient, quantity often gets prioritized over quality. Neither productivity nor optimization necessarily takes well-being or the innate human need for social connection into account.

We can mitigate the human costs that can come when optimization and efficiency take precedence over the human needs of safety, understanding, and belonging. This can be accomplished by guiding remote workers in connecting with others in a meaningful way and maintaining their overall well-being. Encouraging connection is pertinent at a time when people working remotely can seem less engaged. Some employers worry that younger employees aren't learning as quickly as when they are in offices sitting next to more experienced colleagues and observing them do their jobs.[15]

Some companies have recognized that having remote employees necessitates new processes, policies, and entirely new jobs to help create a

Introduction: The Paradox We Created   11

successful, more humanized remote work experience. They recognize that only focusing on efficiency and work output, which will initially be higher, will in the long run have too high a cost on their employees' well-being. Consider for example the path taken by Gitlab, an open-source software firm that has been fully remote since 2011. The company appointed Darren Murph, a 36-year-old former tech editor and communications advisor, as its "Head of Remote Work."[16]

From Murph's home in North Carolina's Outer Banks, he interacts with over 700 Gitlab employees spread throughout the US. One of the many ways Murph serves the needs of the remote workers in the company is by suggesting places to live that have good access to broadband and are more affordable than big cities. He evaluates messaging tools, writes remote work handbooks detailing work-from-home policies, and organizes virtual team-building activities. He also serves as an internal coach to the company's leaders who are structuring new projects. Murph is an example of a company creating an entirely new role to meet the needs of employees who are physically separated. His success underscores the importance of defining ways to create a better, more humanized remote experience.

Gitlab is one example of a company that recognizes the importance of establishing organizational norms, providing technology tools, and creating a shared culture that will support employees working outside the office. Other companies that have added a similar role include Quora, Zapier, Cleveland Clinic, Gong.io, Okta, and Dropbox. More companies will likely join in this trend so they can improve the remote work experience for their employees.

Global Classrooms

Remote learning is another facet of our digital lives that enables people to come together for a shared purpose. We have the ability to learn online about a myriad of subjects and can do so with experts and other learners in any location. There are some online learning opportunities available for free or at a low cost. The field of education has been revolutionized by digital technology.

Quality educational opportunities can be accessed from anywhere by anyone with an internet connection. Entry qualifications are not required. Allowing participants the flexibility to watch brief instructional videos on their own time, rather than at scheduled class times, makes it easier for large numbers of people to learn online. Khan Academy is one example of a free online education platform. It started when Sal Khan made some helpful math videos for his cousin in 2008. When other family members expressed an interest in watching these instructional videos, he posted them online.[17] Fast-forward a few decades, and the 6,500 video lessons of the Khan Academy have been viewed over 1.7 billion times on YouTube.

The lessons have been fully translated into 14 languages and partially translated into 28 more. Khan has piloted many more educational initiatives since those first YouTube videos, including a new venture in 2020 called Schoolhouse.world. This is a free non-profit organization that provides small group online videoconferencing tutorials to students around the world.

Khan's small, localized offering quickly grew to meet the needs of a massive audience with a voracious appetite for educational content. Technology permitted the information to be transmitted rapidly and efficiently, without Khan traveling the world or giving a lecture thousands of times. Similar benefits have occurred with material that originated on college campuses. For example, two professors at the University of Manitoba in 2008 decided to offer their course "Connectivism and Connectivity Knowledge" to an online audience. Their intent was to "exploit the possibility for interactions between a wide variety of participants made possible by online tools so as to provide a richer learning environment than traditional tools would allow."[18] It was attended by 25 students on campus, and 2,300 online students from around the world. This new online classroom format increased in size by 80-fold just three years later when Stanford offered three free online courses. A global audience of 160,000 students from around the world joined one of the courses. These examples show what can happen when a hunger for learning meets the massive connectivity capabilities of a globally connected world.

Over the ensuing years, a whole industry quickly developed to serve this hunger for learning. Several companies started to develop and offer massive open online courses (MOOCs), a term initially coined during the Stanford experiment. Coursera, founded by two Stanford University computer science professors, partnered with top universities to prepare and offer MOOCs. Since its founding in 2012, more than four million students have enrolled for Coursera MOOCs. The same year, MIT and Harvard formed edX, a partnership offering open online courses. It has since developed into a consortium of 140 partners that develop and offer online content. EdX aims to provide high-quality education that anyone can access without barriers of time and location. These and other online learning platforms enable learners to lower the cost of their education, personalize and specialize their studies, and build specific career-enhancing skills and expertise. They also enable educators to reach a large global audience. Whereas traditional classes are limited by the number of seats in a classroom, MOOCs can serve millions.

We can learn about anything from anywhere, without the time and effort required to go to a traditional classroom in person. There are plentiful resources at our fingertips, such as virtual libraries with online books, journals, articles, and databases. Personal and professional development can be completed efficiently from any location, including virtual coaching and virtual training programs.

Human Costs of Efficiency from Technology

Remote work and learning can substantially increase efficiency by reducing distance and time constraints. Employers and educators also need to consider the innate need for human connection and overall wellness. Unless a concerted effort is made to support well-being and human connection, it is left up to individuals to do this on their own. It falls on the individual to avoid feeling isolated and alone, and to stay focused, engaged, committed, and energized.

Many of our remote experiences made possible by digital technology are intended to connect us to achieve work outcomes. However, these experiences can lack a feeling of social cohesion, shared identity, and a sense of belonging. Without these unifying and humanizing forces, there is a risk that remote workers and learners will find it difficult to perform and collaborate effectively.

Digital technology maximizes efficiency in education by providing learners with a vast array of educational tools, resources, and services. Effective teaching and learning strategies and student engagement must remain high priorities despite the push toward optimal efficiency.

Learners learn from each other, as well as from faculty and course materials. To ensure the efficacy of online learning, training, and development activities, we need to consider how educational experiences meet the crucial human need for social connection.

Access

Many of us are experiencing the enormous benefits of having immediate access to people and services from anywhere in the world. We will use the example of access to health and wellness services because these have a huge impact on people's lives. We will talk about the benefits of remote access, and also consider the human costs.

The Road to Remote Access

There has always been a need for remote medical access, but until recently there has not been the technology to meet that need. Long before telemedicine was applied to easy, at-home routine visits, solutions were being sought on a grander scale. NASA, for example, started in the 1960s to explore medicine at a distance in its search for ways to address astronauts' health while they were in space. Back on earth, rural communities struggled with lack of access to healthcare. This led in 1987 to the formation of the Office for the Advancement of Telemedicine (originally called the Office for Rural Healthcare) to address this problem using technology.

14 Doing More Together, Feeling Less Connected

After some slow but significant developments in videoconferencing technology in the 1990s, telemedicine became more and more accessible by the first decade of the new millennium. But just because telemedicine was accessible didn't mean it was readily adopted.

Helping to advance the general acceptance of remote medical care was the power of telemedicine to save lives. This power became clear in essential applications, such as the urgent treatment of strokes.

Remote assessment of strokes can save lives. Every second that brain tissue is cut off from its blood supply is a step closer to irreversible brain damage. There is a life-saving treatment but it can only be delivered within four and a half hours of the stroke onset, or it's too late. Imagine arriving at a local hospital with only two and a half hours left for treatment to avoid irreversible brain damage, and learning there was no neurologist on call. Now with telemedicine, a neurologist can diagnose a stroke remotely and then a non-specialist can administer the treatment. In stroke care, telemedicine can prevent unnecessary deaths.

Other applications of urgent, essential treatments also show the enormous value of telemedicine. Neonatal care, pediatric emergency care, and adult intensive care can require a high level of specialization that is not always available locally. Telemedicine is now being used successfully for neonatal intensive care and emergency consultations for ill or injured children. Tele-ICUs have been created where specialists can manage critical care from afar, communicating with the local physician through video conference and remote monitors. As a result of this increased accessibility, there are improved outcomes, decreased costs, and fewer medical errors.[19]

Despite these life-saving applications of telemedicine, resistance to its use for routine matters remained. This resistance came from two directions: doctors and patients not feeling entirely comfortable with the technology, and insurance companies not being willing to cover remote care. When the global pandemic of COVID-19 hit and whole cities went into lockdown, in-person visits were unsafe or prohibited. Doctors and patients had no choice but to use telemedicine. Existing barriers to telemedicine coverage by insurance companies were quickly removed during the pandemic. As a result, there was a 4,347% increase in telemedicine visits in March 2020 in privately insured patients alone, compared to the previous year.[20] This trend is likely to continue now that telemedicine is widely accepted and used.

Instant Access from Anywhere

We now have access to our doctors and a wide array of innovative tools to help us lead healthy lives. Medical information and advice, remote monitoring, and diagnostic tools easily used at home all provide a sense of self-sufficiency and control. A stronger awareness of our own health data reduces the distance between practitioner and patient and reduces the time between diagnosis and treatment.

The Apple Watch is an example of an innovative tool that enables remote monitoring, including heart rate, heart rhythm, and electro-cardiogram-recorded heart activity. The watch has been approved by the FDA as a medical device. Using this technology, helpful data can be compiled over time and can contribute to a doctor's assessment of a patient's health. Dr. Leslie A. Saxon, Professor of Medicine at Keck School of Medicine of USC, says of the watch, "Apple is democratizing healthcare, providing on-demand access to accurate sensors and software that can help consumers develop real healthcare literacy and inform how daily choices impact their health."[21]

Many companies are working to improve the ability to monitor health from home. AltumView Systems has developed smart medical alert systems for senior citizens. They have remote monitoring capabilities, such as tracking daily activities and alerting the company when falls occur. Babyscripts is a virtual maternity care platform that brings the routine monitoring of early postnatal visits into the home. Weight, blood pressure, and other monitoring can occur at home under a doctor's supervision. Postnatal care is supported in a variety of other ways, such as providing educational content that mothers can easily access. Some companies are innovating to enable more health monitoring from home, such as remote stethoscopes and sleep monitoring devices. A former president of the American Heart Association, Dr. Ivor Benjamin, elaborates on the benefits of remote monitoring technology: "Products that seek to provide deeper health insights... have the potential to be significant in new clinical care models and shared decision making between people and their healthcare providers."[22]

Not only has at-home monitoring changed, the way information is handled once it reaches the doctor has changed too. The digitization of medical information facilitates better healthcare. Quality is improved by eliminating hand-written notes and prescriptions, which reduces mistakes and medical errors considerably. Quality standards and benchmarks for care are easy to set up in an electronic record. Electronic records also have mechanisms for tracking and analyzing these benchmarks over time.

Access is increased as individuals' test results are entered into electronic records that can be easily shared. Providers do not have to repeat tests that were done elsewhere, or spend time tracking down past results. Family members can also be given permission to access medical records for assisting in their loved ones' care. Sharing results saves time and money. Ed Black, President and CEO of the Computer & Communications Industry Association, says, "The ability to monitor the medical records, procedures, medicines of a loved one remotely provides opportunity for quality oversight and rapid response, in contrast to being tied to hospital visits and uncertainty."[23]

Improved access to medical data also extends beyond individual care. It facilitates contributions to the field of science and general knowledge. Medical researchers with a specific question can now easily look through and sort historical data in patient charts with a click of a mouse. An entire field called Biomedical Informatics was created to serve this pursuit. In the past, this instant sorting and compiling task would have required many hours of tedious manual labor.

Access to Wellness Resources

Technological advances and regulatory changes in the field of telemedicine have made many types of health and wellness services more accessible to people anytime, from anywhere. In addition to accessing physicians, we can find nutritionists, therapists, coaches, and meditation instructors without having to leave the comfort of home.

The remote delivery of psychotherapy was already beginning to grow in popularity prior to the COVID-19 pandemic. This was mostly due to the ubiquity of smartphones and the development of accessible, easy-to-use apps. The forced isolation of the pandemic led to even greater use of teletherapy when in-person visits were no longer permissible. The popular online therapy platform Talkspace, for example, saw a 65–70% customer growth rate during the early months of the pandemic.[24] People have appreciated the accessibility and convenience of engaging in therapy from anywhere. The use of teletherapy will likely continue long after the pandemic.

Technological advances that enable remote visits and remote monitoring of treatment plans have increased access to professionals in a variety of wellness-related fields. Nutrition counseling, health coaching, and meditation have joined the app usage trend. For example, more than 2,500 meditation mobile apps have been launched since 2015. In April 2020, the meditation app Calm led the market with 3.9 million downloads, followed by Headspace with 1.5 million downloads, then Meditopia, with 1.4 million downloads.[25]

Public opinion surveys have shown patients' high satisfaction levels with telehealth. People can now access care that they might not have otherwise been able to. They can save time and are no longer limited by geography in choosing a provider. Before remote care, there was nothing quick or easy about going to the provider's office. The trip could involve traveling a long distance, taking time off work, arranging childcare, or spending time in a waiting room with ill people. The benefits are clear. But the human costs are undeniable.

Human Costs of Access through Technology

Increased access through technology has negatively impacted aspects of the patient experience. A JD Power survey showed that doctors are focusing less on effective interpersonal communication when interacting with patients remotely. The survey shows doctors are paying less attention to careful listening and clear explanations.[26] As providers adjust to this new technology, there has been an observable shift of priorities away from meeting human needs for connection.

There is also a human cost for providers themselves. Though electronic charts enable constant access, the technology itself comes with disadvantages for providers' quality of life. A study published in the Annals of Family Medicine in 2017 showed that physicians currently spend more than half their day working on the medical record.[27] They often have to spend more time with charts than with patients. This is due in large part to increasing regulatory and clerical requirements that come along with electronic medical records. Additionally, there are human costs to being able to access medical charts from anywhere at any time. Patient records are no longer located only at the hospital or office, but can be accessed from home as well. This constant access can often make work-home boundaries more difficult to set, a trend that echoes across many fields and industries.

As health and wellness care becomes more accessible through technology, it runs the risk of becoming highly transactional. Patients may begin to share less in virtual interactions, and providers may have less of an opportunity to meaningfully connect. Providers may struggle to maintain a compassionate stance as constant access wears at their work-life balance.

Across all industries, similar patterns are occurring. There is an increased risk of prioritizing quantity over quality. Work-life balance is becoming harder to maintain. Access to anyone from anywhere comes with human costs.

Convenience

When we're not working or learning, we have a seemingly endless array of remote leisure activities from which to choose. These nonwork-related activities are convenient for us because we can do them online with anyone, anytime, often from the comfort of our homes.

Entertainment at Our Fingertips

Gaming communities are virtual hangouts for people who enjoy playing video games. According to Microsoft, there were more than two billion gamers globally in 2019, and the number is continuing to rise. Online games provide a virtual world where gamers communicate with each other by using rich interactive media. Friends from across the world have the convenience of hanging out on a regular basis without getting into cars or airplanes. When games have multiplayer capabilities, they increase the number of people who can connect with each other. They are no longer limited to the video consoles of old where one person sat alone in front of a TV set. Now thousands of people can interact virtually in the fantasy worlds of massively multiplayer online games, such as *World of Warcraft*.

It is much more convenient to hang out in a virtual world without leaving home, than to meet up at an actual location. It is especially convenient for gamers separated by large distances who cannot meet up in person at all.

Convenient Activities of Your Preference

This type of gaming originated online and has always found its home there. There are other types of leisure activities that originated in person but have established an online presence over time. Nearly every personal pastime, hobby, or social activity has some presence in the digital world, from reading and watching shows to dating and doing workouts.

Bibliophiles who prefer the convenience of discussing books from the comfort of their own homes are taking advantage of digital tools. It is now easier to connect with other readers, form discussion groups, and share quotes and passages from books. Goodreads is one popular online book group, which has a book club for practically every genre and discussion groups on nearly every literary topic. Book clubs on this site vary in membership from four people to over 100,000. These clubs provide members with a fun and intellectually stimulating way to enhance their reading experience, as well as a sense of community even when physically apart.

Spending more time with family is another benefit of remote life. The flexibility of working from home means that time previously spent commuting can instead be time spent with family. An organizational development specialist told us, "With reduced commuting time and more flexibility during the day, I find that I can be productive with work and have more balance with my family. It is very meaningful to be able to be present with my son as he leaves for school and arrives home. I think the enhanced balance between my work and home life has generally made remote work more favorable."

A consultant who recently became a parent said, "For me, working remotely has been a positive experience. My commute used to be an hour and a half to two hours each way, which meant getting home at 7:00 pm in the evening at the earliest. I had anticipated having a few weeks of quality time with my newborn daughter, followed by seeing her for only a half hour a day during the week. It was a depressing thought, and luckily it turned out not to be the case. I worked remotely in our apartment while my wife taught art remotely, and we tag-teamed parenting duties. I got to spend much more time with my daughter daily than I ever thought I could and that has been the biggest upside to remote work for me."

Family and friends can spend leisure time together even when physically separated. Digital technology has made it possible to enjoy remote movie and TV nights together. Teleparty (formerly Netflix Party) is one digital tool that enables this by synchronizing video playback and adding a group chat to streaming entertainment services. Family members located in different cities or countries can stream high-quality entertainment together from the comfort of their own homes.

Some people want to extend their network beyond friends and family. They are in search of convenient ways to form new relationships. For this reason, online dating sites and mobile apps are extremely popular. They enable people to expand their dating options beyond their traditional social circles. There is convenience in assessing far more potential partners than can be vetted one in-person date at a time. As of 2019, 23% of Americans say they have gone on a date with someone they met through a dating site or app, and 12% say they have married or been in a committed relationship with someone they met through online dating. This is an increase from 2013 when only 11% of Americans had used a dating site or app and only 3% were in a committed relationship that had started online.[28]

Human Costs of Convenience: Together, Feeling Alone

The average American adult spends over 12 hours per day in front of a digital device, according to the most recent Nielsen total audience report. There is no denying that digital technology has become deeply ingrained in the fabric of our daily lives.

There is no doubt that there is a large quantity of social experiences available online. However, some question whether these experiences are high-quality social interactions where people truly connect. Nicolas Ducheneaut and his group at Stanford's Virtual Human Interaction Lab gathered observational data directly from a massively multiplayer online game to study the patterns of interactions. They concluded that:

> instead of playing with other people, [players] rely on them as an audience for their in-game performances, as an entertaining spectacle, and as a diffuse and easily accessible source of information and chit-chat. For most, playing the game is therefore like being "alone together"—surrounded by others, but not necessarily actively interacting with them.[29]

Constant connectedness through technology enables us to more conveniently gather with others, but we don't always leave it feeling connected or satisfied. A professor at one of the world's leading technological universities wrote:

The ritual of a weekly phone call with friends where there seemed like enough "space" to talk about things in a meaningful way has eroded to texting to "keep up." On the one hand, several of my friends feel more in touch because they are sharing memes, feel they are sharing witty things "on the spot," but there is less going into depth. We don't seem to be able to maintain both. That is what is so curious.[30]

A technology consultant and expert on attention and workflow, previously with a top-five tech company, wrote about the impact of digital technology on our lives: "It's been liberating and enslaving. It takes effort to ignore. We have given it more power than we've given the best parts of our humanity."[31]

Go forward, with this in mind:

1 **The paradox**: The technology we use to connect with others often leaves us feeling less connected.

   - There are benefits on the digital side of the paradox.
   - There are costs on the human side of the paradox.

2 **Social connection**: Human brains are hard-wired for social connection.

   - Humans feel safe and comfortable around other humans.
   - Human brains serve as predictors to help understand other humans.
   - Humans have a biological need to be accepted by a group and to be contributing members.

3 **Three basic human needs**:

   - Safety and comfort
   - Understanding
   - Belonging

4 **Three benefits of digital life**:

   - Access
   - Efficiency
   - Convenience

5 **The human cost of digital life is a diminished focus on the innate need for social connection, but we can humanize the remote experience.**

Notes

1 Lieberman, Matthew D. *Social: Why Our Brains Are Wired to Connect.* Oxford, England: Oxford University Press, 2013, 43.
2 Lieberman, Matthew D. *Social: Why Our Brains Are Wired to Connect.* Oxford, England: Oxford University Press, 2013, 42.

3 Van der Kolk, Bessel A. *The Body Keeps the Score: Brain, Mind, and Body in the Healing of Trauma*. London: Penguin Publishing Group, 2015, 81.
4 Thornton, Mark A., Miriam E. Weaverdyck, and Diana I. Tamir. "The social brain automatically predicts others' future mental states." *Journal of Neuroscience* 39, no. 1 (2019): 140–148, https://doi.org/10.1523/JNEUROSCI.1431-18.2018
5 Eisenberger, Naomi I. and Matthew D. Lieberman. "Why rejection hurts: a common neural alarm system for physical and social pain." *Trends in cognitive sciences* 8, no. 7 (2004): 294–300, https://doi.org/10.1016/j.tics.2004.05.010
6 Oxford University Press. "Altruism." *Oxford Learners Dictionaries*, 2021, www.oxfordlearnersdictionaries.com/definition/english/altruism?q=altruism
7 Filkowski, Megan M., R. Nick Cochran, and Brian W. Haas. "Altruistic behavior: Mapping responses in the brain." *Neuroscience and neuroeconomics* 5 (2016): 65, https://doi.org/10.2147/NAN.S87718
8 Wang, Yilu, Jianqiao Ge, Hanqi Zhang, Haixia Wang, and Xiaofei Xie. "Altruistic behaviors relieve physical pain." *Proceedings of the National Academy of Sciences* 117, no. 2 (2020): 950–958, https://doi.org/10.1073/pnas.1911861117
9 Cascio, Christopher N., Christin Scholz, and Emily B. Falk. "Social influence and the brain: Persuasion, susceptibility to influence and retransmission." *Current opinion in behavioral sciences* 3 (2015): 51, https://doi.org/10.1016/j.cobeha.2015.01.007
10 Cascio, Christopher N., Christin Scholz, and Emily B. Falk. "Social influence and the brain: Persuasion, susceptibility to influence and retransmission." *Current opinion in behavioral sciences* 3 (2015): 51, https://doi.org/10.1016/j.cobeha.2015.01.007
11 Lieberman, Matthew D. *Social: Why Our Brains Are Wired to Connect*. Oxford, England: Oxford University Press, 2013, 290.
12 Anderson, Janna and Lee Rainie. *The Future of Well-Being in a Tech-Saturated World*. Washington, DC: Pew Research Center, 2018: 12. This report is the result of a wide canvassing of 1,150 experts by Pew Research Center and Elon University's Imagining the Internet Center. Technology experts, scholars, and health specialists were asked: "Over the next decade, how will changes in digital life impact people's overall well-being physically and mentally?" We reference relevant quotes from these experts, identified throughout the book by their name and job title.
13 Anderson, Janna and Lee Rainie. *Stories from Experts about the Impact of Digital Life*. Washington, DC: Pew Research Center, 2018, 29.
14 Lund, Susan, Anu Madgavkar, James Manyika, and Sven Smit. "What's next for remote work: An analysis of 2,000 tasks, 800 jobs, and nine countries." McKinsey & Company, November 23, 2020, www.mckinsey.com/featured-insights/future-of-work/whats-next-for-remote-work-an-analysis-of-2000-tasks-800-jobs-and-nine-countries
15 Cutter, Chip. "Companies start to think remote work isn't so great after all." *Wall Street Journal*, July 24, 2020: paragraph 2, www.wsj.com/articles/companies-start-to-think-remote-work-isnt-so-great-after-all-11595603397
16 McGregor, Jena. "Hot new job title in a pandemic: 'Head of remote work.'" *Washington Post*, September 9, 2020, www.washingtonpost.com/business/2020/09/09/head-of-remote-work-jobs/
17 Khan Academy. "What is the history of Khan Academy?" September 2021, https://support.khanacademy.org/hc/en-us/articles/202483180-What-is-the-history-of-Khan-Academy-
18 McGill Association of University Teachers. "A brief history of MOOCs." www.mcgill.ca/maut/news-current-affairs/moocs/history

19 Nesbitt, Thomas S., and Jana Katz-Bell. "History of telehealth." In *Understanding Telehealth*, edited by Karen Schulder Rheuban and Elizabeth A. Krupinski. New York: McGraw-Hill, 2018, https://accessmedicine.mhmedical.com/content.aspx?bookid=2217&sectionid=187794434

20 Lagasse, Jeff. "Telehealth claim lines increased more than 4,000% in the past year." *Healthcare Finance*, June 3, 2020, www.healthcarefinancenews.com/news/telehealth-claim-lines-increased-more-4000-past-year

21 www.google.com/url?q=www.apple.com/healthcare/apple-watch

22 www.google.com/url?q=www.apple.com/healthcare/apple-watch

23 Anderson, Janna and Lee Rainie. *Stories from Experts about the Impact of Digital Life*. Washington, DC: Pew Research Center, 2018, 17.

24 Perrone, Matthew. "Virus drives new demand for Talkspace's online therapy." *ABCnews.com*, May 10, 2020, https://abcnews.go.com/US/wireStory/virus-drives-demand-talkspaces-online-therapy-70603681

25 Perez, Sarah. "Meditation and mindfulness apps continue their surge amid pandemic." *TechCrunch+*, May 28, 2020, https://techcrunch.com/2020/05/28/meditation-and-mindfulness-apps-continue-their-surge-amid-pandemic/

26 Heath, Sara. "Patient satisfaction with telehealth high following COVID-19," Patient Engagement HIT, October 7, 2020, https://patientengagementhit.com/news/patient-satisfaction-with-telehealth-high-following-covid-19

27 Arndt, Brian G., John W. Beasley, Michelle D. Watkinson, Jonathan L. Temte, Wen-Jan Tuan, Christine A. Sinsky, and Valerie J. Gilchrist. "Tethered to the EHR: Primary care physician workload assessment using EHR event log data and time-motion observations." *The Annals of Family Medicine* 15, no. 5 (2017): 419–426, https://doi.org/10.1370/afm.2121

28 Anderson, Monica, Emily A. Vogels, and Erica Turner. "The Virtues and Downsides of Online Dating." Pew Research Center, February 6, 2020, www.pewresearch.org/internet/2020/02/06/the-virtues-and-downsides-of-online-dating/

29 Ducheneaut, Nicolas, Nicholas Yee, Eric Nickell, and Robert J. Moore. "'Alone together?' Exploring the social dynamics of massively multiplayer online games." *Proceedings of the SIGCHI Conference on Human Factors in Computing Systems* (April 2006): 415, https://doi.org/10.1145/1124772.1124834

30 Anderson, Janna and Lee Rainie. *Stories from Experts about the Impact of Digital Life*. Washington, DC: Pew Research Center, 2018: 47.

31 Anderson, Janna and Lee Rainie. *Stories from Experts about the Impact of Digital Life*. Washington, DC: Pew Research Center, 2018: 78.

PART ONE

Doing More Together, Feeling Less Connected

Chapter 1

Confined to the Digital Window

What happens when you enter a remote environment? The brain's first priority when entering any new environment is to establish safety. This evolved as a necessity for survival and remains a part of the human brain's makeup even in the modern day. Without a sense of safety, fully engaging your attention with the task at hand in the remote environment becomes challenging.

> Shay, an executive and team leader, is having a difficult time adapting to working remotely. She works from home and manages a team of six direct reports. She is in back-to-back online meetings throughout the day. Each time a remote meeting starts, she feels disoriented during the first few moments when faces appear on the screen. She is feeling unsettled, uncomfortable, and unfocused.

Focused attention is possible only once a feeling of safety and comfort has been established. When you are not feeling safe and comfortable, your brain will devote a disproportionate amount of attention to that thing you're worried about or afraid of. This can produce anxiety and a hyper-awareness of noises or movements in the environment, also known as hypervigilance. This is the experience for Shay, who feels more alone and prone to hypervigilance in the remote environment, despite seeing other people on her screen. Hypervigilance interferes with the normal process of attention, which goes on to cause other problems in Shay's productivity and wellness throughout her workday.

Shay is an extrovert who has a very social job. Being an extrovert, a lot of her energy and interests are directed outward. She seeks social interaction because this is how she feels energized. Her job used to be an excellent outlet for this social energy. The absence of others is a clear loss for Shay. In contrast, the introverts on her team feel a sense of relief to be working at home alone without the noise of a crowded office. As introverts, they prefer to process the world around them by directing their energy inward. Instead of gaining energy from being around groups of

DOI: 10.4324/9781003170488-3

26 Doing More Together, Feeling Less Connected

people, they can feel exhausted by it and require alone time to recuperate afterwards.

Whether social interactions feel energizing or exhausting, the basic need to be around other humans is hard-wired and it does not go away. In a typical day, social needs are met by casual interactions in an office or even a smile from a stranger. These small interactions add up and reassure the brain that others are around. This is equally true for extroverts and for introverts. Needing a respite at times doesn't mean that the complete absence of other people is a natural state for the brain. The absence of social connections can take a toll on the nervous system despite the day feeling easier overall. Problems can arise, such as Shay's hypervigilance that interferes with her attention.

To understand the problems with attentiveness that the remote experience can cause, it is important to first understand the processes that compose attention. To better appreciate how attention shapes your experience when you are in a remote environment, we will look at the set of processes involved in attention.

The Brain Is Busy Managing the Six Processes of Attention

Your brain selectively chooses what information is relevant in your inner and outer world. William James defined attention as "the taking possession by the mind, in clear and vivid form, of one out of what seem several simultaneously possible objects or trains of thought. Focalization, concentration of consciousness are of its essence. It implies withdrawal from some things in order to deal effectively with others."[1] Although there are multitudes of things happening both in your internal thoughts and in the outside world, there are a finite number of things that you can attend to at any one time.

What you choose to attend to creates your experience at any given moment. You use your five senses to build a meaningful experience of the outside world based on what captures your attention. When confined to a digital window, the sensory information available for actively constructing the picture of your own experience is limited. It is unlike walking through a three-dimensional world filled with rich sensory stimuli that makes it relatively effortless to build a picture of the outside world.

In the two-dimensional space of a computer, your five senses receive less visual and auditory information. It is less clear what to pay attention to. Your senses can become confused and your comfort in the environment will be affected. The confusion originates in the part of the human brain that controls attention, the prefrontal cortex (PFC). The PFC is the seat of attention, as well as many other conscious actions grouped together under the umbrella term "executive functions."

In 1990, cognitive psychologists Steven Peterson and Michael Posner proposed a framework of six key processes that make attention possible in any context. Since then, these six processes have been validated by many other studies using brain imaging technology that can observe in real time what is happening when a person is trying to focus.[2]

The first two processes in this attention framework relate to your state of mind as you get ready to pay attention. These preparatory processes are called alerting and orienting. The remaining four selective processes enable you to focus your attention on specific things in the environment, while tuning out others. These processes are called prioritizing, ignoring, switching, and sustaining.

First, we illustrate how each of the six component processes of attention would unfold in a three-dimensional context full of sensory information: a noisy, in-person social gathering. Then, we examine in more detail what is involved in each of these six processes and how attention can be affected by a remote environment. The challenges that people encounter paying attention in a two-dimensional environment play a significant role in shaping the remote experience.

Prepare to Pay Attention: Alerting and Orienting

Alerting

> At a social gathering, you are sitting on a couch and your mind is wandering. You are worrying about something that you didn't finish up at work. A cell phone rings nearby. The noise causes you to become alert to the present moment, and more aware of what is going on in the room. A minute later, someone walks by and nearly trips over your outstretched legs. You quickly extend a hand to help steady that person. Because you are alert in that moment and ready to receive sensory information, you are able to react fast enough to assist.

Alerting, the first of the two preparatory processes of paying attention, refers to coming into an internal state of mind that is ready to receive and respond to sensory information. Alertness can range from a very low level (asleep) to a very high level (vigilant). It is modulated by a neuro-transmitter (a chemical the brain uses to communicate between cells), called norepinephrine. Norepinephrine is continuously circulating in the blood at varying levels, and will increase in response to perceived danger. When norepinephrine is low, you are either asleep or you would like to be. When norepinephrine is high, you are hypervigilant and on high alert. Neither of these brain states is optimal for complex thought or creative work. Indeed, the brain's concentration abilities are at their sharpest when norepinephrine, and thus alertness, are at a happy medium. At this mid-point, you are alert but not hyperalert, calm but not falling asleep. Here, your brain is able to effectively focus where it needs to.

28 Doing More Together, Feeling Less Connected

That happy medium of alertness can only happen when you feel safe in your environment. Safety is a prerequisite for alertness, just as alertness is a prerequisite for focused attention. If your nervous system deems your environment to be unsafe or threatening, you will be unable to concentrate well. And because humans are wired for connection, safety and comfort often require the actual presence of other people. When the feeling of aloneness is strong enough, anxiety can escalate into a full stress response. This is an acute physical reaction to a challenge or danger.

The stress response will interfere with alerting. Your body's alarm system will automatically prioritize getting away from danger over getting ready to pay attention. This alarm system, the sympathetic nervous system commonly known as the fight-or-flight system, fires under any type of major threat. The main brain chemical this system uses is epinephrine (commonly referred to as adrenaline) that activates the natural responses of fight, flight, or freeze in response to a threat. Through the actions of epinephrine on different cells, the heart can be made to pump fast and hard, the skin to sweat, the lung passageways to widen, and the blood vessels to constrict. The body's resources (oxygen via the bloodstream and glucose for brain and muscle fuel) are diverted away from alerting and toward facing the threat.

When the brain has sensed a threat and decided to act on it, the body enters a reactive survival mode that has no time for alertness and complex thinking. Its focus will be on responding to a danger, disregarding anything that doesn't immediately serve survival. This means that the PFC, the center of attention and other higher reasoning processes, becomes less active.

Only when the stressor is believed to have passed can the PFC come back to an optimal alert state. The frantic and frenzied activity of the sympathetic nervous system is brought to a gentle halt by the opposing system, called the parasympathetic nervous system. This system controls your basic bodily functions, keeping a normal steady heart rate and regular breathing. Signals of calm are sent out and the PFC is able to return to concentrating on other activities.

It is important to note that the stress response can be activated with just as much intensity by any major source of threat, even if it is not actually life threatening. In the remote environment, feeling alone even though other people are on the screen can cause levels of the stress hormone norepinephrine to rise. At its worst, feeling alone can cause not just anxiety but a full-fledged stress response.

These responses happen in the remote environment because humans are wired to connect, and to feel safe and comfortable when around other people. The feeling of being separated from others can cause the brain to respond as if it were in actual physical pain. When virtual interactions are unable to soothe the pain of aloneness and separation, the human need for safety and comfort is not met. Aloneness becomes a major stressor, causing stress chemical levels to increase and interfering with the first process of attention, alertness.

For both extroverts and introverts, the remote environment can cause stress. It can feel comfortable or easy to work at home alone but ultimately all humans need social connection to thrive. A lack of connectedness causes stress for the mind and body, interfering with alertness even if a person is not consciously aware of it.

Optimal alertness can be achieved only when the need for safety and comfort is met. You have to initially enter an alert state when you're ready to start working on something. Then it must be maintained throughout the activity or else you will not remain at your desired level of sharpness and cognitive functioning. Alertness is a continuous process.

Once you are alert, you are ready to move on to orienting. This is the second of the two preparatory processes of paying attention. Orienting gets you ready to direct your attention where you want it to go.

Orienting

> Now you are sitting on the couch with optimal alertness. This makes it easy to notice a friend sit down on the cushion beside you with a deep sigh and then open her mouth to speak. In that moment before the first word even comes out, you orient. You don't spend much time figuring out exactly where your friend is because you felt the shift in the couch, heard the loud exhalation, and saw the movement in your peripheral vision. You turn your head to the correct angle in space, meet her eyes, and your brain is ready to receive the conversation that is about to ensue.

Orienting is moving your attention to a specific location in space during the first moment in a new context. It involves realizing where you are, what is going on, and what your context is.

Your brain takes in the environment using your senses. The process of orienting prepares you for engaging your attention. Orienting can be involuntary and driven by the external environment, such as when your eyes are pulled toward a sound, sight, or sensation in your environment. It can also be voluntary and internally driven when you make a decision to move your attention to a particular place in space.[3] You can think of orienting as a first look at the environment. You scan the scene and take in as much as possible, whether it's a voluntary glance around or an involuntary focus on certain things that attract your senses.

Whereas a two-dimensional remote environment provides a limited amount of external sensory information for orienting, a three-dimensional physical environment supplies a large amount of sensory information. A conference room, a private office, or a noisy bar are all clearly different

30 Doing More Together, Feeling Less Connected

contexts. Orienting does not come as automatically without the sensory richness of contextual information, and you may find that you have to repeatedly reorient during a virtual meeting. Each act of reorienting uses up mental energy.

As you move into new environments, transitions typically give you time to voluntarily orient yourself. For example, a commute to work gives you time to transition your thoughts from home issues to work issues. These transitional periods are lost when working remotely. There is no entering a building, finding the room, taking a seat, and leaving the location when you're done. All you do is click "Join" and you are immediately in the meeting. Appearing in a digital space without a transition can be so abrupt that it makes orienting to a remote environment difficult from the start.

Once you enter a new digital space, there is very little concrete information to be gathered about it. The space lacks relevant aspects of a room that would normally contribute to the ability to orient: the temperature, the furniture, the seating arrangement. In a physical space, a person's location would automatically draw your attention, such as a person speaking from a podium at the front of the room. In a virtual space, none of this relevant information is available when you and others are confined to digital boxes. You must self-direct or push your vision to a location in space when it is time to orient to where you want to pay attention.

In the remote environment, new faces quickly pop up at random all over the screen as people sign on to a meeting. This gives your brain very little time to orient to the new faces and can quickly become over-stimulating. (Imagine how disorienting it would be if colleagues suddenly materialized in the seats next to you in a conference room.) When all participants are presented in a grid pattern of thumbnail images, the brain has too many faces to decode at once and is challenged to find a point of focus.[4] This contributes to the feeling of disorientation that many experience in the first moment of a virtual meeting.

Sounds also contribute to the ability to orient. The human brain is designed to take in sounds coming from all directions in space to form a clear mental map of what's happening in the room. Your brain subconsciously collects and uses sound information so that you know instantly whether a speaker is right next to you or in a distant corner. In the remote environment, all sound comes to your ears from the same computer speaker, as if all the people speaking were at the exact same distance from you. When you don't have accurate sound information, it is impossible to correctly identify where people are in space based on sound.

A user experience researcher spoke about the lack of ambient sound in virtual interactions: "When everyone who isn't currently speaking in the virtual room mutes themselves, which is really common in most group meetings, the information that comes from sounds is just cut off altogether. There's no

Confined to the Digital Window 31

background sound of coughs or chairs scraping. The silence can be jarring and disorienting, like you're talking to yourself."

Like sound, light assists in orienting to the environment. In physical spaces, it is common to interact with the lighting. If you walked into a conference room and it was so dark you couldn't make out other people's faces, someone would surely go and adjust the light switch. If the sunlight were coming straight at you through a window and you couldn't see your colleagues' faces, you'd likely shift your chair slightly. If these adjustments weren't made, the light would interfere with your interactions. Yet you are not able to make any adjustments when you and others are confined to digital boxes. Another piece of information for external orienting, which light normally would contribute, is unavailable.

In the remote environment, a considerable amount of external contextual information that would allow for easy orienting is absent. You have only arbitrary positions on the screen and limited sound and visual information for orienting. The mental picture of space that is formed is like an incomplete jigsaw puzzle. Trying to fill in the pieces of the incomplete puzzle requires voluntary, conscious effort. Orienting is inherently harder when it is driven by conscious effort instead of prompted automatically by the external environment.

To appreciate the difficulty of consciously orienting, think of an instance when you have moved a household object that had been in the same place for a very long time. When you reached for it or turned your attention to the place where it used to be, you found yourself oriented to the wrong place. This caused you to feel a moment of discomfort until your brain caught up to the situation and you stopped trying to orient to that missing target in the wrong place. The environment had changed, but your brain still oriented you automatically based on your expectations and what you were used to. In this example, you needed something and your attention was pushed toward a particular place in space where your brain thought it was located. That push failed and your brain had to reorient elsewhere. Instead of being automatic, orienting became a conscious, active process.

Orienting is often more effortful in the remote environment. More energy is required to frequently reorient and this can get exhausting over the course of a day. Reorienting is required each time you prepare yourself to proceed to the next steps of selecting where to pay attention.

Select Where Your Attention Goes to Enable Sustained Focus

Your brain receives a tremendous number of stimuli and has to select what will be focused on and what will be ignored. Some of this stimulation enters the brain from outside the body, in the form of sensory input from the environment. Other stimulation comes from within the body, including thoughts, memories, and internal sensations. Your brain cannot focus on all of this at once. Attention is a finite resource, and the four selective processes of attention decide how it will be allocated. These four processes are: prioritizing, ignoring, switching, and sustaining. They are modulated by the neurotransmitter dopamine.

Dopamine, one of the main chemicals that reinforces rewarding experiences, makes activities and sensations feel enjoyable or even addictive. It helps the brain to identify what is relevant in the environment. It also links that relevant item or action to a feeling of reward or satisfaction. Dopamine is one of the main targets for medications that treat deficits in attention. In attention-deficit/hyperactivity disorder (ADHD), the brain has difficulty selecting and settling on only one relevant factor in the environment. Increasing dopamine through medication helps to decrease that difficulty and enable the selective attention processes.

Only after becoming alert and oriented can you decide what to pay attention to using the selective attention processes. Alertness readies the inner state for proper attention and orienting brings that alert state to the current task. In this prepared state you can begin to prioritize what is relevant.

Selective Attention: Prioritize What Is Relevant and Ignore What Is Not

Prioritizing

> You begin a conversation. You are primarily focused on the story your friend is telling you. Changes in your friend's tone of voice and her physical gestures catch your attention because they are relevant to what she is saying. In contrast, you do not pay any attention to the facial expressions of a person nearby. Even though the nearby person is also in your visual field, your brain determines he does not have relevance so you don't notice him at all.

Your brain must prioritize what will be focused on and what will be ignored. There is too much stimulation in the external and internal world for one brain to process it all at once. Deciding what to prioritize is the role of a specialized brain system, known as working memory. Working memory holds what is on your mind at the moment (as opposed to the past, which is stored in long-term memory). All of the perceptual information the brain takes in from the outside world gets funneled toward your working memory. The information is filtered along the way and only some of it advances all the way to working memory. The information that enters working memory is evaluated and assigned priority. This determines where attention will be directed.[5]

You can think of working memory like a container. Whatever is in the container at the moment is what's on your mind and what has already been assigned top priority. The capacity of working memory is quite limited. Most humans can only think about one thing at a time. Whatever your mind is on right now (hopefully this book), it cannot be simultaneously on something else. While reading this book, your working memory is dedicated to processing what you are reading. If you start to think about what to have for dinner tonight, that decision will take over the space in your working memory and you will no longer be thinking about this book. You cannot read this book and think about dinner at exactly the same time. Even if you switch back and forth quickly, one topic must bump the other one out of the container of your working memory.

Fortunately, working memory is also somewhat flexible. It has just enough wiggle room to let another thought in briefly when it is necessary to compare or make decisions. If random thoughts make it all the way into your working memory, it is able to make the decision whether these thoughts will take over the space or get bumped back out again. This process involves working memory briefly considering both thoughts at once, and making a decision about which gets priority.

To see the range of working memory's capabilities to make these types of decisions, it is helpful to consider a few examples. An example of an easy task is deciding between two simple items. Other tasks, such as thinking about a simple decision while listening to someone speak, are more difficult. Doing two very similar tasks at once is often impossible.

An easy task for working memory is deciding between two menu items to order for lunch. You can hold these two items in your working memory at once, considering the pros and cons of each. You can also imagine what it would be like to eat each one, and then decide which you prefer for lunch that day.

A more difficult task, although it can be done, is choosing between two menu items while listening to your friend talking from across the table. You are working on two things at once, but this is possible because working memory has separate spaces for auditory and visual information. There may be just enough room to hold the food decision and follow the conversation at the same time, as long as neither is too complicated.

The previous example is difficult but not impossible, because there are separate spaces to work on auditory and visual information. However, the brain cannot work on multiple auditory or visual inputs at once. An impossible task would be simultaneously listening to your friend's story and listening to the waiter read the specials, or reading a menu and reading a magazine. There is no room for two auditory tasks, or two visual tasks, to hold a place in working memory at the same time.

In remote experiences, the limitations of working memory become evident. When you are in a meeting leading a discussion, you are tracking a

34 Doing More Together, Feeling Less Connected

lot more than the content of what is being discussed. For example, you think: What are they seeing right now? Am I still sharing my screen? Can they hear me? Where are they looking? What email just came in? Where should I be looking? Is my internet dropping out? There is much more for working memory to monitor. Some thoughts about the meeting content are bumped out of the working memory space by competing concerns unique to the remote experience. Prioritizing can be difficult or faulty.

Working memory cannot make priority decisions on everything that comes into the brain. This would be too much work and you would not be able to function efficiently if you were constantly prioritizing a whole world of stimuli. Fortunately, your brain has ways to control which perceptual information captures your attention strongly enough to make it into working memory.

Your brain has filters that help it weigh the relevance of perceptual information. You will likely respond preferentially to certain qualities of stimuli, such as intensity, motion, novelty, or size. A sudden high-volume, intense noise will typically arouse more interest than a quiet, constant, steady hum. A moving image will capture your eye over a stationary one. You will pay more attention to the face of someone that you've never seen before than other faces that are familiar to you. Your attention will be drawn automatically to an oversized face on a screen of smaller faces. These filters are hard-wired and most people have them in common.[6]

Other filters are learned over time, rather than hard-wired. There are certain stimuli in the environment that will have personal or emotional significance to you alone. Your attention might be drawn to a particular cell phone ringtone you know well or your partner's voice. Activating one of these filters will give a stimulus more relevance, making the stimulus more likely to reach the working memory system.

One of the main challenges to prioritizing with limited contextual information in the remote environment is deciding how different priorities should be weighed. The human brain and its filters evolved in a three-dimensional environment, so they don't always work as well in a two-dimensional one. On a flat screen of two-dimensional images, or simply a name in a black box if the camera is turned off, the spatial relationships between people are not what the brain expects. This affects which information is delivered to working memory and how priority decisions are processed.

Another challenge to prioritizing is the active search for more contextual information in the remote environment. It results in attention being drawn to both relevant and irrelevant stimuli. As an example, the leader of a meeting looking at the participants' still faces might quickly pick up on any movement in a search for relevance. Even simple gestures, such as a person fixing his hair or adjusting his computer monitor, might be picked up by this search. The shortage of relevant contextual information is in contrast to in-person settings where there is much more information that can be used to prioritize what is relevant. With limited information coming in from the environment, decision-making must be generated using more internal information. Decision-making has to rely more on past knowledge, thoughts, feelings, and inferences.

In any particular moment, you have one main thing in your working memory that is your central focus. Successful prioritizing prevents competing stimuli from breaking into the container of working memory and bumping the current focus out. Then, within the space of working memory, you can consciously decide where to focus.

Ignoring

There are 20 other conversations going on in the same room while you converse with your friend. Yet you are not paying attention to any of their content. You are ignoring all of that sensory information because your prioritizing system decides it has no relevance to the conversation on your own couch. However, if one of the people on the other couch called out your full name, you would probably turn to look. Even though your active attention is ignoring that part of the room, your brain is also aware on some level of what is going on over there. Though this processing is happening on a level outside of your consciousness, your brain is holding on to things that might interest you. In the process of ignoring information, you have awareness of other noises but are not giving them your attention.

Ignoring what is irrelevant and tuning it out as background noise is the other side of prioritizing relevant stimuli. If information doesn't make it into working memory, it isn't actively processed. But that doesn't mean it is completely lost; the brain still continues to monitor it on some level in case anything relevant comes up. That is why you could hear a person calling your name in the example above, even without actively paying attention to the conversation of the person who said it.

"The Invisible Gorilla," an experiment conducted by Daniel Simons and Christopher Chabris in 1999, is one of the most famous illustrations of the ignoring process. Participants completed a high-concentration video task: counting the number of rapid basketball passes between three players dressed in white, while being distracted by crisscrossing basketball passes from three other players dressed in black. In the middle of the video, a black gorilla walks ostentatiously through the group of six players who are passing the balls. When asked about it afterwards, half of the experiment participants had completely missed the gorilla. Their attention was so focused on the task that they had completely blocked out both the irrelevant black-clad players and the highly unusual stimulus of the black gorilla. By ignoring information irrelevant to the task, they missed something

36 Doing More Together, Feeling Less Connected

potentially dangerous. The other half of the experiment participants had ignored the irrelevant players while still monitoring the background. They were aware of background stimuli enough to pick up on something out of the ordinary; that is, the gorilla in the middle of the group.[7]

When a person is not able to monitor background information like those who missed the gorilla, it is referred to as inattentional blindness. As described by Daniel J. Simons of the Visual Cognition Lab at the University of Illinois at Urbana-Champaign, "Inattentional blindness is the failure to notice a fully-visible, but unexpected object because attention was engaged on another task, event, or object."[8] The inattentional blindness of the gorilla participants illustrates that ignoring is not an all-or-nothing process. Ignoring is a more complex process than completely turning off certain noises in the environment, which could result in missing important information. Both focusing attention on a task and being flexible enough to see what else is coming at you are important.

The gorilla experiment demonstrates the differences in the way people are able to ignore visual information. Other experiments have studied how ignoring takes place in the auditory system. The "dichotic listening task" is one way to study how the ears process background noise. Participants wear a set of headphones and listen to two different auditory messages simultaneously, one in each ear. They are told to pay attention to one ear and ignore the other. Then the researcher examines how much of the content presented to the ignored ear actually reaches the brain. Some content, such as a message spoken in a different language or played backward, is not noticed or recalled at all. Other content, such as a change in volume or tone,[9] a mention of the listener's name,[10] or any sexual content,[11] is usually noticed by the listeners. It will catch their attention even though they were focused on the sounds in the opposite ear. This demonstrates once again that the process of ignoring is not all-or-nothing. Certain information is still able to reach working memory to be consciously noticed.

The brain takes in a lot of information and uses it to make decisions, often out of conscious awareness. Evolution and survival of the fittest required a safe balance between tuning out background stimuli and continuously monitoring surroundings. If ancient humans were focused on the task of foraging for berries in the forest, for example, it would not benefit them to devote 100% of their attention to the task. If all their brain power were used to hunt for red berries from among green leaves, like the gorilla subjects distinguishing black from white, then a predator could go unnoticed. This would not lead to survival in the wild.

In the modern day, there is less need to monitor for mortal threats than in ancient times. Yet the environment contains more stimuli than ever. Deciding what to pay attention to is a complex interplay of processes. One process ignores much of the stimuli in the environment while still keeping an eye out for anything of interest. Another process prioritizes the information that does make it through to working memory, and decides where attention should be directed.

Prioritizing is not a simple process and it becomes even more complicated the more stimuli there are in the environment competing for attention. In modern digital life, there are multiple screens and constant notifications. It becomes very tempting to switch frequently from one stimulus to another. Yet sustaining attention in one place is necessary to get work done effectively.

Selective Attention: Switch Only When Necessary and Sustain Whenever Possible

Switching

> You now turn away from your friend who is telling you the story and look toward the person who called out your name. Your attention goes to identifying him and then greeting him. You switch to a new conversation with a different person. Then you switch back to your friend who was mid-sentence and apologize. You direct your attention to introducing your two friends to each other and bringing the two conversations together into one.

Switching is possible because the brain is able to remember where it left off on an incomplete task and pick up again at the same spot later. Humans have the capability to switch from one focus of attention to another. This ability to switch attention makes humans more adaptable, ready to confront the unexpected and act on it immediately.

Flexible attention means that you can unhook your attention from one point, engage and readjust at a different point, and then come back to the original point without losing your place. However, every movement comes at a cost. The switch cost is the amount of extra reaction time required when changing to a new task. For example, you will have a slower reaction time when you have just switched your eyes from your cell phone back to the road than if you were watching the road all along.

Many people do not realize how often they are switching attention because they believe they are effectively multitasking. In fact, multitasking, the idea that one can complete multiple goals simultaneously, is a myth.[12] There is no such thing as parallel processing of multiple tasks except when one of the tasks is completely habitual, such as walking.

By attempting to do two things at once, people make approximately twice as many errors and take twice as much time overall.[13] One of the most deadly applications of this misattribution of capabilities is driving while doing other things. It is not possible to pay full attention to both. In fact, you are switching. That higher switch cost when returning your

38 Doing More Together, Feeling Less Connected

attention to the road can be the time it would have taken to stop short and avoid an accident.

As Daniel J. Levitin describes in his book *The Organized Mind: Thinking Straight in the Age of Information Overload*:

> the kind of rapid, continual shifting we do with multitasking causes the brain to burn through fuel so quickly that we feel exhausted and disoriented after even a short time. We've literally depleted the nutrients in our brain. This leads to compromises in both cognitive and physical performance.[14]

Research has shown that there are long-term consequences to heavy so-called multitasking. One study asked chronic heavy media users (people used to having many computer browser tabs and multiple devices open) and low media users to do simple experimental tasks. Then the researchers compared their reaction times. They found that the heavy media users actually had a higher switch cost. Their reaction time was slower on switching tasks than those who were unaccustomed to frequent switching. The research showed that over time, heavy multitaskers become worse and worse at filtering out irrelevant information; and therefore, their ability to quickly switch becomes less refined.[15]

This has powerful implications. The more people attempt to multitask, the worse the effect on their attention. People who attempt to multitask all the time rarely use the ignoring process. They switch from one stimulus to another and another. Just like an underused muscle, the capacity for ignoring can weaken. But when that ignoring muscle is flexed, irrelevant information can be tuned out. There will be little need for switching because tuned-out irrelevant information no longer threatens to grab attention. Appropriate choices for prioritizing can be made. Now the path is cleared for sustained attention.

Sustaining

> The conversation you are having with your two friends on the couch is so engaging that nothing else in the environment distracts you for a good long time. You are now devoting all your attention to this lively three-way conversation.

Sustaining, the process of holding attention on one subject for a significant period of time, is required to effectively complete tasks. Sustaining attention occurs when you have a good level of alertness and are oriented to your context. You have prioritized the stimuli relevant to your task, ignored the irrelevant ones, and avoided switching away from the task at hand.

It is naturally difficult to keep attention on one thing for an extended period of time. The ability to do this varies from person to person and in each individual over time. In infancy, sustained attention can be held for about a minute. By toddlerhood, ten minutes of focusing on one thing can occur.[16] Because the brain is not fully developed until the late twenties, adolescent brains are still wired very similarly to children. Often their brains are unable to work efficiently enough to sustain attention as long as their school and home lives demand.[17]

The adult brain has completed the development process and can work more efficiently. It is better able to avoid distraction, switch less, and sustain attention. There are some adults who still struggle with sustaining attention for prolonged periods of time, such as those suffering from ADHD. Others excel at sustaining attention. For example, professional athletes, surgeons, and chess players have been described as achieving such focused, sustained attention that they enter a flow state of complete absorption in their activity. Artists have also described reaching a flow state when deeply immersed in their craft. Meditation practice is one way to train and exercise sustained attention abilities.

Many factors can affect the process of sustaining attention, including sleep, nutrition, level of alertness, and levels of distraction in the environment. In the remote environment, sustaining attention and limiting the amount of switching can be especially difficult. Some of these difficulties relate to distractors that are different in each person's physical environment.

In a physical space with others, people tend to share the same distractors. If there is a loud noise in the next room, or something interesting is happening out the window, you won't be alone if your attention is diverted. It is likely that many people in the room will switch their attention to the new stimuli, and then the group's attention will eventually refocus. But this is not possible in the remote environment where everyone is in their own digital window. You may be distracted by something in your space while everyone else continues on with the conversation. No one is aware that you have switched your attention, and you can easily lose the thread of the group's conversation as a result.

If you work from home, you likely have more distractions in the form of external stimuli competing for your attention. For example, hearing your children or pets in the next room, regardless of how well or poorly they are behaving, is a distraction. This increases the likelihood that you will switch your attention and have trouble prioritizing the meeting you are leading. Avoiding attention switches can be even trickier if you do not have the luxury of a completely dedicated space in your home for remote work. A repurposed or shared space comes with its own distractions.

Aside from distractors in the physical surroundings, a brand new distraction has been introduced with videoconferencing tools: your own image. Entrepreneur Steve Blank writes,

Before meeting in person, you may do a quick check of your appearance, but you definitely don't hold up a mirror in the middle of a meeting constantly seeing how you look. Yet with the focus on us as much as on the attendees, most video apps seem designed to make us self-conscious and distract from watching who's speaking.[18]

How often do you attend an in-person meeting with a mirror propped up right in front of you? You might glance in a mirror a few times during a typical in-person workday, but in a remote meeting your image is constantly available to you. It can be extremely distracting to see your own face in this way. You stop focusing your attention on those who are speaking, aware only of yourself and the adjustments you want to make to your appearance. When looking at yourself, there is a tendency to evaluate your own facial expressions and then modify them to change how you appear to others.

An educator we spoke with reflects on these distraction issues:

> Digitally mediated formats bring us back into ourselves. They center around you, your digital being, instead of what else is out there, who else to focus your attention on. The default setting on this platform is you see yourself, whereas in person the default setting is never seeing yourself, unless you are in a room of mirrors.

If available, an excellent option is to turn off self-view in the videoconferencing software. This will eliminate the distraction of your own image and keep you from becoming self-conscious. Nevertheless, many people choose not to turn off self-view because they value being aware of how they appear on camera to others.

A consultant commented on his colleagues' distractibility in remote conversations:

> In person, I think people felt like taking their phone out to answer emails in the middle of a meeting would be too obvious and reflect poorly on themselves. When everyone is communicating on a laptop, though, I think people feel they can get other work done without others noticing they are looking at an email and not their colleagues' faces. For me, it's still quite obvious when I notice someone's eyes darting around the screen following their mouse cursor. It's extremely distracting as I'm trying to speak or listen. I've begun addressing it by saying things like "It looks like something came up. Do you need a minute to take care of it?"—which works. It lets them know I noticed without accusing them of doing anything wrong, preventing a defensive response most of the time.

Confined to the Digital Window 41

There are ways the use of digital technology impacts the process of sustaining attention. People often exchange chat messages in a side window and think they are still focused on the content of the main conversation. In reality, they are switching. A professor reflects on how switching occurs when people chat during online classes and remote meetings: "The private chat function can be problematic. I have disabled it and students complain. However, when it is enabled, it can cause them to be distracted. In faculty meetings too, lots of private conversations are going on in the chat window."

For effective sustained attention, switching must necessarily stop. The two are mutually exclusive. If you are working from home surrounded by distractors that are unrelated to work, there are many more temptations to switch back and forth. As long as distractors are present and you engage with them, you are not sustaining attention.

Successfully paying attention requires:

- An optimal level of alertness, neither too sleepy nor too worked up and elevated
- A clear orientation to the surroundings, without the need for frequent reorienting
- The ability to prioritize items in working memory and select the most relevant ones
- The ability to ignore irrelevant stimuli, while still able to notice unexpected stimuli
- The ability to switch attention when it is needed and resist switching when it is not
- The ability to sustain attention on one task for prolonged periods of time

Attention in Remote Environments: A Hard Process Becomes Even Harder

In this chapter, we discussed how the failure to meet the basic requirements for safety and comfort set the stage poorly for focused attention. Attention is a complicated interplay of processes. Understanding what these are can increase awareness of what you are asking of your brain and why some things are more challenging to accomplish. Identifying where attention difficulties are encountered in remote experiences highlights areas where changes could be made to mitigate these challenges.

Humans are wired for safety and comfort. The human brain evolved in dangerous environments, and our species is still hard-wired to feel most comfortable around other humans. This need is not always fully met in remote experiences. If the brain thinks it is alone and responds with alarm, humans feel distressed. It doesn't matter if it is logically unnecessary. This

42 Doing More Together, Feeling Less Connected

feeling of distress can impact all of the six components of attention when working in remote environments.

Alerting, the first of the two preparatory processes of paying attention, gets your system ready to receive and respond to sensory information. If it is consistently difficult for you to maintain the optimal amount of alertness in the remote experience, you won't have a stable baseline for creating a focused experience. Too little alertness leads to sluggishness or sedation. A high level of alertness creates an anxious feeling that is not conducive to focus. When the alertness level is excessively high, it can trigger a full stress response in which calm, productive focus will not be possible.

Safety is required for proper alertness. Alertness is challenging when the hard-wired need for safety is not met. If you are separated from other people and the remote environment does not convince your brain that you are still safe and comfortable, your system will have difficulty staying optimally alert. If your alertness is very low, you more likely feel sluggish or spaced out. If your alertness is very high, you more likely feel hypervigilant or proceed to have a full stress response. Staying alert and assessing your environment for safety is an ongoing process. With fluctuating levels of alertness throughout the day, you might feel frustrated and uncomfortable.

Orienting, the second preparatory process, brings your attention to where you want to focus. Unlike the continuous processes of alerting and assessing for safety, orienting happens in one individual moment. Your brain is skilled at locating people in three-dimensional space based on physical cues that are not present in the remote environment. Information about the people around you that comes only from the flat screen doesn't match what your brain expects. This mismatch causes the need for frequent reorienting throughout the day. For example, you need to reorient when someone speaks or leaves the meeting and faces on the screen change position. Having to reorient frequently is disruptive and tiring, but reorienting is necessary in order to prepare yourself for the four selective attention processes: prioritizing, ignoring, switching, and sustaining.

Prioritizing the stimuli in your environment allows for good focus. When it is not easy to find what is relevant in the environment because it is a flat, digital landscape, the brain will keep scanning. It will act like a searchlight continuously sweeping back and forth across the field of vision, unable to settle on any one thing as the most relevant.

Working memory, temporarily storing and managing a limited amount of information, is normally dedicated to making priority calculations between two things. Without reliable contextual information, inputs can't be filtered properly. Working memory can become flooded with content. Rather than focusing on one thing, it bounces from one focus to the next as it unsuccessfully searches for clues to help prioritize. Prioritizing is more challenging in the flat remote environment and it can be exhausting.

Ignoring irrelevant background information is essential for focused attention. The brain works hard to ignore extraneous stimuli, monitor what might be important, and decide what background information should be allowed in for further processing. These actions can be considerably more challenging in the remote environment. The absence of shared contextual information in remote spaces leaves out information necessary for deciding what is relevant and what is background. The brain gets tired without its ignoring capabilities fully intact, and ends up attending to too much at times and not enough at other times.

Switching attention happens frequently as a result of insufficient prioritizing and ignoring. In remote environments, there is an increase in distractors that come from each person working in a separate environment, instead of in shared spaces with shared stimuli. Missing spatial cues also make it harder to settle on one stimulus. Video platforms introduce many new distractions that result in frequent switching, such as the chat function and the ever-present self-view. Every switch from one stimulus to another takes extra time.

Sustaining attention is the culmination of each of the previous processes functioning properly. It requires that one focus of attention is the priority, the rest are ignored, and switching ceases. Maintaining sustained attention on one focused task is rewarding to the brain. It allows you to get through your day with a sense of direction, and complete the tasks that you set out to accomplish.

In the remote environment, it can be difficult to manage all six components of attention, making periods of sustained attention more rare. Oftentimes, the level of alertness isn't sufficient. Reorienting happens repeatedly. Prioritizing is near impossible. Switching is frequent and ignoring is challenging. All of this results in tasks becoming more difficult for the brain to complete. Putting your brain through this struggle on a daily basis can feel stressful. It is exhausting when each small task is hard.

When tasks are more effortful, stress hormone levels gradually rise. The negative effects of an unresolved stress response build up in your body, depleting your energy over time. A lack of focused attention can snowball into a larger problem, leading to feelings of physical, mental, and emotional exhaustion. This can make it difficult to engage with others in a meaningful way.

Research has confirmed that humans have a strong drive to connect, an essential survival instinct. The human species is not only wired to feel safety and comfort around others, it is also wired to understand others. We have looked at some of the emotional and physical challenges of being situated in a flat, two-dimensional environment where it is possible to feel alone and stressed. There can also be significant cognitive challenges in a remote environment when our intention is to interact in ways that create shared understanding with others.

Human interaction is complex in any environment but the remote environment has unique challenges. We have seen that people face

44 Doing More Together, Feeling Less Connected

attention difficulties simply by being confined to a digital window. Next, we examine what happens when we start interacting with other people in this remote environment.

Go forward, with this in mind:

1 **Basic need:** Safety and comfort.

- The brain's first priority when entering a new environment is to establish safety.
- Focused attention is possible only once a feeling of safety has been established.

2 **Attention**: Your experience is shaped by what you choose to attend to at any given moment.

- There is a limited number of things that you can attend to at any one time.
- Your brain selectively chooses what is relevant in your inner and outer world.

3 **Attention framework**: Attention is a complex interplay of processes.

- Two processes are preparatory—alerting and orienting.
- Four processes are selective—prioritizing, ignoring, switching, and sustaining.

4 **Preparing to pay attention**:

- Alerting—coming into an internal state of mind that is ready to receive sensory information.
- Orienting—moving your focus to a specific location and adjusting to what is going on during the first moments in that new context.

5 **Selective attention**:

- Prioritizing what is relevant
- Ignoring what is not relevant
- Switching from one focus of attention to another
- Sustaining attention on one subject for a significant period of time

6 **People face attention challenges simply by being confined to a digital window.**

Notes

1 James, William. *Principles of Psychology*. New York: Dover Publications, Inc., 1950, 626.

2 Petersen, Steven E. and Michael I. Posner. "The attention system of the human brain: 20 years after." *Annual review of neuroscience* 35 (2012): 73–89, https://doi.org/10.1146/annurev-neuro-062111-150525

3 Raz, Amir. "Anatomy of attentional networks." *The anatomical record Part B: The new anatomist* 281, no. 1 (2004): 21–36, https://doi.org/10.1002/ar.b.20035

4 Sklar, Julia. "'Zoom fatigue' is taxing the brain. Here's why that happens," *National Geographic*, April 24, 2020, www.nationalgeographic.com/science/article/coronavirus-zoom-fatigue-is-taxing-the-brain-here-is-why-that-happens

5 Knudsen, Eric I. "Fundamental components of attention." *Annual review of neuroscience* 30 (2007): 57–78, https://doi.org/10.1146/annurev.neuro.30.051606.094256

6 Ormrod, Jeanne Ellis. *Human Learning.* England: Pearson Education Limited, 2016.

7 Simons, Daniel J., and Christopher F. Chabris. "Gorillas in our midst: Sustained inattentional blindness for dynamic events." *Perception* 28, no. 9 (1999): 1059–1074. doi:10.1068/p281059.

8 Simons, Daniel J. "Inattentional blindness." *Scholarpedia* 2, no. 5 (2007): 3244, www.scholarpedia.org/article/Inattentional_blindness

9 Gandour, J.T. "Tone: Neurophonetics." In *Encyclopedia of Language & Linguistics* (second edition), edited by Keith Brown. Amsterdam: Elsevier, 2006, https://doi.org/10.1016/B0-08-044854-2/04796-9.

10 Moray, N. "Attention in dichotic listening: Affective cues and the influence of instructions." *Quarterly journal of experimental psychology* 11 (1959): 56–60, doi:10.1080/17470215908416289.

11 Nielson, Stevan Lars, and Irwin G. Sarason. "Emotion, personality, and selective attention." *Journal of personality and social psychology* 41, no. 5 (1981): 945–960, doi:10.1037/0022-3514.41.5.945.

12 Kubu, Cynthia and Andre Machado. "Why multitasking is bad for you." *Time*, April 20, 2017, https://time.com/4737286/multitasking-mental-health-stress-texting-depression/

13 Wallis, Claudia. "The multitasking generation." *Time Magazine*, March 19, 2006, http://content.time.com/time/magazine/article/0,9171,1174696,00.html.

14 Levitin, Daniel. *The Organized Mind: Thinking Straight in the Age of Information Overload.* London: Dutton, 2014, 219.

15 Ophir, Eyal, Clifford Nass, and Anthony D. Wagner. "Cognitive control in media multitaskers." *Proceedings of the National Academy of Sciences* 106, no. 37 (2009): 15583–15587, https://doi.org/10.1073/pnas.0903620106

16 Neville, Helen. *Is This a Phase? Child Development & Parent Strategies from Birth to 6 Years.* Seattle, WA: Parenting Press, 2007.

17 Hill, Amelia. "Why teenagers can't concentrate: Too much grey matter." *The Guardian*, May 31, 2010, www.theguardian.com/science/2010/may/31/why-teenagers-cant-concentrate-brains

18 Blank, Steve. "What's missing from Zoom reminds us what it means to be human." Steve Blank (blog). April 27, 2020: paragraph 10, https://steveblank.com/2020/04/27/whats-missing-from-zoom-reminds-us-what-it-means-to-be-human

Chapter 2

Missing the Signals

The human brain is wired to be able to understand others. During infancy, our brains are instinctually driven to work hard to understand other people in order to bond with caregivers. This continues throughout life so we can thrive in our communities. We rely on nonverbal and verbal signals to generate meaning and figure out what others are trying to convey in a social context.

> Shay, who spends most of her days in back-to-back Zoom meetings, described a particular meeting when she was giving feedback to a team member named Ava. While Shay was speaking, Ava's facial expression did not change at all. Shay thought perhaps she had gotten something wrong. After shuffling through her notes to confirm that her information was correct, Shay looked back at the screen and saw that Ava was looking off to the right. She thought Ava was avoiding looking at her and might be about to cry. Shay then asked if Ava was all right. Shay learned that Ava's video had been frozen so she missed all of the introductory remarks. Then Ava had to look to the right at her second monitor to make sure her internet had reconnected securely. Ava apologized for missing the remarks and asked Shay to start over.
>
> Shay reflected on the experience: "The missed signals, like not having full body language, add to my cognitive load. When people are staring at me and I'm trying to figure things out without having information, my brain is guessing but making mistakes. It's jarring and exhausting."

Verbal and nonverbal signals would normally assist Shay in making predictions about how interactions will unfold. Her brain, like all human brains, anticipates what will come next after considering what has come before. Prediction saves the brain time and energy. Unfortunately, in a virtual interaction like Shay and Ava's, many of the signals used for prediction are distorted or missing altogether. Distorted signals like Ava's

DOI: 10.4324/9781003170488-4

frozen expression and eye gaze diverted off to the side were misinterpreted by Shay's brain. They were not accurate representations of Ava's feelings or intentions. Many signals were missing entirely: Shay and Ava didn't enter the same room, use visible hand gestures and other body movements, or look directly at one another.

Perceiving meaning and understanding others has become harder for Shay because interacting virtually takes extra time and concentration. Shay finds herself more exhausted at the end of the day than she used to be, despite working from home and being spared a long commute.

In this chapter, we will first examine how using verbal and nonverbal signals to predict what others mean saves the brain time and energy. Then, we will demonstrate how prediction errors occur when signals are missing or distorted during virtual interactions. Lastly, we will explain the extra work that the human brain has to do to understand others during remote interactions, and why mental fatigue is a common result.

Signals Are Used for Prediction, a Time-Saver and Energy-Saver for the Brain

Humans use verbal and nonverbal signals to communicate. The brain uses these signals to make predictions. For example, when someone is looking directly in your eyes, this gives the appearance that the person is paying attention to you. The brain jumps to this conclusion rather automatically without putting too much thought into it. Similar jumps are made throughout a typical day as the brain processes signals in current experiences and compares them to what it knows from past experiences. By operating based on expectations of what will probably happen next, the brain saves time and energy.

Prediction evolved as a shortcut to aid the energy-intensive process of understanding. It is a way for the brain to stay energy-efficient, using the least number of calculations to come to a conclusion. We will look more closely at the process of understanding to fully appreciate the energy that it requires. This will show why prediction is needed and why it is problematic when it doesn't work as intended.

A vast amount of energy-intensive brain work is required to understand complex human interactions. Millions of extremely fast communication signals and calculations must be made among different brain regions during the process of understanding. Brain cells talk to each other using chemicals that send messages through synapses, the small gaps between cells. They also talk to each other using electrical signals that can travel longer distances, such as the path from the brain all the way down the body to the big toe. All of this is a lot of work and requires a constant energy supply. In fact, a fifth of the body's daily energy supply is devoted to keeping the brain running.

48 Doing More Together, Feeling Less Connected

You can think of energy in this context as a fuel supply which can run out. The body gets energy by consuming food, which is broken down by digestion into energy sources. One byproduct of digestion is carbohydrates that are burned immediately for energy. The brain must receive a constant steady supply of a carbohydrate called glucose, via the bloodstream, to work. You can't function properly when your glucose supply is insufficient. You may have experienced the early consequences of low glucose when you are hungry and feel a bit lightheaded.

We can look at the example of listening to a friend's spoken words to appreciate how extremely complex and energy-intensive it is to understand another human. Your ears transmit the sound of your friend's voice through a complicated pathway that ends at your auditory cortex on the surface of your brain. Your eyes transmit the motions of her face and body. This spatial information is sent via a pathway that ends at your visual cortex. All of these auditory and visual cues coming from your friend need to be assembled together to make a coherent meaning.

The information gathered from the cues goes zipping around different centers of your brain, making connections and comparisons via specialized centers. One center specializes in faces and their meaning, one is designed for receiving and understanding words and nonverbal signals, and another generates words in response. Parts of your memory are accessed. Information is provided from your memory regarding things you know about this friend in particular and about interactions in general, to help determine how you should act. Then there are other distinct neural structures which talk amongst themselves to build a concept of what you imagine your friend might be thinking and feeling, to help you respond appropriately.

Clearly a lot of energy goes into these multitudes of steps. Energy is a precious resource. As the human brain evolved, it was important to conserve energy for procuring food and staying safe. Communicating with one another was also vital to achieve these survival goals, and it was necessary to do this without wasting too much energy.

The theory of predictive processing[1] explains how humans process information in a way that is energy efficient. The brain constantly thinks about the outside world and makes predictions about the incoming information based on what it already knows. It continuously modifies its expectations and seeks out more information as needed when those expectations are not met. You have learned throughout your life to associate signals with the meaning that they represent. These are predictions that help your brain save time and energy. Your brain is a prediction generator that is active throughout your lifetime.

To understand another person and avoid having to newly figure things out each time they are encountered, the brain relies heavily on predictions based on prior knowledge. Throughout a lifetime, these expectations are constantly built upon to create a sort of database about all the things out in the world. Predictions are very useful in the task of understanding others because of the complexity of human interactions. When incoming information about people's actions or behaviors doesn't match with expectations, it is called a prediction error.

Missed Signals Trigger Prediction Error Messages

Humans evolved as social creatures who rely on verbal and nonverbal signals to understand one another. Many nonverbal signals, including body movements (kinesics), interpersonal space (proxemics), touch (haptics), and nuances of the voice (paralanguage) are missed or distorted when interacting virtually. We have to rely more heavily on verbal signals. As a result, it is more difficult to make predictions and the number of prediction errors increases.

"It's not just what you say, it's how you say it." This expression emphasizes the critical importance of both the verbal signals (words spoken) and many nonverbal signals that we respond to during human interactions. Among these nonverbal signals are facial expressions, eye contact, body movement and posture, gestures, speaking rate, and volume. During in-person conversations, the brain derives meaning from the spoken words and many nonverbal cues. These cues help the listener understand what is being conveyed and decide how they might respond.

Listeners will trust nonverbal cues over the actual meaning of the speaker's words when there is ambiguity or an obvious mismatch between these two elements of communication. Researcher Albert Mehrabian emphasized the importance of nonverbal elements of communication. His research focused on how people send and receive feelings or form attitudes of liking or disliking another person. He offered an equation for how humans communicate feelings: 7% words (verbal), 38% tone of voice (nonverbal), and 55% body language (nonverbal). As Mehrabian states, "Generalizing, we can say that a person's nonverbal behavior has more bearing than his words on communicating feelings or attitudes to others."[2]

Many nonverbal cues are missing on a typical video call. The camera is adjusted to have only your head (and sometimes your head and shoulders) fill the screen. Distorted cues, perhaps caused by poor video quality, also occur. You have to fill in the blanks yourself instead of being able to rely on predictions. Missing and distorted nonverbal cues in virtual interactions make it harder to form predictions and easier to make prediction errors.

My Eyes, Your Eyes

Nonverbal communication includes the physical behaviors you use to convey meaning and information to other people. These observable behaviors

50 Doing More Together, Feeling Less Connected

include facial expressions, head movements, hand gestures, physical posture, muscle tensions, breathing patterns, touch, the use of space, and eye contact.

Eye contact is an especially important nonverbal social signal in human interactions. Visually engaging with others who are speaking acknowledges their presence and shows that you care about receiving their message. It can make the people you're talking with feel they can trust you. When speaking to others, you ideally look directly in their eyes for at least a full (short) thought and that usually takes more than a few seconds. This projects confidence and conviction in your ideas, and can convey a host of emotions. Eye contact also plays an important role in maintaining the flow of a conversation and monitoring the interest of the other person.

The experience of mutual eye contact, each person holding the other in the center of their gaze and attention, is so profound that it causes identifiable changes in the brain. When this nonverbal signal that is deeply hardwired into the species is missed, there is a significant cost to its absence. The usual predictions that are made using eye contact signals become more difficult to make, or are made with errors.

Both the appearance of the eyes and the quality of eye contact are important cues that humans use to interpret and predict one another's behavior, often subconsciously. A large body of research has explored different facets of eye contact and how it guides interactions and predictions about others. Research has shown that people are better at remembering the faces of those who are making direct eye contact with them than those with an averted gaze.[3] The brain makes predictions about what faces will be more relevant and useful to remember for later based on information conveyed in gaze direction. When eye contact information is distorted in virtual interactions, these automatic predictions about relevance will be erroneous.

Other research studies have shown that when humans encounter appealing people or things, the pupils dilate; that is, the size of the black central part of the eye gets larger than normal. Larger pupils convey more interest and arousal. Even without prior knowledge of this effect, participants in scientific studies were able to make accurate judgments about the interest level of sample faces that varied only in their amount of pupillary dilation.[4] Participants in paired tasks tended to trust pupil-dilated partners more than undilated ones, and participants' pupils will actually change to match their partners.[5] The brain can't make informed predictions about others as easily when this pupil information is not visible on the screen. Without this shortcut, the brain will either take more time to gather information from other cues or jump to conclusions that can lead to more errors.

Neurologists have found that the brain draws information from both the distance and directness of eye contact to predict the behaviors of others. In one study, a researcher stood at varying distances from the subject and

Missing the Signals 51

measured the intensity of electrical signals coming from the brain. The signal was most intense when the researcher was at a distance of two feet and making direct eye contact. This signal decreased in intensity as the researcher moved further away from the participant. It was always more intense for direct eye contact than indirect eye contact.[6] The brain responds strongly to direct eye contact at a close distance. Predictions about the world will be adversely affected when information about another person's distance or the directness of their eye contact is not available in the remote experience.

During virtual interactions, you are supposed to look directly at the camera and not into another person's eyes on the screen. This gives the appearance that you, the speaker, are connecting with the listeners. But you are not actually looking into their eyes. You also don't know where they are actually looking. If you look directly into the image of their eyes as it appears on the computer screen, they may not be looking back into your eyes. Mutual gaze is virtually impossible. As a result, the benefits of eye contact cannot be experienced.

A consultant reflects on the loss of eye contact in remote meetings: "I miss being able to know if someone is looking at me or not. I now find myself assuming all eyes are on me all the time which is draining. In person, I could make eye contact with someone when something funny happened and know that someone else noticed it too." Most of the information that eye contact is supposed to give the brain to help make informed predictions about others is lost. As a result, people are more prone to making prediction errors.

Errors will be augmented by the technical difficulties that sometimes occur in videoconferencing. Facial expressions, for example, don't always appear clearly enough to convey emotions or indicate intentions. The human face, the most expressive part of the body, may be too far away, too close, not visible at all, or frozen. A person with a fixed image on a screen can appear to be lifeless for a moment.

Further complicating the issue is the intense and unnatural prolonged eye contact in the remote environment. Listeners in an online meeting often stare directly at the speaker for long periods of time, whereas in person they might be sitting side-by-side or looking around the room. For some people, prolonged eye contact can feel extremely uncomfortable. It can be perceived as an aggression and can even activate the fight-or-flight response. Natural compensations, such as adjusting gaze direction or increasing interpersonal distance, are not available.

The Space between Us

In virtual interactions, you perceive your interpersonal and environmental space differently than you do in your in-person interactions. The spatial signals you receive in virtual interactions are either missing or distorted. Since predictions are based on signals, this will lead to more errors.

Picture the space between people on a screen during a video meeting where everyone can be seen from the shoulders up. They appear to be the same distance from one another. The position of the little boxes with individuals inside them can move on the screen. The size of the boxes can even get a little larger when fewer people are present. However, these spatial changes are not based on any active choices you make. The space you would choose to maintain between yourself and others during in-person social interactions would be extremely different.

The cultural anthropologist Edward T. Hall writes in *The Silent Language*, "Spatial changes give a tone to a communication, accent it, and at times, even override the spoken word. The flow and shift of distance between people as they interact with each other is part and parcel of the communication process."[7] Due to missing interpersonal spatial signals in remote interactions, predictions will be harder to make or will result in errors.

Hall's concept of proxemics, described in detail in *The Hidden Dimension*, focuses on how distance and space influence communication and behavior. He identified four distance zones used in human interactions: intimate, personal, social, and public. According to Hall, the amount of distance between those who are communicating varies depending on the proxemic patterns of people in different cultures, personality, and environmental factors. Hall's work shows that the use of space and distance influences human interactions.[8]

However as Robby Nadler, an academic director at the University of California at Santa Barbara, states bluntly, "Try as we might to create physical interactions, virtual space plays by different rules."[9]

Entrepreneur Steve Blank elaborates on the lack of contextual clues in virtual space:

> In the physical world the space and context give you cues and reinforcement. Are you meeting on the 47th floor boardroom with a great view? Are you surrounded by other animated conversations in a coffee shop or sitting with other classmates in a lecture hall? With people working from home you can't tell where the meeting is or how important the location or setting is. In a video conference all the contextual clues are homogenized. You look the same whether you are playing poker or making a sales call, in a suit or without pants.[10]

Interactions in virtual space differ from in-person interactions in many ways. Besides the much smaller distance between people on a video call, side conversations and shared sidelong glances are not possible during virtual interactions. You cannot engage in the rituals of sharing food or drink with others or the shared experience of talking about the temperature of a meeting room. Also, you are not able to use your sense of touch or smell. Without the sense of touch, people miss out on important social bonding reinforcements. These include a reassuring pat on the arm or shoulder and a knowing nudge of an elbow during a shared joke, among others. Without the sense of smell, you miss out on the social information carried in a person's perfume, cologne, or body odor.

In virtual interactions, you lose many nonverbal signals that convey important messages. The human brain cannot simply ignore environmental and spatial information that it thinks is relevant when trying to understand interactions. This is especially true for people from high-context cultures[11] that use an implicit, indirect communication style. They rely heavily on nonverbal cues, body language, and contextual cues that are missing in virtual interactions. The brain will continue to take in the available spatial signals and make faulty predictions based on it. The same applies to vocal signals.

Sounds and Silences

When people interact in the same physical space, their individual voices are separated by distance. Each voice comes from a different place in the room and you can easily identify who is talking when and to whom. In a digital space, all of the virtual voices are heard at the same distance from the listener. Spatial audio cues are missing when all virtual voices emanate from one direction, either through the same speaker or pair of headphones. You are unable to locate a speaker using your ears. Figuring out where people are creates extra work since your auditory system can't predict locations in space as easily as it normally would.

Paralanguage, the elements of speech aside from the words themselves, is an aspect of nonverbal communication that conveys shades of meaning. These elements include speaking pace, pitch, volume, inflection, articulation, and the use of silence, pauses, hesitations, and expressiveness. All of these paralinguistic signals that accompany spoken words help express your attitude and are used consciously or unconsciously to modify meaning, give nuanced meaning, or convey emotions. In virtual interactions, some of these vocal cues are missing or distorted.

Silence, meaning the absence of speech, occurs during in-person interactions when the speaker comes to a full stop. When speakers allow a moment of silence at the ends of sentences, it gives the listeners time to process what has just been said. This increases the impact of the verbal messages. However, in virtual interactions, the silence that listeners receive is not necessarily related to the verbal message at all. It can be difficult to differentiate deliberate silence from unintentional silence caused by internet connection problems. Many people we interviewed commented on the

54 Doing More Together, Feeling Less Connected

difficulty of using humor when there is unintentional silence immediately after telling a joke. Although this silence is usually the result of a sound delay, it causes them to feel uncomfortable and anxious.

A lag in a person's response can also cause the listener to make an incorrect judgment about the speaker. Sound delays of more than 1.2 seconds affect how people think about a speaker. A research study found that long sound delays result in people judging the speaker as less attentive and less conscientious. People tend to incorrectly assign the cause of the delay to personal characteristics of the speaker, rather than technology issues.[12] Your brain does not immediately consider that the cause of a long pause could be a technical issue. Instead, it is more likely to make wrong predictions about speakers and their intentions. These prediction errors cause more work. Building erroneous predictions due to missing or distorted signals during virtual interactions can negatively affect interpersonal relations.

Science Confirms Challenges to Prediction in the Remote Environment

Scientific studies have confirmed that prediction capabilities are flawed in remote environments. One example is a research study in which participants were asked to judge whether a supposed criminal's confession was truthful or not. When reading a confession statement, or listening to an audio recording, participants made fairly accurate predictions of the criminal's truthfulness. But when analyzing video recordings of confessions, their predictions were even worse than the random error rate of simply guessing.[13] It turns out that people are inherently worse at making judgments based on information conveyed by video.

Other studies came to the same conclusion about the difficulty humans have making accurate judgments based on video information. One study showed that videoconferencing participants are more influenced by the personality traits of a speaker, while in-person participants are more influenced by the content of the speech itself.[14] Another found that people in videoconferences were significantly more suggestible and biased when forming social opinions than those listening to information via audio only.[15] These studies, and many others like them, demonstrate that the information transmitted about a speaker via videoconference is not always processed reliably by the human brain.

The brain seems to have trouble with interpreting communication in video interactions despite the vocal and visual signals that are available. "And while the technology allows us to conduct business, see friends and transfer information one-on-one and one-to-many from our homes, there's something missing," writes Steve Blank. "It's just not the same as connecting live at the conference room table, the classroom or local coffee shop. And it seems more exhausting. Why?"[16]

When relying primarily on verbal signals because nonverbal signals are missing or hard to discern in the remote environment, prediction errors are more common. More errors cause your brain to do more work. As a result, you are likely to feel more fatigued and less able to connect virtually with others in a meaningful and satisfying way.

More Mental Work Can Lead to More Mental Fatigue

The Brain Wants Error Resolution

The human brain is very uncomfortable with prediction errors. These are mismatches between previous expectations and objective reality. The brain works hard to resolve prediction errors using two main strategies: internal corrections and external corrections.

Using the internal correction strategy to resolve prediction errors, the brain thinks, "This prediction did not match what I was expecting so the prediction must have been wrong. I will modify it to better match what actually happened." The prediction gets modified and the mental-expectations map is updated to better fit the world it is encountering.

Using the external correction strategy to resolve prediction errors, the brain thinks, "This prediction did not match what I was expecting so the information received must be wrong. I will take action to gather more information so the problem can be resolved." Physical action is taken to clarify the information that is being received. This can be accomplished, for example, by squinting to get a clearer view, looking around for more contextual information, or using language to ask for clarification.

Both strategies provide more information to help the brain resolve prediction errors, but they also cause the brain to do more work. The internal strategy requires a change in thoughts and expectations. The external strategy involves taking entire extra steps to clarify confusing information.

Imagine that you make a comment to a colleague sitting in front of you and there is an awkward silence. Your brain predicted a response and did not receive what was expected. A big error message flashes. Because the brain dislikes errors so much, it will scramble to resolve the discrepancy between the response it expected and what it actually received.

Using the internal strategy would mean changing your own perspective to match the incoming information. You might adjust your thoughts about how you come across or re-examine your words and behavior. You are correcting your internal representation of this interaction. If instead your brain uses the external strategy, you would need to take some additional action to resolve the error. You might continue speaking to try to explain yourself better, or refer to your notes and find where you might have made a mistake.

56   Doing More Together, Feeling Less Connected

Now imagine that this interaction is virtual, and the silence after the comment was due to your colleague's internet dropping for a moment. In this case, it is not an awkward silence and you did not misspeak. However, your brain still has to work hard to resolve the prediction error because it did not get the response it was expecting. By the time your brain goes through all the internal or external strategy steps, your colleague has reconnected to the internet, explained the problem, and continued the conversation. But there was still a momentary discrepancy between the expected response and the one you received. Resolving the discrepancy required extra mental steps that your brain had to take using mental energy.

The human brain is equipped with prediction-generation and error-resolution strategies because they are useful. They developed to save time by building a representation of the surrounding world that is easy to navigate. Understanding others is an energy-intensive process and prediction is intended to make it more efficient. However, prediction errors are more common in virtual interactions. The extra energy required to resolve the errors adds up.

The Brain Is Vulnerable to Overload

More work for the brain caused by an increase in prediction errors is a problem because the brain has limits. It can become overloaded. Cognitive load is a measure of how much processing capacity your brain has at any given moment. Processing new information takes a lot of work and requires the use of working memory, whereas doing things automatically does not. Cognitive overload is the point where the demands being made on the working memory are more than your brain is able to meet. There is no extra room to process or hold more information. Your working memory is pushed to its max.

The potential for getting overloaded makes prediction an essential way for the brain to save energy and mental space. Life is complicated and the brain has a lot to deal with moment-to-moment. Every extra demand that is made on the brain adds up, bringing it closer to overload. In the remote experience, interactions are complex and demands on brain processing are high. The time and energy that can be saved with prediction is precious. Yet with missed and distorted signals, prediction is harder and more likely to be faulty. This means less energy saved, and more time spent correcting the errors.

Tasks can add an intrinsic cognitive load when there is complex new information coming into working memory. A high intrinsic cognitive load might come from the challenge of trying to understand a new language or a technical skill. It involves tracking what you already know and integrating it with new information. Tasks can also add a large extrinsic load.

This refers to the way in which information is presented. The clarity of instructions will determine the level of extrinsic cognitive load. Extrinsic cognitive load might be very high for a remote meeting in which new information is presented in a challenging way. For example, if you are receiving instructions from a colleague with a bad internet connection, you might find that every few words are lost. The video is choppy and her verbal and nonverbal communication is incongruent. This makes the information she is conveying extrinsically more difficult to process.

A high intrinsic cognitive load will be present when information or tasks are new, complex, uncertain, or ambiguous. There will be more of an extrinsic cognitive load when the required information is conveyed in ways that are more difficult to immediately understand. Remote workdays are more populated with situations that increase cognitive load:

- *Videoconferencing.* Decades of research has shown that videoconferencing itself causes a higher cognitive load than other forms of remote communication, such as phone calls.[17]
- *Self-monitoring.* A recent study suggests that watching yourself on camera throughout a workday increases cognitive load in several ways. Self-monitoring of your own expressions and actions, the sense of being watched, and the presence of one's own image in the video field all take extra mental energy. The researchers found an increased amount of fatigue during camera-on days compared to camera-off days. The fatigue effect from self-focus and self-evaluation was strongest in this study in women and new hires. These are two populations that often feel additional pressure to achieve a desired impression on others.[18]
- *Overcompensation.* In virtual interactions, your cognitive load is further increased by the acts of overcompensation that often occur to make up for prediction errors. One way that people overcompensate is to emote more than usual. People also tend to speak 15% louder on video calls to make up for missing cues.[19] All overcompensating behaviors increase the cognitive load as they present more for the brain to work on. This requires a lot of energy.
- *Technology updates.* Frequent technology updates mean there is almost always something new to learn about communication technology tools. A professor told us about the extra work she had to do during Zoom class sessions to find her teaching assistant among the 62 boxes on the screen. This added task was a direct consequence of the technology, since the teaching assistant's location would have been easy to find in a physical classroom. Having to scan all the boxes on the screen to find a specific person increased her cognitive load. Later in the semester, the professor learned that it was possible to move the

on-screen boxes to any location. She put her teaching assistant's box alongside hers so she didn't have to spend time searching for him on the screen. The location issue was resolved by learning a new way to navigate the technology. However, both the problem and the solution added to the professor's cognitive load in a way that would not have occurred were she in a physical classroom.

- *False conclusions and misunderstandings.* People rely on predictive processing more in virtual interactions when nonverbal signals are limited. Shortcuts are necessary to prevent cognitive overload but can lead to false conclusions about someone's intentions on a video call. The tendency toward false inferences and assumptions due to limited information can lead to misunderstandings and miscommunications, which need to be sorted out. This can end up causing much more work in the long run.

These cognitive load issues are reflected in the experiences of many people we interviewed who work and learn remotely:

> Participants losing internet connection causes disruptions for learning and is one more thing to think about for the instructor. I find teaching remotely especially exhausting.
>
> —Corporate trainer

> There's so much lost in the virtual experience. You feel like you're not actually bringing 100% of yourself. That makes me uncomfortable. It's exhausting. I feel like I'm performing and inauthentic.
>
> —Graduate student

> It feels so much more exhausting to be on video calls all day than to sit in an office and move around to different meetings.
>
> —Advertising executive

> Having my camera on hastened my Zoom fatigue because I spent so much mental energy being hyperaware that I was on camera.
>
> —Graduate student

> Processing virtual interactions takes more work and energy. We get fatigued because there are less cues that are relevant here, but our brains are still processing.
>
> —Professor

When working memory is at capacity, there is no leftover cognitive load. This can lead to a state of cognitive overload for a majority of the day, which will cause feelings of mental exhaustion. Cognitive overload

Missing the Signals 59

happens more often in virtual interactions when our brains have more to juggle. Just one more task, big or small, might be insurmountable to take on. The brain says, "I can't." It has already hit the limits of its capacity. There is no working memory space left. There is no cognitive load left to even think about other tasks. You are maxed out and fatigue sets in as a result.

Running on Empty

Mental fatigue is perceived as a subjective sense of tiredness that usually occurs after prolonged periods of cognitive overload. According to a multitude of studies, mental fatigue is often accompanied by decreased commitment or unwillingness to continue the present activity, and decreased performance.[20] This research shows that mental fatigue can have numerous consequences, including difficulties in concentrating, planning, adapting to adversity, sustaining attention, ignoring irrelevant stimuli, avoiding errors, and correcting mistakes.

As Daniel Goleman explains in *Focus: The Hidden Driver of Excellence,*

> Tightly focused attention gets fatigued—much like an overworked muscle—when we push to the point of cognitive exhaustion. The signs of mental fatigue, such as a drop in effectiveness and a rise in distractedness and irritability, signify that the mental effort needed to sustain focus has depleted the glucose that feeds neural energy.[21]

The brain, which has a finite energy supply, chooses wisely what is worth engaging with and what is not worth the energy it will require.

Think of your brain's energy supply like a car's gas tank that gets used throughout the day. Your brain is always making calculations to protect its energy supply. It has to weigh the energy required for each action and decide if it is worth the expected benefits. At the beginning of the day, on a full tank of gas, this is easy decision-making. But as your tank gets emptier, your brain must be more discerning. If the expected rewards of an activity are low, your brain will be less willing to use up gas.

An expected reward could be a paycheck, a promotion, or feelings of purpose and mastery. A reward can also come in the avoidance of negative outcomes, such as getting fired, letting down colleagues, or feeling shame. Some activities will provide their own rewards, such as enjoyable or fun tasks. The significance of the reward, not the time spent on an activity, is what determines when fatigue occurs. One person could go all day long on a rewarding, engaging job and leave it with a decent amount of gas left in the tank. Another person might slog through unrewarding work for only a few hours and feel completely spent. The difference is in the reward.

60 Doing More Together, Feeling Less Connected

Scientific studies have confirmed that rewarding work leads less often to mental fatigue, while unrewarding work can lead quickly to mental fatigue regardless of duration.[22]

This important link between rewarding feelings at work and susceptibility to mental fatigue is vital to consider in the remote experience. Many of the rewarding parts of work come in the form of mutual understanding and feeling connected to colleagues. These more fulfilling aspects are affected when signals are missed and distorted in virtual interactions. The gas tank will tend to be less filled up with rewards. At the same time, the energy required for action is much higher in the remote experience because the brain has a lot more work to do. The gas is burned through more quickly in the course of the day. Fewer rewards and more work mean fatigue will be reached earlier in a workday.

Mental fatigue happens when your brain decides that any additional effort is not worth the gas it will require. The gas tank is too close to empty and none of the rewards are appealing enough to convince the brain to use up more gas. Working through your fatigue feels grueling because you are trying to push forward when your brain has already decided that it has no capacity for further action. It is like getting out of a car that has run out of gas, and commencing to push it down the road.

It is worth noting that fatigue can operate in unexpected ways. At times, you might have experienced fatigue suddenly disappearing or reappearing. If something comes up later in the day that you are very excited about, such as going to a social engagement or hearing an inspiring speaker, that high reward will provide a bit of extra gas. You feel reinvigorated and your brain is suddenly ready for action. If you encounter trouble, you will also get a burst of energy in the form of adrenaline. But adrenaline-driven energy will be short-lived and followed by even deeper fatigue when you are left with an empty tank after the trouble is over.

The fact that fatigue can be overridden by highly appealing or highly stressful things has important implications. It confirms the reality that fatigue is not simply running out of energy. Fatigue is a decision your brain makes and a message it sends to the rest of your body to stop, rest, and recover. Yet it is a message that is often ignored. If it were the legs that were being pushed to their capacity, the muscles would collapse and there would be no choice but to stop. The brain, however, doesn't have the option to collapse and stop action. Because the brain can never fully stop action, collapse is instead experienced as the sensation of fatigue. The reaction to the fatigue message is often to drink more coffee and push through it.

Mental fatigue will affect not only mental performance, but also physical performance. For example, in a 2009 study Samuele Marcora and colleagues tested performance on a stationary bike in two groups of subjects. The test group performed a mentally challenging task for 90 minutes.

The control group watched an emotionally neutral movie for 90 minutes. Then both groups were put on bikes. The results clearly showed that the mentally taxed people reached a state of physical exhaustion on the bikes faster than the control group.[23] The brain's fatigue message applies to both mental and physical activities that draw on the same supply of gas.

An Empty Gas Tank in the Remote Experience

An academic administrator told us about feeling exhausted after trying to connect with others during Zoom calls:

> I believe that every human has at least one superpower. I think that my superpower lies in connecting with people. When I meet someone, or a group of people, I'm often able to pick up on spoken and unspoken cues that can help build rapport (in most cases, at least). Before remote work, I never realized how much I rely on live, in-person communication to activate my connection powers. The Zoom world quickly exposed me. While on a webcam, I would often strain incredibly hard to pick up on the same cues that used to come so naturally during face-to-face interactions. To the contrary, I found myself absolutely exhausted after a day of Zoom calls, where I used to feel energized after in-person meetings (in most cases, at least).

As social creatures, we are wired for understanding other people. During virtual interactions, we often search so hard for missing signals that our brains can get overloaded and fatigued. As a result, we feel drained, frustrated, and exhausted. Entrepreneur Steve Blank writes,

> We're exhausted because of the extra cognitive processing (fancy word for having to consciously do extra thinking) to fill in the missing 50% of the conversation that we'd normally get from nonverbal and olfactory cues. It's the accumulation of all these missing signals that's causing mental fatigue.[24]

The term "Zoom fatigue" was coined when remote work became the norm during the COVID-19 pandemic. It describes the mental fatigue and exhaustion associated with overusing virtual communication platforms. Zoom fatigue can be experienced in many ways. It has been described as fogginess, tiredness, intense worry, and brain overload. It can lead to less productivity, less effective learning, and less satisfying interactions.

In an editorial review article on the subject, Dr. Brenda Wiederhold describes the experience of leaving yet another remote meeting: "You click 'Leave Meeting' and blink, bleary-eyed from yet another video call. It was only an hour long, just like the in-person meeting you used to have each

62 Doing More Together, Feeling Less Connected

week, but gathering online has left you tired and irritable, ready to swear off the internet for good."[25]

Social scientists have pointed out that the way we interact virtually is altering the instinctual and fine-tuned way of communicating that humans developed in order to survive.[26] Humans are wired to connect with one another.

Meeting the human needs for safety and comfort, understanding, and belonging are what has allowed our species to survive and thrive. We will look next at how humans are wired for belonging and how virtual group dynamics affect our remote experience.

Go forward, with this in mind:

1 **Basic need**: Understanding other human beings

- The human brain is constantly processing incoming sensory information.
- Humans are social creatures who rely on verbal and nonverbal signals to convey messages and understand one another.

2 **Prediction**: Energy-intensive brain work is required to understand human interactions.

- Generating predictions is a brain function designed to save energy.
- Your brain makes predictions about what it expects from people based on previous experience.

3 **Prediction errors**: Missed or distorted signals can result in prediction errors.

- Scientific literature confirms that prediction errors are more frequent when interacting on video platforms than when interacting in person.
- Resolving prediction errors involves more work for the brain.

4 **Cognitive load**: This is a measure of how much processing capacity your brain has at any given moment.

- Cognitive overload happens when the demands being made on your brain are more than it is able to process.
- Virtual interactions take more work and extra energy that can cause fatigue.

5 **Fatigue**: Mental fatigue occurs after prolonged periods of cognitive overload.

- Mental fatigue affects physical functioning as well.
- Zoom fatigue refers to the exhaustion caused by overuse of virtual platforms of communication, particularly videoconferencing, that overtaxes the brain.

- Feeling foggy, anxious, irritable, and mentally drained results in less productivity, less effective learning, and less satisfying interactions.

Notes

1 For a review see: Hutchinson, J. Benjamin, and Lisa Feldman Barrett. "The power of predictions: An emerging paradigm for psychological research." *Current directions in psychological science* 28, no. 3 (2019): 280–291.
2 Mehrabian, Albert. *Silent Messages*. Belmont, CA: Wadsworth Publishing Company, 1971, 44.
3 Mason, Malia, Bruce Hood, and C. Neil Macrae. "Look into my eyes: Gaze direction and person memory." *Memory* 12, no. 5 (2004): 637–643, doi:10.1080/09658210344000152.
4 Lick, David J., Clarissa I. Cortland, and Kerri L. Johnson. "The pupils are the windows to sexuality: Pupil dilation as a visual cue to others' sexual interest." *Evolution and human behavior* 37, no. 2 (2016): 117–124, https://doi.org/10.1016/j.evolhumbehav.2015.09.004.
5 Kret, M.E., A.H. Fischer, and C.K.W. De Dreu. "Pupil mimicry correlates with trust in in-group partners with dilating pupils." *Psychological science* 26, no. 9 (2015): 1401–1410, https://doi.org/10.1177/0956797615588306.
6 Gale, Anthony, Graham Spratt, Antony J. Chapman, and Adrian Smallbone. "EEG correlates of eye contact and interpersonal distance." *Biological psychology* 3, no. 4 (1975): 237–245, https://doi.org/10.1016/0301-0511(75)90023-X.
7 Hall, Edward Twitchell. *The Silent Language*. India: Doubleday, 1990, 175.
8 Hall, Edward Twitchell and Edmund T. Hall. *The Hidden Dimension*. London: Doubleday, 1966.
9 Nadler, Robby. "Understanding 'Zoom fatigue': Theorizing spatial dynamics as third skins in computer-mediated communication." *Computers and composition* 58 (2020), https://doi.org/10.1016/j.compcom.2020.102613.
10 Blank, Steve. "What's missing from Zoom reminds us what it means to be human." Steve Blank (blog). April 27, 2020: paragraph 6, https://steveblank.com/2020/04/27/whats-missing-from-zoom-reminds-us-what-it-means-to-be-human
11 Anthropologist Edward T. Hall classifies cultures as high context and low context. In high context cultures, communication is mostly in the setting, not in the words. Meaning can be found in the use of space and nonverbal signals, such as silence and gesture. In low-context cultures, communication is mostly transmitted in words.
12 Schoenenberg, Katrin, Alexander Raake, and Judith Koeppe. "Why are you so slow? Misattribution of transmission delay to attributes of the conversation partner at the far-end." *International journal of human-computer studies* 72, no. 5 (2014): 477–487 https://doi.org/10.1016/j.ijhcs.2014.02.004
13 Bradford, Deborah, Jane Goodman-Delahunty, and Kevin R. Brooks. "The impact of presentation modality on perceptions of truthful and deceptive confessions." *Journal of criminology* (2013), http://dx.doi.org/10.1155/2013/164546
14 Ferran, Carlos and Stephanie Watts. "Videoconferencing in the field: A heuristic processing model." *Management science* 54, no. 9 (2008): 1565–1578. doi:10.1287/mnsc.1080.0879.
15 Hinds, Pamela J. "The cognitive and interpersonal costs of video." *Media psychology* 1, no. 4 (1999): 283–311, https://doi.org/10.1207/s1532785xmep0104_1
16 Blank, Steve. "What's missing from Zoom reminds us what it means to be human." Steve Blank (blog). April 27, 2020: paragraph 4, https://steveblank.com/2020/04/27/whats-missing-from-zoom-reminds-us-what-it-means-to-be-human

17 For a review see: Ferran, Carlos and Stephanie Watts. "Videoconferencing in the field: A heuristic processing model." *Management science* 54, no. 9 (2008): 1565–1578. doi:10.1287/mnsc.1080.0879.

18 Shockley, Kristen M., Allison S. Gabriel, Daron Robertson, Christopher C. Rosen, Nitya Chawla, Mahira L. Ganster, and Maira E. Ezerins. "The fatiguing effects of camera use in virtual meetings: A within-person field experiment." *Journal of Applied Psychology* 106, no. 8 (2021): 1137.

19 Croes, Emmelyn A.J., Marjolijn L. Antheunis, and Alexander P. Schouten. "Social attraction in video-mediated communication: The role of nonverbal affiliative behavior." *Journal of social and personal relationships* 36, no. 4 (2019): 1210–1232, https://doi.org/10.1177/0265407518757382

20 For a review see: Habay, Jelle, Jeroen Van Cutsem, Jo Verschueren, Sander De Bock, Matthias Proost, Jonas De Wachter, Bruno Tassignon, Romain Meeusen, and Bart Roelands. "Mental fatigue and sport-specific psychomotor performance: A systematic review." *Sports medicine* 51 (2021): 1527–1548, https://doi.org/10.1007/s40279-021-01429-6

21 Goleman, Daniel. *Focus: The Hidden Driver of Excellence*. New York: Harper, 2013, 56.

22 For a review see: Boksem, Maarten A.S., and Mattie Tops. "Mental fatigue: Costs and benefits." *Brain research reviews* 59, no. 1 (2008): 125–139.

23 Marcora, Samuele M., Walter Staiano, and Victoria Manning. "Mental fatigue impairs physical performance in humans." *Journal of applied physiology* 106, no. 3 (2009): 857–864.

24 Blank, Steve. "What's missing from Zoom reminds us what it means to be human." Steve Blank (blog). April 27, 2020: paragraph 17, https://steveblank.com/2020/04/27/whats-missing-from-zoom-reminds-us-what-it-means-to-be-human

25 Wiederhold, Brenda K. "Connecting through technology during the coronavirus disease 2019 pandemic: Avoiding 'Zoom fatigue.'" *Cyberpsychology, behavior, and social networking* 23, no. 7 (July 10, 2020): 437–438, https://doi.org/10.1089/cyber.2020.29188.bkw, 437.

26 Morris, Betsy. "Why does Zoom exhaust you? Science has an answer." *The Wall Street Journal*, May 27, 2020, http://wsj.com/articles/why-does-zoom-exhaust-you-science-has-an-answer-11590600269

Chapter 3

Lost in the Group

Humans have an evolutionary need to belong to a group. We can trace the human need to belong back to our prehistoric ancestors. Living in small groups and sharing jobs like hunting and gathering were essential for survival and safety. A person alone was unlikely to last very long. As social creatures, belonging was and always will be necessary for our survival.

There are very few people in modern society who are not a member of some social, familial, occupational, or other group. Jane Howard writes in *Families*, "Call it a clan, call it a network, call it a tribe, call it a family. Whatever you call it, whoever you are, you need one. You need one because you are human."[1] This is how the human species evolved. The pressures of survival dictated that certain beneficial qualities would be favored and carried on through the generations. One of these qualities was the ability to work cooperatively with others in a group. Although human beings in modern times have the means to survive safely on their own, the basic need to belong is a deep-seated drive that has not gone away.

> Shay feels that her team doesn't connect well in remote meetings. Some of her team members are not contributing as much as they had in person, or are silent during entire meetings. Other team members are outspoken and seem to carry the conversation in every meeting. She is told privately by one of her team members that he is feeling unseen and lost in the group. He feels uncertain about when to jump in and make it known that he's ready to contribute. Shay knows that she has to make some changes so that all her team members feel as psychologically safe in remote meetings as they did when meetings were in person. She recognizes that creating a more positive team climate and ensuring that all her team members feel a sense of belonging is necessary.

Belonging, a personal experience associated with the longing to connect with others, has been studied by scientists from a variety of fields. They have looked at how people function in groups and teams, as well as how belonging is essential for our psychological and physical health. We will

DOI: 10.4324/9781003170488-5

66 Doing More Together, Feeling Less Connected

look at the human brain's evolutionary adaptations to facilitate bonding and belonging, and consider how they can sometimes serve us poorly in virtual interactions. The consequences of insufficient trust and a lack of psychological safety in groups will also be discussed. In the final part of this chapter, we will examine the elements of burnout and outline ways that you can identify burnout in yourself and others.

Social Is the Brain's Resting State

Belonging is critical to our survival. Scientific studies show that the human brain's preferred state from birth onward is to be socially connected with others.

Affective neuroscientist James Coan's Social Baseline Theory explains that thinking about social issues is the human brain's resting baseline. "The human brain *expects* access to relationships characterized by interdependence, shared goals, and joint attention." Coan goes on to describe what happens when this baseline of belonging to a group is disturbed. The sense of being alone requires more mental and physical work "as the brain perceives fewer available resources and prepares the body to either conserve or more heavily invest its own energy."[2]

The idea that belonging with others in a group is the brain's resting state receives support from neuroscientific research and numerous brain imaging studies. Social cognitive neuroscientist Matthew Lieberman and others have discovered that there is a region of the brain that spends most of its time on social thinking, or thoughts about the self or others. It is called the default mode network (DMN). In his book *Social: Why We Are Wired to Connect*, Lieberman offers examples to show how the DMN prefers social thinking over all other kinds of activity. He shows how the human brain enters a default state when it's at rest, engaging in thoughts about other people and relationships.[3]

One of Lieberman's studies examined the brain activation patterns in infants. He found that they tend to have thoughts about self or others whenever they're not actively engaged with anything else. This is remarkable since infants don't yet understand social interaction and they can barely discern a face. The fact that infants are automatically thinking socially provides compelling evidence that it is the default state of the system from day one. Humans are born to belong. Another of Lieberman's studies looked at where people's minds wandered to when they were participating in an experiment with a specific task. With only seconds-long breaks between tasks, the participants' thoughts were expected to be on what they just did or were about to do. Instead, in those seconds of rest, their brain patterns showed that they went directly to social thinking. Lieberman's data show that thinking about others "is the brain's preferred state of being, one that it returns to literally the second it has a chance."[4]

Even when people are physically apart, they are still driven to seek a sense of togetherness and connectedness. To connect with others in a group or team involves forming bonds, feeling interpersonal trust, and being in a climate of psychological safety.

We Belong Together but Can Feel Apart

Individuals satisfy their need for belonging by joining groups. When group members can effectively work together, they can achieve goals that might not be possible by working alone. This requires building bonds between the people in the group or team.

Forming Social Bonds

Driven by social brains that do not want to be alone, there are basic ways that humans bond with one another. Some of these, including meeting eyes, listening to and looking at the same things, and sharing physical space are not available in the remote environment. This can make bonding more challenging when most interactions are virtual.

Chatting casually with someone when walking down the hall to get a cup of coffee isn't just wasting time. Chemicals in our social brain, including oxytocin, endorphins, and dopamine, are released in response to this and many other encounters with other people throughout the day. These brain chemicals influence the individual's willingness to bond.

Oxytocin is dedicated to ensuring that social bonding will happen. It keeps you feeling relaxed and comfortable when you interact with other people. Best known for its role in childbirth and maternal bonding, oxytocin is important for bonding in many other situations as well. Levels of oxytocin increase when engaging in activities such as connecting with other people, walking outside, listening to relaxing music, laughing, and helping others. Direct eye contact with other human beings causes a surge of oxytocin.

Most people have a natural aversion to getting too close to a stranger. In order to form new relationships, oxytocin helps overcome this aversion by promoting closeness and bonding. To prove this idea, researchers at the University of Zurich tested the effect of oxytocin on trust levels during an experimental trust-based game that simulated risky investing. They found that by giving people extra oxytocin, trust levels increased among participants.[5]

Another role of oxytocin is to moderate the amygdala, the orchestrator of the fight-or-flight response. While a variety of regions across the brain and body act in concert during the fight-or-flight response, the amygdala is in charge of emotions. Its primary role is to pick up on strong emotions like fear, activating the release of the stress hormone norepinephrine. Norepinephrine increases the vigilance level of the whole brain. By calming the fight-or-flight response, oxytocin reduces this vigilance and makes it safer and more comfortable to form human bonds. Oxytocin augments the positive feelings of being with others and motivates people to interact socially.

While oxytocin helps initial bonding, endorphins help to maintain long-term relationships. To ensure that humans stay with the people they've bonded with, endorphins produce a euphoric feeling. Endorphins provide the added benefit of reducing the perception of pain. Many people experience euphoria from increased levels of endorphins during exercise. Endorphins can create the same feeling of excitement and happiness when a person bonds with others.

Belonging is also reinforced by dopamine, a brain chemical which sends messages like, "This feels good, we should do it again!" Dopamine makes experiences rewarding and motivates a lot of what people do socially. It can affect our experience of the world by first alerting us to what might be interesting and then motivating us to act on it. Dopamine is also what makes humans crave things when they are not available, including other people. Researchers at MIT looked at the small dopamine-rich region deep in the brain that causes humans to crave food when hungry. They were curious if this area would respond to ten hours of social isolation in the same way it responded to food deprivation. They did in fact find that an isolated person craves social interactions in a way similar to how a hungry person craves food.[6]

Sitting alone in front of a screen does not activate these brain chemicals the same way that three-dimensional human interactions would. Working in a remote environment can make bonding more difficult, especially when establishing new relationships. New relationships require building and earning mutual trust and respect.

Without the physical presence of other familiar people or direct eye contact with others, less oxytocin will be released. Lower oxytocin levels mean a more reactive fight-or-flight system and more hypervigilance. This negatively impacts the willingness to trust and the ability to feel empathy for others. Naturally circulating endorphins will be lower during a day spent at a computer, alone in a room without socializing during coffee breaks or in-person work events. Dopamine will be lower without the small natural rewards of in-person interactions throughout the day.

These difficulties with bonding are unique to the remote experience. The limited availability of chemical messengers makes it more challenging to form bonds in groups. If group members cannot establish a bond, it is hard for their brains to get on the same wavelength.

Brain-to-Brain Synchrony

When people are socially connected and oxytocin levels are high, individuals' brainwave patterns actually begin to resemble one another. Neuroscientists have found that the higher the oxytocin levels of individuals in a group, the more likely their brains will be to synchronize.[7]

Research studies have shown that group members whose brains exhibit synchrony perform better.[8] Interacting brains do not operate on a completely individual basis, rather they influence each other. To visualize the synchrony effect, imagine a rowing team sitting in line with their oars in the water. All the rowers are aware of each other and work at the same rhythm to propel the boat in the same direction through the water. It is the same when people are together, matching rhythms and aware of the same things in the environment. Their brains synchronize.

Numerous studies have been conducted in a variety of contexts to understand how brains sync as people interact. Suzanne Dikker, a research scientist at the NYU Department of Psychology, studied the electrical activity in the brains of multiple students while they participated in their high school biology class. She and her colleagues found several interesting correlations between the matching up of students' brainwaves and their behaviors in the classroom. More synchrony was observed when students were more engaged in the material, and felt positive about their teacher and the other students. Synchrony was higher in the students who had interacted with each other just before the class. Importantly, students who exhibited synchronous activity with their classmates had better focus, felt more connected to the group, and had more empathy.[9] These conclusions have important implications for how to engage students and can be generalized to many types of work groups.

Neuroscientist Uri Hasson of Princeton used brain scans to examine brain synchrony of the speaker and the listener during storytelling. He found evidence that the brain of the speaker and the brain of the listener exhibit similar activation patterns. The more their two brains were aligned, the more the listener comprehended the story.[10]

Synchronized brains have even been shown to provide each other with more comfort and reduce each other's pain. This demonstrates just how powerful an effect connection with others can have on an individual. To show this, social neuroscientist Simone Shamay-Tsoory looked at brain electricity readouts of pairs of people to see how they responded when one was given a mildly painful stimulus. She found that there was a matching pattern of brainwaves in both participants, the one who was in pain and the one who was comforting. The better the pair knew each other, the more strongly their brains synchronized. And the more their brains synchronized, the less pain they felt from the stimulus.[11] The human brain is built to synchronize with other brains.

Many of the behaviors that affect the phenomenon of brain-to-brain synchrony are not possible during virtual interactions. For example, it is not possible to look into someone's eyes and know that they are looking back into yours. It is also difficult to experience joint attention, the experience of two people looking at and responding to the same thing at the same time. As a result, it will be significantly harder to achieve brain synchrony when working virtually in groups. Group cohesion and performance then suffer.

Like social bonds and synchrony, the element of trust has a major impact on group functioning because it provides a sense of safety with others. Trust enables members of groups and teams to feel comfortable opening up, taking moderate risks, and relying on others to respect their ideas.

Building Trust

Trust enables the individual in a group or team to be honest, expose vulnerabilities, ask for help if needed, and give others the benefit of the doubt. More people can get more done efficiently when individuals trust one another to contribute part of the work. Trust is a feeling that convinces the brain to take the risk of being open and honest.

Patrick Lencioni, an American management consultant, believes that teamwork without trust is all but impossible. In his book *The Five Dysfunctions of a Team*, he identifies the absence of trust as the first dysfunction teams need to overcome. If this dysfunction is allowed to flourish, teamwork deteriorates. When there is an absence of trust, the other dysfunctions follow: fear of conflict, lack of commitment, avoidance of accountability, and inattention to results. According to Lencioni, trust is the foundation of teamwork. Once trust is established, team members can: speak their opinions and have candid debates, disagree when making a decision and then commit to the decision once it is made, hold each other accountable to team standards, and focus on the team's results.

Trusting team members genuinely admit to weakness or error and ask for help. They offer feedback and support to others, and accept feedback and support from others. Trusting team members recognize and tap into others' strengths, and importantly give each other the benefit of the doubt before jumping to a conclusion. When trust is present, team members are able to depend on each other, collaborate, and achieve goals.

Trust is essential for team success. A professor we interviewed discussed distributed work teams:

> I had students in California, Jamaica, London, and different parts of China, all time zones. I said to them, "Some of you have never met each other. Some of you will never meet each other. What are the things that you need? What's important now that you are in distributed work teams?" Ultimately, the teams that functioned best and had the best deliverables were the ones who developed their own strategies to build trust.

Lencioni differentiates predictive trust, which requires knowing or working together over time, from vulnerability-based trust. Being vulnerable runs counter to what many people learn in the course of their career advancement and education. Many people learn to look out for their own interests and be protective of their reputations. Rather than show vulnerability, they cover up weaknesses, mistakes, and failures. They also avoid asking for help when it's needed. In contrast, Lencioni encourages team members to be willing to make mistakes and acknowledge their vulnerability. Understanding the vulnerability of team members and trusting that it won't be used against them is the first step to building a great team.[12]

There are two main factors that make it harder to build trusting relationships among team members in remote environments: lower oxytocin levels when people are physically apart and higher cognitive loads during virtual interactions.

When you are not working with others in the same physical space, there is less oxytocin circulating. Typically, oxytocin levels increase when someone trusts you. Then, in turn, your higher oxytocin levels make it more likely you will trust others.[13] This chain reaction of trust leading to more trust, facilitated by oxytocin, occurs less readily in virtual interactions.

Social bonding and building trust can feel forced in a remote environment where conversations only occur when they are scheduled. Formally requested virtual meetings lack the spontaneity of an in-person encounter. In contrast, being in-person and bouncing an idea off someone in the hallway is likely to make them feel confided in and trusted. As a result of being trusted by another person, the colleague's oxytocin levels will increase. Then this makes it more likely that the colleague will trust someone else, perhaps turning to them for help later that day and continuing the chain reaction of trust.

The lack of casual, spontaneous conversations was a common complaint we heard when we spoke to people about their remote experiences:

> I feel somewhat disconnected from most of my colleagues, particularly ones I didn't know in the office. I think this must have to do with the lack of "water cooler" talk. I don't know anything about most of their lives. When we get on a video call for a meeting, we have a set amount of time to accomplish what we are there for and the culture of my company is not to waste any time. Small talk seems more strained in these conversations even than they do with strangers who I've spoken with in person.
>
> —Advertising executive

> One of the biggest downsides to remote work for me has been the challenge of connecting with people both in depth and breadth. The informal interactions I used to have simply passing by a conversation

72 Doing More Together, Feeling Less Connected

in the hall and joining in are a thing of the past. Conversations typically only happen when scheduled as meetings and the ability to overhear something relevant to me and join a conversation physically can't happen anymore.

—Consultant

I just feel isolated, like I'm working alone. There are all these different things I'd usually be bouncing ideas off other people about—and yet that doesn't exist. In order to get feedback on anything, I have to make some kind of formal appointment to discuss it.

—Healthcare worker

The challenges of understanding one another virtually can interfere with building trust because it increases our cognitive load. That same healthcare worker reported, "Just today alone I've had to send several emails that would have been a simple five second question in the office." Rather than quick in-person conversations, each virtual interaction carries the additional cognitive load of attending to a computer screen, opening an email account, translating thoughts into words, and formatting a readable email. As these cognitive demands add up over the course of a workday, there is less processing capacity left over in the brain to consider whether to give someone the benefit of the doubt and decide to trust them.

Without increases in oxytocin for bonding and sufficient mental capacity to analyze whether it is safe to be open with others, it will be difficult to feel trust. Despite this difficulty, it is extremely important to establish team trust. Research shows that trust among team members improves performance,[14] and trust is especially necessary in groups that meet virtually.[15]

Building a climate of trust and respect facilitates a sense of acceptance and belonging among team members. They feel free to share their ideas, questions, and even mistakes. High performing teams need psychological safety.

Psychological Safety in Work Groups and Teams

Psychological safety is defined by researcher and Harvard Business School Professor Amy Edmondson as "the belief that the environment is safe for interpersonal risk taking." She explains that in a psychologically safe environment, "people feel able to speak up when needed—with relevant ideas, questions, or concerns—without being shut down in a gratuitous way. Psychological safety is present when colleagues trust and respect each other and feel able, even obligated, to be candid."[16]

Whereas trust is established when an individual gives others the benefit of the doubt, psychological safety is a climate the group establishes to support individuals to freely express themselves. It can be fostered by a team leader, but ultimately is created by the way members of a work group or team behave toward one another. Psychological safety is the group members' shared belief that they can have challenging conversations, be vulnerable in front of each other, and be themselves without fear of negative consequences. Research has shown that psychological safety among teams results in a greater willingness to acknowledge mistakes and learn from them, as well as confront difficult issues and find solutions to them.[17]

We spoke to a graduate student about her negative experience in a professional development program that lacked a culture of psychological safety:

> The program asked you to be very open and vulnerable in a group setting, but a safe environment cannot be created out of thin air. I felt that the moderator, who was integral in making that environment psychologically safe, was uncomfortable herself and visibly nervous. At first, it provoked me to want to comfort her. But when I shared a problem, she responded with such a lack of compassion that I realized I could no longer be psychologically safe sharing vulnerable things in front of her. As a result, I quit the program. I would have been fine continuing the work with the other participants but I couldn't trust her.

To discover the key traits that effective teams share, researchers at Google conducted a two-year study they called Project Aristotle. This study was launched in 2012 to understand what makes teams effective. Google statisticians, organizational psychologists, sociologists, engineers, and researchers studied many different characteristics of 180 teams (115 in engineering and 65 in sales) distributed across the whole company. Some of these groups performed well and others did not. Every time they thought they'd found a set of characteristics common to effective teams, it failed to apply consistently. No evidence pointed to a combination of personalities, skills, or backgrounds. The success of effective teams was entirely based on the presence of psychological safety.[18]

Google validated the findings of previous researchers at Carnegie Mellon, Union College, and MIT, who had identified two key characteristics of successful teams. Anita Williams Woolley and her colleagues found that teams performed best when two conditions were met. First, team members take equal turns talking. Woolley refers to this as "equality in distribution of conversational turn-taking." Second, group members recognize and understand each other's emotions. Woolley refers to this as "average social sensitivity."[19] Project Aristotle researchers noticed that the most effective teams generally shared these two behaviors.

Equal conversational turn-taking is a group norm that fosters psychological safety. Teams perform better when individual members feel they can freely participate and have an equal chance to contribute their thoughts and

74   Doing More Together, Feeling Less Connected

ideas to the collective intelligence. But this can be more difficult when teams are working remotely because individuals can easily lose attention or disengage if they are not encouraged to speak. Team members need to know when to speak and feel safe enough to speak up.

Knowing when to join the conversation in virtual group interactions can be challenging at times. Some of the nonverbal cues you rely on to indicate when you want to speak, such as a simple intake of breath or posture shift, are not easily noticed by others. It can seem like there's not an easy or clear opening to take a turn to speak. Complicating the issue is the fact that video software generally can only support one microphone input at a time. All participants are essentially muted while one person is talking. Those who take their turn to speak are likely the most extroverted and most willing to break silences or start talking unannounced. Because these qualities are specific to only some individuals in a group, equal turn-taking is less likely to occur.

Psychological safety provides an environment in which team members are willing to express their views openly, admit mistakes, and ask questions. There is no need for team members to remain silent, retreat and let others talk, or disengage. Sometimes in remote environments, equal conversational turn-taking happens naturally if the members tend toward this behavior on their own. But equal conversational turn-taking doesn't always happen naturally, especially when some members are inherently more outspoken than others. In that case, the team will need to establish specific processes to ensure that everyone gets an opportunity to speak. Equality in distribution of conversational turn-taking is critical for team effectiveness.

Google's Project Aristotle confirmed that social sensitivity is also essential for creating a climate of psychological safety. Social sensitivity means having the ability to use cues to perceive and understand the behavior, feelings, and viewpoints of others. This is an important social skill that is sometimes referred to as interpersonal sensitivity.

Being aware of how teammates feel about the team's processes and productivity makes it possible for the team to adjust for optimal functioning. For example, there may be one member who is clearly uncomfortable with how another member is pushing the team to go in a certain direction. A team member with a high level of social sensitivity would pay attention to this and be willing to openly address the situation as it's occurring. Another example is when one individual on a team seems self-conscious about sharing her own ideas and tends to keep quiet. A socially sensitive team member would notice this and could draw out the quiet member, who might be able to make a significant contribution to the team's success.

Despite the best intentions, individual members are sometimes less sensitive to the social pulse of the team when their interactions are confined to a digital window on a screen. It can be harder to accurately gauge feelings by observing an individual's eye contact behaviors and body language. Similarly, reticence and hesitation to share an idea can be harder to distinguish when the audio is muted and eyes appear to be looking straight ahead. Individual team members are then unaware of the need to draw their teammates out and address their concerns. The result is a decrease in social sensitivity when interacting virtually even though team members care about how others in the team are feeling.

Google's data confirmed the same conclusion that many effective managers have realized: successful teams rely on members listening to each other and being sensitive to feelings and needs.

Even though it can be harder to create psychological safety in remote work environments, it must be fostered anyway. Without a climate of psychological safety, teams will have a harder time collaborating and achieving collective results. This difficulty and frustration drives some team members to disengage from the group, which will be detrimental to the team in the long run.

Disconnection Is Painful

A team environment that lacks psychological safety negatively impacts performance and can cause individual team members to feel disengaged. When equal turn-taking does not occur and no one notices that a person is silent for a whole meeting, that individual can feel unseen and unheard. This can result in feeling as if the meeting and the work could go on without them and no one would notice. The pain of feeling insignificant can cause an individual to feel disconnected.

A graduate student that we interviewed experienced this disconnection:

> Not knowing people at the start of my MBA program and feeling a little imposter syndrome because of my non-traditional background, I felt nervous asserting myself. I felt uncomfortable because delayed reactions on Zoom mean sometimes being met with silence. This caused me to contribute less than I was used to. In person, to feel comfortable, I could jump in with a funny comment or a quip or a joke to let people know I'm engaged. On Zoom, people couldn't get to know my personality. When more than one person spoke on Zoom, I couldn't make small comments that didn't add value because it felt like interrupting. I felt disconnected from the group. It was very isolating and made me feel like I didn't belong there.

The way the brain perceives the emotional pain of social disconnection is similar to how it perceives physical pain. Being excluded from a group and feeling disconnected can cause emotional pain, activating the same part of the brain that processes physical pain. This underscores how much it hurts to be left out. Scientific studies have even shown that remembering an incident of being left out will cause a greater pain response in the brain than remembering an incident of getting physically hurt.[20] Other studies have shown that it doesn't matter what causes the individual's feeling of disconnection and isolation, whether it's something done intentionally or accidentally by the group. It is perceived by the brain in the exact same painful way regardless.[21]

Without a sense of belonging, a person can lack the bonded feeling that oxytocin supplies, the rewarding feeling provided by dopamine, and the pain-relieving effects of endorphins. Feeling isolated from others can be as distracting and uncomfortable as hunger, and as distressing and hurtful as physical pain.

When feeling like an outsider causes pain, one option is to get emotional distance. People try to convince themselves that it's not important to engage with others. These attempts are most often in vain. The social brain is not comfortable separating from other people because of the hard-wired biological drive to belong.

Disengaging from the group is intended to avoid pain but has the reverse effect of causing increasingly more emotional distress for the individual. Being alone for long periods can start to make a person highly sensitive to social slights, whether they are real or only imagined. This can lead to a self-fulfilling prophecy of expecting rejection and seeing it everywhere, making it even harder to connect.[22] It also means losing access to other people's resources and support. People working together can combine efforts, share expertise, pool resources, and achieve common goals. Alone, they lose the benefits of collaborating, supporting each other through challenges, and tapping into all the energy, creativity, and resources of the group. As a result of these losses, there is more emotional strain on the individual and stress builds.

The buildup of stress was apparent in the experience of a graduate student we spoke to: "I was stressed in my online course because I had no one to talk to and didn't know what other people were feeling. I was alone in my room trying to learn statistics, not knowing if anyone else was struggling, or if I was the only one not getting it."

Prolonged and Excessive Stress Builds Up to Burnout

Fulfilling the basic human needs for safety and comfort, understanding, and belonging can be stressful in the remote experience. An overwhelming amount of stress often leads to an acute stress response, also known as a fight-or-flight response. Short of an acute stress response, a state of chronic stress can still cause physical, mental, and emotional harm.

When the need for safety and comfort is not met, some people feel constantly on guard. People are more prone to feeling this in the remote environment when others are not around. Trying to work or focus despite a heightened state of physical alertness is highly demanding. Accomplishing tasks will take more mental effort as a result.

When the need to understand other people is not met in virtual interactions, the brain has to do a lot more work. The brain has tools such as prediction generation that are intended to enable clear and energy-efficient understanding. When prediction generation is faulty in the remote environment because of missed and distorted signals, understanding others requires more work. People can reach a state of cognitive overload more quickly when they ask their brain to process in a less energy-efficient way. This causes mental fatigue.

When the need to belong to a group is not met, there can be a feeling of not being fully seen or heard. Levels of dopamine, endorphins, and oxytocin run low. With less oxytocin, it is harder to feel bonded with others. With less dopamine, things feel less rewarding. With less endorphins, physical and emotional pain can feel more intense. It can become difficult and frustrating to stay motivated under these conditions.

Over time, the fatigue and frustration that accumulate from failing to meet these basic needs can take a heavy toll. Undergoing prolonged and excessive stress can lead some people to feel overwhelmed and unable to cope. One possible reaction to this extreme stress is mental and physical exhaustion. Another possible reaction is emotional distance or detachment from work and colleagues. A third possible reaction is a self-evaluation of reduced professional efficacy, a lack of achievement, and feelings of incompetence. The combination of exhaustion, detachment, and feelings of inefficacy at work is referred to as burnout.

The Burnout Experience

Humans burn out when they don't have sufficient resources, support and connection with others, just as fire burns out without enough fuel. The condition of burnout occurs when the natural capacities of a person are continually exceeded by the demands of work.

Human burnout is so rampant that in 2019 it was given an official classification as an occupational phenomenon in the International Classification of Diseases, 11th revision: "Burn-out is a syndrome conceptualized as resulting from chronic workplace stress that has not been successfully managed. It is characterized by three dimensions: feelings of energy depletion or exhaustion; increased mental distance from one's job, or feelings of negativism or cynicism related to one's job; and reduced professional efficacy."[23]

Everyone experiencing burnout will have some combination of the three symptoms: exhaustion, detachment, and feelings of inefficacy. Each symptom describes a unique personal experience that can be uncovered by self-reflection. Burnout can happen in any work context but can be reached more quickly when working remotely. This is due to the unique demands of remote work that can leave a person more vulnerable to a state of prolonged and excessive stress.

Exhaustion

The first symptom of burnout, exhaustion, comes from continually having a high level of work demands. Exhaustion occurs when work requires you to invest more emotional, mental, or physical energy than you have to give. It can feel difficult to concentrate. Even tasks you previously enjoyed feel difficult and tiring.

The demands of work increase in the remote environment. Working harder to maintain focus often leads to physical exhaustion. Communicating when signals are missing and distorted can result in mental exhaustion and cognitive overload. Lacking group support and social connection can cause overwhelming emotional exhaustion.

Exhaustion, the stress dimension of burnout, can be experienced as emotional, physical, or mental fatigue, or sometimes all three. It refers to a kind of constant tiredness that doesn't go away with a good night's sleep, a hearty meal, or even time off from work. Physical fatigue has been shown to increase levels of pain in the muscles and joints.[24] It can also leave people more prone to gastrointestinal disorders, increased blood pressure, and viral illnesses. Mental fatigue makes moving forward extremely difficult. It can be associated with headaches and disturbances in sleep patterns. Emotional fatigue brings with it a sense of being drained with little more to give. Anxiety and irritability are common results of emotional fatigue, and depression can develop.[25]

Are you experiencing exhaustion? Ask yourself:

- Do you feel tired when you wake up and have to face another workday?
- Do you sometimes find it hard to think straight?
- Do you feel you have little emotional energy left at the end of a workday?
- Do you feel like you reach your endpoint before your obligations are completed?
- Are you too tired to do things you enjoy after work?
- Do you spend a great deal of time worrying?
- Do you have trouble sleeping at night?

Detachment

The second symptom of burnout, detachment, is a self-protective way of finding distance from a job that is demanding more than you can give.

Common causes of detachment include an unmanageable workload, unfair treatment, unreasonable time pressures, a lack of role clarity, poor communication, and insufficient support. Rather than confronting these issues, it can feel safer and easier to distance yourself from work and have a general negative outlook about others, yourself, or your job.

The feeling of detachment can manifest as emotional separation from work and an attitude of not caring about performance or colleagues. When detachment is used as a coping mechanism, people become less invested in their projects and feel indifferent or even cynical about their colleagues, collaborators, and clients. They might become irritable, inclined to speak sharply, short-tempered, or not even feel like contributing or listening to others. For example, a computer programmer working remotely said, "I can't easily align with my colleagues. There's no stopping by each other's desks—everything is a formal invite or a text chat. We're getting terse and irritated with each other." The feeling of detachment is a way of coping with extreme stress.

Detachment, the motivational and interpersonal distancing dimension of burnout, puts people into a self-protective mode. They convince themselves that the job causing them stress doesn't really matter and the colleagues they find annoying don't mean that much to them anyway. People start to believe that they don't really care about their performance. Telling themselves these things separates them emotionally from the causes of their stress.

Using detachment as a way of coping with chronic stress also leads to a decrease in positive behaviors, such as cooperation, sharing, and generosity. It can cause more interpersonal conflicts among people who work together. Job satisfaction and commitment to the organization can decrease. Research has shown that detachment is the burnout factor that most strongly predicts whether someone will quit their job altogether.[26]

Studies have shown that lacking high-quality relationships with colleagues and supervisors is a major cause of burnout. Without a shared space and the shared experiences that come with it, camaraderie suffers and there can be a loss of emotional involvement with work. Missing cues and lack of direct eye contact that lead to misunderstandings during virtual interactions also negatively impact the quality of relationships. Positive social encounters are less prevalent when people are not physically around each other and rarely interact outside of scheduled meetings that have a particular focus. Two of the foremost researchers in burnout, Christina Maslach and Michael P. Leiter, state that "in sum, negative social interactions seem to drain energy and distance people from their job, and the absence of positive social encounters is discouraging."[27]

Are you experiencing detachment? Ask yourself:

- Have you lost some of the passion for your work?
- Does your patience run out by the end of the workday?

80 Doing More Together, Feeling Less Connected

- Are you becoming more insensitive or irritable with your colleagues?
- Are you counting the hours until the day is done?
- Do you put off work that you once would have addressed without hesitation?
- Do you find yourself caring less about outcomes at work?

Inefficacy

Inefficacy, the self-evaluation dimension of burnout, develops when the overwhelming demands of work cause changes in the way people evaluate their own performance on the job.

Demands can feel overwhelming when you don't have enough time, information, or resources to do your job appropriately. The lack of frequent feedback and supportive relationships can lead to feeling undervalued and ineffective.[28]

Inefficacy describes a sense of inadequacy and lack of accomplishment. This can lead to a lack of motivation, low morale, and poor performance. If work demands exceed a person's ability to meet them, it can feel like a personal limitation.

These feelings can exacerbate a condition known as impostor syndrome, defined as "chronic feelings of self-doubt and fear of being discovered as an intellectual fraud. Despite evidence of abilities, those suffering from impostor syndrome are unable to internalize a sense of accomplishment, competence, or skill. Overall, they believe themselves to be less intelligent and competent than others perceive them to be."[29] Impostor syndrome is a common experience for people who feel pressure to be successful and to achieve. It results in intellectual self-doubt that resurfaces frequently, especially in response to intimidating situations. Burnout can cause these feelings to resurface.

Regardless of actual capabilities, people experiencing the symptom of inefficacy feel inadequate and incompetent. Instead of pride in their work, they feel disappointed with the quality of their work outcomes. People also doubt that they have the necessary skills to produce high-quality work. Eventually, they begin to question their job fitness despite being highly qualified and extremely competent.

Are you experiencing a reduced sense of efficacy? Ask yourself:

- Are you feeling less effective and less productive than usual?
- Do you feel bad about not functioning at your optimal level?
- Are you disappointed in yourself and your work output?
- Are you feeling like you aren't contributing anything meaningful?
- Do you feel like you'll never get on top of your to-do list?
- Do you experience self-doubt and a sense of failure?

Burnout Brings Us Back to the Paradox

More and more, people are feeling overworked, overstressed, and exhausted. In the digitally reliant world that humans have created, we have not only increased our efficiency, speed, and access, we have also made ourselves more susceptible to the harmful effects of disengagement and disconnection.

As humans, we are wired to connect. We seek out safety and comfort and know that it is best achieved in the presence of others. When this human need is not met, we feel stress that interferes with the ability to focus on a task and hold sustained attention. We are wired to understand other people. Our brains generate predictions to facilitate understanding others in an energy-efficient way. When prediction errors increase in virtual interactions, we have to work harder to understand each other and we become fatigued. We are also wired to belong to a group. When this human need is unmet, we feel unseen and unheard. This leads to disengagement from the group, a sense of not being productive, and low morale.

Prolonged stress can be the result when unmet human needs for connection are combined with technology that feels exhausting and intrusive. When we keep trying to meet work demands despite this stress, it can lead to burnout. Burnout in the workplace is on the rise. A 2015 Deloitte survey found that 77% of full-time US workers had experienced burnout at their current job; 91% of respondents identified an "unmanageable amount of stress or frustration" that negatively impacts the quality of their work.[30] In the United States, poor management of workplace stress contributes to more than 120,000 deaths per year and 5–8% of annual health costs by some estimates.[31]

This brings us back to the paradox with which we began Part One of this book: the technology we use to connect with others often leaves us feeling less connected. The remote experience often fails to satisfy the need for social connection. It falls short of fully capturing the complexity of human interactions. Seeing many faces on a screen is not enough to make us feel that we are truly connecting with other human beings. When we behave in remote environments just as we would in person without any adaptations, meaningful human connections are often not achieved.

In Part One of this book, we have explained the domains where technology has had the most detrimental effects on human connectedness. By identifying specific needs that must be met for humans to feel content and connected with others, we have pinpointed where our current ways of interacting virtually fall short.

In Part Two, we will suggest ways to strengthen human connections and improve virtual interactions. We will offer perspectives on how to establish a sense of well-being, raise engagement, and support meaningful human

82 Doing More Together, Feeling Less Connected

connections in our increasingly remote lives. The perspectives and suggested strategies for fostering connection at a distance come from our personal and professional experiences, supported by scientific evidence. Humanizing the remote experience calls for focusing not only on the quantity and efficiency of our interactions, but also the quality and depth of our human connections.

Go forward, with this in mind:

1 **Basic need**: Belonging to a group or community

- Humans are social creatures by nature.
- Belonging is a feeling of connectedness with a group and identification as a member of a group.

2 **Social brains**: The human brain is hard-wired to connect with others.

- Brain chemicals play a major role in facilitating social bonds.
- Brain-to-brain synchrony occurs when people do activities together.
- Psychological safety is present when group members trust each other and show sensitivity to each other's feelings and needs.

3 **Social disconnection**: The brain perceives social pain and physical pain in a similar way.

- Exclusion from groups can be as distracting and uncomfortable as hunger.
- Feeling isolated from others can be as distressing and hurtful as physical pain.

4 **Burnout**: The combination of exhaustion, detachment, and inefficacy at work is referred to as burnout.

- Exhaustion can be experienced as emotional fatigue, physical fatigue, mental fatigue, or all three.
- Detachment is a self-protective way of finding distance from a job that is demanding more from you than you can give.
- Inefficacy describes a diminished sense of effectiveness and a feeling that you are not accomplishing anything worthwhile at work.

5 **Back to the paradox:**

- Part One focuses on how the technology that has beneficial effects can also detract from human connections.
- Part Two suggests ways to strengthen human connections and improve virtual interactions, focusing on wellness, engagement, social connection, and choices.

Notes

1 Howard, Jane. *Families*. New York: Simon and Schuster, 1998, 234.
2 Coan, James A., and David A. Sbarra. "Social Baseline Theory: The social regulation of risk and effort." *Current opinion in psychology* 1 (2015): 87–91, https://doi.org/10.1016/j.copsyc.2014.12.021, 87.
3 Lieberman, Matthew D. *Social: Why Our Brains Are Wired to Connect.* Oxford: Oxford University Press, 2013.
4 Lieberman, Matthew D. *Social: Why Our Brains Are Wired to Connect.* Oxford: Oxford University Press, 2013, 42.
5 Kosfeld, Michael, Markus Heinrichs, Paul J. Zak, Urs Fischbacher, and Ernst Fehr. "Oxytocin increases trust in humans." *Nature* 435, no. 7042 (2005): 673–676, https://doi.org/10.1038/nature03701
6 Tomova, Livia, Kimberly L. Wang, Todd Thompson, Gillian A. Matthews, Atsushi Takahashi, Kay M. Tye, and Rebecca Saxe. "Acute social isolation evokes midbrain craving responses similar to hunger." *Nature Neuroscience* 23, no. 12 (2020): 1597–1605, https://doi.org/10.1038/s41593-020-00742-z
7 Mu, Yan, Chunyan Guo, and Shihui Han. "Oxytocin enhances inter-brain synchrony during social coordination in male adults." *Social cognitive and affective neuroscience* 11, no. 12 (2016): 1882–1893, doi:10.1093/scan/nsw106
8 For a review see Reinero, Diego A., Suzanne Dikker, and Jay J. Van Bavel. "Inter-brain synchrony in teams predicts collective performance." *Social cognitive and affective neuroscience* 16, no. 1–2 (2021): 43–57, https://doi.org/10.1093/scan/nsaa135
9 Dikker, Suzanne, Lu Wan, Ido Davidesco, Lisa Kaggen, Matthias Oostrik, James McClintock, Jess Rowland, Georgios Michalareas, Jay J. Van Bavel, Mingzhou Ding, and David Poeppell. "Brain-to-brain synchrony tracks real-world dynamic group interactions in the classroom." *Current biology* 27, no. 9 (2017): 1375–1380, http://dx.doi.org/10.1016/j.cub.2017.04.002
10 Denworth, Lydia. "'Hyperscans' show how brains sync as people interact." *Scientific American*, April 10, 2019, www.scientificamerican.com/article/hyperscans-show-how-brains-sync-as-people-interact/
11 Sukel, Kayt. "In sync: How humans are hard-wired for social relationships." Dana Foundation, November 13, 2019, https://dana.org/article/in-sync-how-humans-are-hard-wired-for-social-relationships/
12 Lencioni, Patrick M. *The Five Dysfunctions of a Team: A Leadership Fable.* Berlin: Wiley, 2010.
13 Kosfeld, Michael, Markus Heinrichs, Paul J. Zak, Urs Fischbacher, and Ernst Fehr. "Oxytocin increases trust in humans." *Nature* 435, no. 7042 (2005): 673–676, https://doi.org/10.1038/nature03701
14 De Jong, Bart A., Kurt T. Dirks, and Nicole Gillespie. "Trust and team performance: A meta-analysis of main effects, moderators, and covariates." *Journal of applied psychology* 101, no. 8 (2016): 1134, doi:10.1037/apl0000110.
15 Breuer, Christina, Joachim Hüffmeier, and Guido Hertel. "Does trust matter more in virtual teams? A meta-analysis of trust and team effectiveness considering virtuality and documentation as moderators." *The journal of applied psychology* 101, no. 8 (2016): 1151–1177, doi:10.1037/apl0000113.
16 Edmondson, Amy C. "How fearless organizations succeed." *Strategy+Business*, November 14, 2018: paragraph 2, www.strategy-business.com/article/How-Fearless-Organizations-Succeed
17 Grant, Adam. "Building a culture of learning at work." *Strategy+Business*, February 3, 2021, www.strategy-business.com/article/Building-a-culture-of-learning-at-work

84 Doing More Together, Feeling Less Connected

18 Duhigg, Charles. "What Google learned from its quest to build the perfect team." *The New York Times Magazine*, February 25, 2016, www.nytimes.com/2016/02/28/magazine/what-google-learned-from-its-quest-to-build-the-perfect-team.html?smid=pl-share

19 Woolley, Anita Williams, Christopher F. Chabris, Alex Pentland, Nada Hashmi, and Thomas W. Malone. "Evidence for a collective intelligence factor in the performance of human groups." *Science* 330, no. 6004 (2010): 686–688.

20 Chen, Zhansheng, Kipling D. Williams, Julie Fitness, and Nicola C. Newton. "When hurt will not heal: Exploring the capacity to relive social and physical pain." *Psychological science* 19, no. 8 (2008): 789–795, https://doi.org/10.1111/j.1467-9280.2008.02158.x

21 Eisenberger, Naomi I., and Matthew D. Lieberman. "Why rejection hurts: A common neural alarm system for physical and social pain." *Trends in cognitive sciences 8*, no. 7 (2004): 294–300, https://doi.org/10.1016/j.tics.2004.05.010

22 Entis, Laura. "How COVID-19 and technology that connects us may be making us lonelier." *Vox*, May 26, 2020, www.vox.com/the-highlight/2020/5/26/21256190/zoom-facetime-skype-coronavirus-loneliness

23 World Health Organization. "Burn-out an 'occupational phenomenon': International Classification of Diseases." May 28, 2019, www.who.int/news/item/28-05-2019-burn-out-an-occupational-phenomenon-international-classification-of-diseases

24 Armon, Galit, Samuel Melamed, Arie Shirom, and Itzhak Shapira. "Elevated burnout predicts the onset of musculoskeletal pain among apparently healthy employees." *Journal of occupational health psychology* 15, no. 4 (2010): 399.

25 Maslach, Christina, and Michael P. Leiter. "Understanding the burnout experience: Recent research and its implications for psychiatry." *World psychiatry* 15, no. 2 (2016): 103–111, https://doi.org/10.1002/wps.20311

26 Maslach, Christina, and Michael P. Leiter. "Understanding the burnout experience: Recent research and its implications for psychiatry." *World psychiatry* 15, no. 2 (2016): 103–111, https://doi.org/10.1002/wps.20311

27 Maslach, Christina, and Michael P. Leiter. "Understanding the burnout experience: Recent research and its implications for psychiatry." *World psychiatry* 15, no. 2 (2016): 103–111, https://doi.org/10.1002/wps.20311, 107.

28 Valcour, Monique. "Beating burnout." *Harvard Business Review*, November 2016, https://hbr.org/2016/11/beating-burnout

29 Villwock, Jennifer A., Lindsay B. Sobin, Lindsey A. Koester, and Tucker M. Harris. "Impostor syndrome and burnout among American medical students: a pilot study." *International journal of medical education* 7 (2016): 364, doi:10.5116/ijme.5801.eac4.

30 Deloitte. "Analysis: Workplace burnout survey." www2.deloitte.com/us/en/pages/about-deloitte/articles/burnout-survey.html

31 Goh, Joel, Jeffrey Pfeffer, and Stefanos A. Zenios. "The relationship between workplace stressors and mortality and health costs in the United States." *Management science* 62, no. 2 (2015): 608–628, https://doi.org/10.1287/mnsc.2014.2115

PART TWO

Connecting and Thriving

Chapter 4

Wellness Matters

The increasing use of digital technology that enables constant connectedness has introduced new stresses and challenges. Thankfully, there are ways to make your digital life better. It is possible to approach the remote experience from a healthy state that addresses the basic human need for safety and comfort. To achieve overall wellness, it is necessary to learn how to intercept stress early and control it. Wellness enables you to interact in a way that is positive for you and for others.

As employees, clients, students, friends, and family struggle to adjust to the remote experience, you can address their uncertainties, ambiguities, and causes for anxiety in a way that supports them. Your support can come from leading by example or suggesting strategies to establish and maintain wellness, engagement, and social connections. You can facilitate their learning and encourage them to take intentional actions that will enable more meaningful and fulfilling interactions in the remote experience.

This starts at the most basic, essential level with a focus on your own health and wellness. Once you have achieved this, you can support the health and wellness of the people with whom you interact.

Wellness Is Whole-Self Health

Wellness is the presence of health in multiple aspects of your life. Research has identified six facets of a healthy lifestyle that make up a state of wellness for an individual.[1] To feel good, you have to achieve some element of each of the six facets in a combination that works for you.

1   A state of physical health is one in which you are either free of illness, or feel in control of your illness, symptoms, or pain. You put nutritious things into your system and keep toxic things out of it. You are comfortable in the way your body moves. Either you can move freely or you are able to adjust well to any physical limitations.

2   A state of emotional health refers to the reactions that are produced by your brain in response to the outside world. When you have health

DOI: 10.4324/9781003170488-7

88 Connecting and Thriving

in this realm, you are able to identify and regulate your emotions to some extent. The emotion does not control you, ruin your day, or negatively impact the way you approach relationships or your activities in the world. Instead, you can use your strengths and your emotional responses to increase self-esteem, communicate more effectively, and understand the emotions of others.

3 A state of cognitive health refers to how well you use your brain for thinking and learning. You will feel healthiest when you use your brain's capabilities and exercise it to its full potential. This could be in the form of thinking hard about problems: those in your personal and professional life, world issues, even the problems in crossword puzzles. It could come from creativity, such as making things for yourself or reading fiction to expand your thoughts to a world that is different from your own. With cognitive health, you are able to use your brain to learn new things and then properly store them in your memory to be accessed later. You can explore life's questions and sit comfortably with them even when you don't have the answers.

4 A state of occupational health is one in which you gain personal satisfaction through the work that you do. Your work provides a sense of purpose that keeps you engaged and enriches your life. With occupational health, you are able to prevent the symptoms of burnout. Maintaining enough energy and vigor in your purpose allows you to avoid exhaustion. Staying engaged and invested in the work you do prevents detachment. Holding on to enough confidence in your own abilities keeps you from experiencing feelings of inefficacy.

5 A state of social health refers to all the connections you form with other people. When you have health in this area, you have satisfying relationships and feel like your actions have an impact on others in some way. You feel like you are a contributing part of a group or community and are able to adapt to different social situations. Social health comes with a sense of harmony with the world around you. The environment in which you interact matters to you, and in turn you feel that you matter to that environment.

6 A state of spiritual health refers to your inner life, the part that is separate from all material things. When spiritually healthy, you feel a sense of confidence about your place in the universe. You are able to find meaning in your life. You either discover this on your own or find guidance from the practices and beliefs of a certain philosophy, religion, or other tradition that resonates with you. With spiritual health, you are able to think positively and maintain a healthy outlook regardless of external circumstances.

A healthy lifestyle does not require 100% health in all of these areas, but rather some combination. The weight and significance of each facet of health will vary from one individual to the next, and will vary over time and circumstances as well. For example, a person with a chronic medical illness may experience poor physical health. Yet he can still feel a sense of wellness most of the time because he has healthy emotional and social connections. Another person may enjoy a life of solitude because she draws on a healthy spiritual life that allows her to focus on her physical and cognitive health.

Maintaining a diverse mix of the six facets of health gives you resources to draw from when one facet weakens. This means staying attuned to how heavily you are relying on certain types of health at the expense of others. As an example, you might be completely driven by your purpose at work at the expense of your health in other areas. This means that you maintain your wellness as long as occupational health continues to serve you. But if problems arise at work or you lose your job, there will be little else to fall back on. It is beneficial to diversify your sources of health and not to rely too heavily on only one.

Having diverse sources to fuel your health builds your capacity for resilience. According to the American Psychological Association, resilience is "the process of adapting well in the face of adversity, trauma, tragedy, threats, or significant sources of stress."[2] With resilience, you can withstand the challenges life throws at you and bounce back from these difficult experiences.

The more you can be fueled by any of the six types of health, the more energy you will have to face challenges.

Stress Is Here to Protect You

Your wellness is affected by the personal and professional challenges that you inevitably face. These challenges are often difficult enough that they can cause a stress response. In response to a threat, your sympathetic nervous system releases the stress hormones adrenaline and cortisol into your bloodstream. These stress hormones protect you by giving you a burst of energy and increased mental clarity to confront the problem you face.

Once the perceived threat is thought to be over, your parasympathetic nervous system acts to rein in the stress hormones and move the body into a recovery phase. In this phase, you can heal and recuperate, and get prepared for the next threat that comes along. Once you resolve the stress response and move into this process of recovery, you are able to emerge stronger and more resilient.

As an example of facing and resolving the stress response, imagine experiencing the stress of interacting with a demanding client. When you see this client's name pop up on your phone, your heart rate suddenly quickens as stress hormones are released into your bloodstream. This surge of energy will serve you well when you answer the phone call. You can use the boost of mental clarity and focus to face the stressor and effectively communicate with the client about the demands.

Once the call ends, the threat is over. However, you might still feel revved up since your sympathetic nervous system doesn't yet know there is nothing to worry about anymore. You can use physical actions to calm yourself and convey to your sympathetic nervous system that the threat has, in fact, passed. These actions can be as simple as taking a few deep breaths, gazing out the window at a natural scene, or glancing at a pleasing photo on your desk. Taking these actions will convey to your nervous system that you are not in danger now. Your parasympathetic nervous system will then kick in, resolve the high-energy state, and move you into recovery. Your heart rate and breathing will slow down to a normal pace.

You have let the stress response resolve. As a result, you will be recharged and ready for the next challenge. Additionally, since you overcame the stressor without coming to any harm, you will likely have a less robust stress response the next time this client calls. If you had chosen to jump into the next call immediately, the adrenaline might have buzzed through your veins for the next few hours. This could have colored your interactions with others or distracted you from your next task. Instead, you have experienced stress through its beginning, middle, and, most importantly, its end.

Chronic Stress Does Not Protect

Chronic stress occurs when stressors continue over a long period of time without resolution. To avoid chronic stress that detracts from wellness, it is important to understand how to move through the stress response and resolve it.

We will refer here to the initial boost of energy that stress provides as the Drive Phase. The stress response exists to protect us by ensuring our chance of surviving a perceived threat. Drive is characterized by a period of increased focus, clarity, and energy. In this phase, you have identified a challenge and have energy from your stress response to protect you from that challenge.

Stress itself is not a problem. It only becomes a problem when it is prolonged, unresolved, and moves into what we will call the Drain Phase. This phase is harmful to your overall health. Stress is supposed to be a time-limited response to perceived danger. Its initial benefits will wane if it continues for too much time without resolution. Stress will begin draining you and detracting from your health instead of driving you.

Once you enter the Drain Phase, you will start to feel mentally foggy instead of sharp. Negative physical responses occur as a result of chronic exposure to stress. These include body aches, a decreased immune response, and increased cardiovascular risk. Prolonged stress can also cause emotional responses such as anxiety, irritability, and loneliness. Cognitive responses to continuous stress include poor attention, slowed thinking, poor memory, decreased sharpness, and less productivity.

The Drive Phase of stress is like a sprint: a short period of high-power energy. Sprinters use all their energy at once to get to the finish line as quickly as possible. Then, they require some time to recover from the intense use of their muscles and lungs. Extended time in the Drain Phase is like attempting to sprint over very long distances.

By taking advantage of the burst of energy that the stress response initially provides, you can focus your efforts to resolve a challenge while you're still in the Drive Phase. This will prevent you from ever having to enter the Drain Phase.

Stress Can Be Used to Drive Action and Change

To ensure wellness, you can address stressors in the Drive Phase when you have high levels of physical energy and mental clarity. Action during the Drive Phase prevents stress from becoming prolonged to the point where you are exhausted, energy depleted, and have reached Drain. Even if the stressors are still present, you can resolve your stress response.

You can ask yourself two simple questions to figure out if you are still in Drive or have entered Drain.

1   **What exactly are you stressed about?**

- If the answer comes immediately to mind, you are likely in Drive. Your energy is focused on the task at hand so the answer to this question seems simple to you.
- If you can't quite identify what is bothering you without some deeper thought, you are more likely in Drain. The initial energy your body has provided to fight a problem has now become diffused. Now you are a little worried about a lot of things. Perhaps now small things can set off your temper or you feel a sense of unease and tension throughout your body. You still have stress hormones in your body but there is no longer anything directed or useful about your stress response. The response has become generalized and is no longer protecting you from a specific perceived challenge.

2   **Do you know what steps would make you feel better?**

- If the answer is clear, you are likely in Drive. Your energy is focused so you know where the problem is. Even if you don't know exactly how to fix the issues you are facing, you are aware of what they are. You know what might need to happen next for you to resolve the problem (e.g., "I'll feel better once we've figured out how to complete this project on time").

- If you're not quite certain, you are more likely in Drain. The energy that your body provided to face the challenge no longer has a clear target. You're not focused on how to meet the challenge. Stress is not functioning to protect you anymore and is making things more difficult instead (e.g., "Everything in life feels overwhelming and I don't even know where to begin").

In the Drive Phase, stress stimulates action or change. It draws your attention to the stressor, meaning whatever is threatening enough to cause the release of stress hormones. Stress is intended to make you address the issue and resolve it or make peace with it. Think of it like a smoke alarm. If you treat a clanging alarm like a nuisance to be ignored, it will probably distract you and perhaps cause a headache. If you address the issue it is alerting you to, you can resolve the source of the smoke and prevent it from becoming a full-fledged fire.

When stress tells you something is wrong, you can use that message to address the problem. Ignoring it will permit the stress response to slowly deplete you and send you into Drain. Often, stress is thought of as a constant state that must be endured rather than a temporary one that is seeking resolution.

You can use stress to recognize which problems in your life are causing the most difficulty. Stress can help you to identify how your challenges are affecting the various facets of your health and what the best way to address them might be. If you are in Drive when a lot of adrenaline is flowing, this is an ideal time to attack the stressor head-on.

If instead you are in Drain and feel fatigued and mentally foggy, the stress response is no longer helpful. Rather than being pointed at the problem, your circulating stress hormones are wearing you down. The state of chronic stress can cause you to react negatively toward almost everything, not just the thing that triggered the initial stress response. Here is where stress is an unhelpful state.

Without being aware of what exactly your individual stress response looks like, it's hard to intercept it early and control it. Everyone responds to stress differently. A deeper understanding of how you experience stress will enable you to develop better control over it.

Understand Your Stress Subtype So You Can Use It Effectively

Stress can look different in different people. This is based partly on genes (commonly called nature), and partly on learning and environment (commonly called nurture).

Genes are microscopic packets of instructions that are carried within all the cells in your body. It is the differences in these instructions as they are carried out by your body that determine your characteristics. Eye color is an example of a gene variation that is visible. Response to stress is a gene variation that is invisible.

Various genes have been identified that predict how a person will respond to stress. As an example, we can look at the story of one particular gene called COMT (catechol-O-methyltransferase). Variations among the way individuals express this gene result in differing responses to stress, experienced by two subtypes of people that scientists have dubbed as warriors and worriers.[3]

If your gene variation puts you in the warrior subtype, your brain tends to perform better under stress. You actively seek out the feelings that come with the Drive Phase of stress. This means that you probably thrive when you are under a tight deadline. You might even seek out these thrills and high-pressure situations.

If you are in the worrier subtype, you require a calm and low-stress environment to effectively manage tasks that require high levels of memory and attention. Compared to a warrior, you are likely to have worse cognitive performance under stress.

You can use the information about your performance under stress to identify your brain's preferred environment for optimal functioning. The presence of these two subtypes shows that some responses to stressful situations are genetically predetermined (nature), which is out of your control.

Other responses to stress are learned (nurture). As a young person, you probably coped with stress the same way you saw the people around you coping with it. For example, if your caregiver responded to adversity by talking things through, you might be more prone to turn to this constructive strategy. You're likely to then respond to stress in a similar way throughout your life. However, some of the strategies you learned earlier in life may no longer be appropriate for new situations. As an adult, you might eventually need to identify the behavioral responses to stress that are maladaptive and then replace them with more productive ones.

In addition to the genetic and environmental variations, people experience stress in different ways. Some people experience stress in a physical way. In these people, the gearing up of the fight-or-flight system can have negative effects on the normal functioning of the body. Stomach aches can occur when the body does not devote enough energy to the full digestion of food. Headaches might come from tension in the jaw or continually clenching other facial muscles. The heart races or the breath shortens and quickens to such a degree that it requires a conscious effort to sometimes take a deep breath. There is a sense of tension or a shaky feeling when carrying stress in the body.

Other people are more prone to carrying stress in their minds rather than their bodies. For these people, the fight-or-flight system believes there is a mortal danger out there and does not want to let the mind forget it for even a second. Whatever is perceived as threatening or unresolved takes a position in the forefront of the mind where it is hard to budge. Attention repeatedly gets pulled back to the stressor and leads to ruminating about it all day and into the night. Just when the brain is supposed to be calming down for rest and recuperation, it is instead highly active. An overactive brain is antithetical to the relaxed state of sleep, leading to tossing and turning all night long. This kind of preoccupation, obsession, and restlessness is a common way that the mind is affected by stress.

Take a moment to identify your unique responses to stress. Start by considering whether you might carry the worrier gene or the warrior gene. You can determine this by reflecting on how your brain functions under stress. Then, reflect on the way that stress manifests in your everyday life.

Are you a warrior?

- Do you thrive working under a deadline?
- Do you think best under pressure?
- Is it hard to formulate plans and take action when you have a lot of unstructured time?

Are you a worrier?

- Does your thinking get cloudy when there is a lot of external pressure on you?
- Do you work best when you are following a clear plan of action?
- Do you think best when you can stay focused on one thing at a time?

Do you manifest your stress physically?

- Do you tend to get more physical ailments when you are working hard or worried about something?
- Do you feel tension in your body when stressed?
- Do you get easily run down when you are under stress?

Do you process your stress emotionally or cognitively?

- Is it hard to fall asleep at night when you are stressed?
- Are you able to refocus your attention when necessary or is it too difficult to focus on anything other than the problem you are stressed about?
- Is your stress often accompanied by negative emotions, like irritability or sadness?

Preventing Negative Impacts of Stress in the Remote Experience

Whether physical or emotional, chronic stress takes up a lot of the body's energy and the mind's mental space. It is hard to feel a sense of wellness when stress is draining your energy. Stress can wear away at physical health if you carry it in your body, or emotional health if you carry it in your mind. Cognitive health suffers because a prolonged stress response makes mental clarity difficult and discourages exploration outside of the focus on the stressor itself. Occupational health is hard to achieve without an engaged mind, and decreased productivity can be the result. Social health is neglected since most mental energy is focused on a threat with little to spare for engaging meaningfully with others. Spiritual health becomes difficult because a preoccupation with stress can shift your focus away from positive thoughts.

Stress levels can be significantly higher in the remote environment, increasing the challenge of maintaining the six facets of health and wellness. As stressors build up and compete for your attention, you are prone to reach the Drain Phase of stress more quickly. In Drain, your thoughts and efforts go toward the immediate problems your stress is working to manage. As your physical and emotional resources eventually become depleted, you will have little energy left to get anything done or to care for yourself. And you certainly can't help others until you have cared for your own health and wellness.

Science-Based Strategies: Suggestions to Control Stress and Achieve Wellness

Instead of simply saying, "I'm so stressed out" and carrying on, it is in each individual's best interest to first acknowledge stress and then take steps to resolve it. Remember, stress is a call to action.

In the stress response, there is an interplay between activating to fight a challenge and relaxing to recover from fighting a challenge. The relaxed recovery phase is when there are opportunities for personal growth and for productivity. We will look next at how to increase the amount of time spent in this relaxed recovery phase. Reducing stress will improve your health and wellness, creating the conditions for connection. We suggest particular body-based strategies and mind-based strategies that are all grounded in scientific research.

Body-Based Strategies

While it is possible for stress to control you, it is also possible for you to control stress. Humans are all endowed with a secret stress-reduction

96 Connecting and Thriving

weapon known as the vagus nerve. Remember the parasympathetic nervous system that calms the body back down to normal after a fight-or-flight response? This system is primarily under the control of a very long nerve called the vagus. The vagus nerve originates in your brain, snakes down past your carotid arteries, and sends out extensions to your heart, lungs, and all the way down to the colon. It takes in sensory information from most organs to convey to the brain and also sends out information to the organs. In general, it sends one loud and clear message to all of these different body parts: Relax.

You can control this relaxation to some extent. The vagus nerve receives sensory input from many parts of your body. This means that you can use the parts of your body that you can control to send your vagus nerve the message that it is a good time to relax. There are multiple ways to stimulate the vagus nerve, which will be mentioned in the list of strategies below.

It is possible to convince your sympathetic nervous system that you are calm and in control, even if you don't entirely feel that way. You can do this by cultivating a sense of calm and control through the ways you physically interact with the world around you. We suggest the place to start is with your breathing.

• Focus on Your Breathing

If you are a little scared or tense, you can change the fear message by breathing as if you were not nervous at all. The vagus nerve that reduces stress comes into play when you control your breathing. Slow, deep, diaphragmatic breathing directly stimulates this relaxation nerve. That means at any point in the day, you have the power to deactivate your fight-or-flight system by taking deep breaths.

The Relaxation Response is a term coined by Harvard physician Herbert Benson that refers to a physical state of deep rest and recovery from the effects of stress. Benson compares it to the fight-or-flight response as "a second, equally essential survival mechanism—the ability to heal and rejuvenate our bodies." He goes on to explain:

> In modern times, the Relaxation Response is undoubtedly even more important to our survival, since anxiety and tension often inappropriately trigger the fight-or-flight response in us. Regular elicitation of the Relaxation Response can prevent, and compensate for, the damage incurred by frequent nervous reactions that pulse through our hearts and bodies.[4]

Benson found in his research that a focused mind causes the heart rate and breathing rate to decrease. The more you practice focusing, the better you will become at calming your body in response to stressful situations. Your physical health improves as you deliberately deactivate your fight-or-flight response and calm the body's state of high alert.

Key actions: Spend five to ten minutes per day letting your mind and body rest by harnessing your Relaxation Response. Practice proper diaphragmatic breathing to stimulate your relaxation system. Place one hand on your chest and one hand on your stomach. Inhale through your nose as you count to four. The hand on your stomach should rise, while the other hand on your chest moves very little. Exhale through your mouth as you count up to eight, pushing out as much air as you can while contracting the abdominal muscles. The hand on your stomach moves in, while the other hand on your chest moves very little. Spending a greater amount of time in the exhale phase than the inhale phase delivers a message to the parasympathetic nervous system to relax.

• Get Physical

Moving your body in deliberate and controlled ways is another way to convince your nervous system that there is no threat to be found. This is another way to deactivate your fight-or-flight response and calm the body's state of high alert.

Exercise can directly increase the activity of the vagus nerve, which will shut down the fight-or-flight activation and promote relaxation. Yoga, for example, involves putting the body into specific positions while maintaining slow, diaphragmatic breathing. Dr. Navaz Habib explains in his book *Activate Your Vagus Nerve: Unleash Your Body's Natural Ability to Heal* that "if we train ourselves to handle voluntary stressors by maintaining our breath, then we can be trained to maintain composure and handle other stressors with significant ease." He writes that breathing-focused exercise can beneficially activate the vagus nerve.[5]

There is extra adrenaline and cortisol flowing through your body to get you moving when you are under stress. You can make good use of the energy these stress hormones provide by engaging in physical activity, such as running, walking, weight training, sports, yoga, and others. Moving your body is an effective way to feel in control during the Drive Phase of stress and avoid progressing into Drain. You will come back to the task more refreshed and ready for action.

Key actions: Incorporate some type of physical movement into your day. Turn to it when you start to feel stress building up in your system. This can be an organized sport, a full workout, a brisk walk, or taking time to stretch your muscles. Notice how using your physical energy brings your stress level down. A more active lifestyle will have long-lasting benefits for your overall physical health.

98 Connecting and Thriving

• Make Healthy Food Choices

Making healthy choices about what goes into your body is another way of telling your stress response that there is nothing to be worried about in the present moment. Grabbing a quick unhealthy high-calorie snack and insufficiently hydrating as you run from one obligation to the other does not send a message of calm. Your stress response is taking in messages from the environment to decide if your body is in danger or not. A slow nutritious meal is what someone under no threat has time to consume and digest, while scarfing down food in a hurry is the marker of someone who is on the run.

Besides choosing what you eat, you can choose what you do while you eat. Your actions during mealtimes can also convey to your body that there is no cause for concern. If you are eating lunch every day while working on your computer, you are losing a daily opportunity to pause from your stressors and cultivate calm. If you eat dinner every night accompanied by a TV show or scrolling through your phone, you are not taking time to check in with your body or the people around you. You can use mealtimes to center yourself as you focus on the sole task of nourishing yourself. Even if it's only for a few minutes this can still help to deactivate your stress response.

Key actions: Consume healthy food and hydrate. Take your time eating and focus on the nourishment that you're giving your body. This sends a signal of calm to your brain.

• Get Eight Hours of Sleep Each Night

Sleep provides time for the recovery phase of stress to be fully carried out. Healing and rebuilding occur in the brain during sleep. If you shortchange yourself on sleep, your physical health will suffer during the daytime hours. Skimping on sleep is like wearing out your muscles in a high-intensity workout and then not giving them sufficient recovery time before the next high-intensity workout. Without letting the muscles recover, you will not experience the desired increase in strength. By letting your brain recover each night, you will be much more effective the next day.

In his fascinating book *Why We Sleep: Unlocking the Power of Sleep and Dreams,* neuroscientist Matthew Walker explains that "sleep is the single most effective thing we can do to reset our brain and body health each day— Mother Nature's best effort yet at contra-death."[6] Walker presents a compelling argument that humans need to get eight hours of sleep every night. He dispels the myth that we can catch up on missed sleep. Many people sleep only a few hours at night during the work week and think they can make up for it by sleeping longer during the weekend. But that's not how it works. Once you have a sleep deficit, it will continue to act on your brain and body and worsen each day. Research has shown that your physical, cognitive, and emotional health suffer when you get less than six hours of sleep every night.[7]

Napping can also be good for your health, although doing it too much during the day can interfere with a good night's sleep for some people. Researchers at NASA studying pilot performance and alertness showed that short naps resulted in a 34% improvement in task performance and over 50% increased overall alertness. They concluded that the ideal nap time, to reduce the problem of grogginess on awakening, is 10 to 20 minutes.[8] Another study conducted by Harvard scientists measured the sleeping habits of a population of people that tended to nap often. They found that the occasional nap lowered the risk of dying from heart disease in that population by 12%, and regular napping lowered the risk of dying from coronary heart disease by 37%.[9]

Not only does sleep keep you healthy, it also can contribute to keeping you socially connected. Healthier sleep leads to increased productivity and an improved mood. This can lead you to be more present with people at work and with friends and family.[10]

Key actions: Get seven or eight hours of sleep each night. Supplement with a 10 to 20 minute nap during the day when needed. Sleep promotes physical health by helping you recover from the day's stressors and preparing your body for the upcoming ones.

• Be Aware of Light

Sunlight is important for your health. The type of light that you receive from spring and summer sunshine actually travels through the eyes and is received by cells on the front of the brain. These cells are involved in making serotonin (a brain chemical that regulates mood) and melatonin (a brain chemical that regulates your circadian rhythm of sleeping). During the winter and fall, the full spectrum of sunlight needed for production of serotonin and melatonin is not available unless you live close to the equator.

A lack of sunshine can actually translate into lower mood, poor concentration, and decreased interest in activities. This type of reaction can be alleviated by sufficient time outside during the spring and summer. Sun exposure can be replaced artificially during the winter and fall. Home-use sun lamps that provide greater than 5,000 lux have been proven to be highly effective in treating this type of low mood (unless this is a clinical depression that requires medical attention).[11]

While the right kind of light can give your brain a boost, the wrong kind can be detrimental. Electronic devices emit a blue-spectrum light that your brain interprets as sunlight. When you expose yourself to this kind of blue light in the evening, you interfere with the natural process of winding down. As the sun sets, changes occur in your brain in preparation for sleep. You block these changes if you expose yourself to blue light right up until the moment you try to go to sleep. This will keep you awake because your brain has not been given the necessary notice to wind down for sleep. It's best to either avoid using any

100 Connecting and Thriving

electronic devices before sleep, or use only devices that come with blue-light filters to block the detrimental light. Many cell phones and e-readers now have this feature. You can also purchase blue-light blocking glasses. The less blue light your brain receives at night, the easier it will be to fall asleep.

Key actions: Get as much sunshine during the daylight hours as possible. If low light in the winter and fall affects your mood or concentration, consider purchasing a device to simulate full spectrum sunlight. Minimize exposure to blue light as you approach bedtime. By not working against your natural daily rhythms, you will sleep better and improve your physical and cognitive health.

Mind-Based Strategies

Stress can significantly impact the way that you think, process, communicate, and form memories, just as it impacts your everyday physical functioning. The following suggested strategies involve using your mind to filter and make sense of your experience in the world. Actively filtering your experience allows you to enrich your health and live in a way that promotes thriving.

• Practice Focusing

The therapeutic practice commonly referred to as mindfulness involves focusing awareness on the present moment, letting each feeling and thought pass through the brain without judgment. In Eastern traditions, this type of focused awareness has been practiced for thousands of years. Over the past few decades, it has been embraced universally and rigorously studied using brain scans and controlled trials of novice and expert practitioners.

One of the most prominent American voices on the topic is Jon Kabat-Zinn. He has worked to integrate Buddhist principles with scientific findings and has written invaluable books that provide guidance in the practice of mindful living. In *Wherever You Go, There You Are: Mindfulness Meditation in Everyday Life*, he defines mindfulness as "paying attention in a particular way: on purpose, in the present moment, and nonjudgmentally."[12]

Here are instructions Kabat-Zinn gives for one way to start practicing mindfulness:

> Try: stopping, sitting down, and becoming aware of your breathing once in a while throughout the day. It can be for five minutes, or even five seconds. Let go into full acceptance of the present moment, including how you are feeling and what you perceive to be happening. For these moments, don't try to change anything at all, just breathe and let go. Breathe and let be.[13]

Kabat-Zinn goes on to explain that mindfulness helps to grow "an appreciation for the present moment and the cultivation of an intimate relationship with it… It is the direct opposite of taking life for granted."[14] Researchers have found that cultivating this relationship with the present moment with even a brief daily practice of mindfulness has widespread benefits to health and wellness. Meditation through mindfulness makes measurable changes in multiple parts of the brain associated with positive emotion, memory, awareness, and emotional control.[15] Over time, practicing mindfulness improves a person's ability to control their own stress and focus their attention. Improved psychological and immune system functioning can also occur with regular mindfulness meditation.[16] There is even evidence that it slows down the normal process of aging in the brain.[17]

If you prefer to focus on something other than your breathing, you can select a different point of focus. The focus can be on a word, or a short phrase. It can also be a sound or rhythm: the beat while dancing, the slap of the feet while running, the up and down of the pedals while biking. Activities such as knitting, coloring, flower arranging, or any such pursuit can also supply a steady point of focus for the meditating mind.

Taking time to practice mindfulness means that you will experience more cognitive health throughout your day. More cognitive health will be available for focusing on tasks, working through challenging problems, or being present in conversations.

Key actions: Strengthen your ability to be fully present by setting aside at least ten minutes in your daily schedule for focusing practices, such as mindfulness. Use the following practice suggested by Kabat-Zinn:

> Try staying with one full inbreath as it comes in, one full outbreath as it goes out, keeping your mind open and free for just this moment, just this breath. Abandon all ideas of getting somewhere or having anything happen. Just keep returning to the breath when the mind wanders, stringing moments of mindfulness together, breath by breath.[18]

Choose an alternative point of focus if breath doesn't work for you, such as a sound, rhythm, or simple activity. These practices not only activate awareness of the present moment, but also cause positive changes in the brain's ability to focus, regulate emotion, and retain information.

• Name Your Emotions

To maintain emotional health, it is necessary to understand what emotions are and where they come from. Emotions are not verbal. They are visceral, experienced in the body. By naming your emotions, you are able to make them verbal. Psychiatrist Daniel J. Siegel explains this process:

> In the brain, naming an emotion can help calm it. Here is where finding words to label an internal experience becomes really helpful.

We can call this "Name it to tame it."... Your inner sea and your interpersonal relationships will all benefit from naming what is going on and bringing more integration into your life.[19]

By using the naming process, you are linking the emotion in your body with a conscious experience in your rational human brain: a feeling that you can describe and talk about.

Emotions live in a deep, primitive part of the brain called the amygdala. The amygdala is a brain region that humans have in common with other animals. A rabbit can experience fear, and this drives its instinctual behavior to escape a predator. But a rabbit doesn't know it feels scared. It just knows to run. What makes humans different is that we have the capacity for language. We can use our highly developed and specialized cortex to identify what we are afraid of, talk about it, and work through it as a mental problem. By naming emotions and making them into verbally represented feelings, we increase our awareness and understanding of situations.

Consider the emotion of fear, an orchestrated response of your nervous system to something threatening that increases your heart rate and adrenaline levels. You can experience this fear response without conscious awareness of it. Alternatively, you can have the thought, "I am scared." These words describe the conscious experience of the response occurring in your body. The simple act of naming the response as a feeling changes the way you experience it. Studies have shown that the act of naming a fear response will lessen the body's hyperarousal and decrease blood flow to the amygdala.[20]

By naming your emotions, you are increasing communication between the amygdala and cortex. This increases control over an emotion because you are making sense of what you are feeling and can think your way through it.

Key actions: When you have a strong feeling, write it down on a piece of paper. Continue to jot down your feelings throughout the day. Observe the overall effect this naming activity has on your stress level by the end of the day. The regular practice of transforming the visceral experience of emotions into the conscious, understandable experience of feelings gives you greater control over your emotional health.

• Reframe and Reappraise

Reframing is used in a number of different types of psychotherapies. It is also an activity you can do on your own. Reframing involves changing the way you view a particular situation, experience, idea, or emotion by looking at it from a different perspective. Reappraisal means not just changing how you think about a situation, but also giving it a new name or description to reinforce the change in perspective. Both reframing and reappraisal are powerful cognitive tools.

They are possible because "reality is created by the mind. We can change our reality by changing our mind," as Plato noted.[21]

Strong emotions are usually preceded by some type of thought. While emotions are hard to change (in the amygdala), thoughts are more malleable and under conscious control (in the cortex). That's why reframing, changing your perspective and altering your thoughts, can improve your feelings. For example, you might think, "I'll never get this project done" and then feel stress. You can reframe this by changing that thought to, "This is going to take a long time. What's the next part I can tackle successfully?" Alternatively, you can think to yourself, "My colleague has offered to work together on projects like this. I should enlist her help." Changing your thoughts about the situation can actually change the way that you feel about it.

Your thoughts can be changed by exploring the same situation through a different lens or finding alternative explanations for why a certain situation has come to be. This change in perspective can significantly modify negative feelings. Psychologist Carrie Steckl writes about the reframing she practices in her own life:

> When either my husband or I find ourselves viewing something in a negative light—or feel stuck in a problem—we will try to reframe the problem for the other. For instance, I might feel discouraged that I'm such a slow runner. My husband will encourage me by saying something such as, "I know you feel like you're running too slowly, but you're still in great shape and you're avoiding injury by not pushing yourself too hard." This is when I thank him by saying, "Good reframe!"[22]

Giving the emotion a new name can create a new experience. Many research studies have confirmed that reframing the way you are thinking about a particular emotion can change how you feel that emotion, and in turn the experience you are having. "Compared with those who attempt to calm down, individuals who reappraise their anxious arousal as excitement feel more excited and perform better," states Alison Woods Brooks in a 2013 study. She goes on to say that "individuals can reappraise anxiety as excitement using minimal strategies such as self-talk (e.g., saying 'I am excited' out loud) or simple messages (e.g., 'get excited'), which lead them to feel more excited, adopt an opportunity mind-set (as opposed to a threat mind-set), and improve their subsequent performance."[23]

Key actions: Write down a negative feeling and then write down an alternative, more positive way to describe it. You can also write down the advice you would give to a friend in that same situation. Notice how it changes the way you experience the feeling. Your emotional health improves as you develop more control over the way feelings affect you in your daily life.

104 Connecting and Thriving

• Journal

There are many different kinds of journaling, including stream of consciousness journaling, what-is-going-well journaling, gratitude journaling, one-sentence journaling, and others. All of these involve writing down your thoughts and feelings to understand them more clearly.

The physical act of writing, putting pen to paper, allows you to slow down and process your experiences in more depth. Reflecting on your experiences and then collecting your thoughts and ideas on paper is an effective way to learn. It allows you to see the bigger picture and connect with the issues you're encountering. Today, it's possible to feel bombarded by all the news and information there is to consume. Journaling provides an opportunity for you to process and understand things in your own words.[24]

Another benefit of journaling is strengthening the immune system. Researchers have found that journaling about illnesses, such as HIV/AIDS in one study, can help reduce the stress of the illness and can actually temporarily increase the number of immune cells in circulation.[25] A study exploring other chronic illnesses such as asthma and arthritis showed that writing about stressful and emotional events significantly decreased the physical effects of the disease after four months compared to control groups.[26] Journaling about stressful events helps people come to terms with them. In other words, journaling acts as a stress management tool.

Journaling can also bring to your awareness the small positive social interactions you've had throughout the day. In addition, you see more clearly the steps you took toward solving a problem. These reflections will help you avoid the natural human tendency to put too much weight on negatives or to assume that positive outcomes come by chance alone.

Key actions: Record the day's events and any thoughts or feelings you are having. Make it a regular practice, either before you go to bed or as soon as you wake up. Use your journaling practice as a tool for increasing self-awareness, processing events, and acknowledging your growth. You can also use journaling for problem solving and engaging with ideas. Your physical, cognitive, and emotional health all benefit from the clarity that results.

• Read

Reading is good for your brain. Learning new things and making new connections between brain cells improves cognitive health. Researcher Anne-Laure Le Cunff writes:

> The main benefit of reading is that it puts your brain to work. This is why it's probably one of the healthiest hobbies for your mind. Reading is not only educational and informative—which is a great benefit in itself as learning something new is good in itself for your brain—it

actually actively rewires the connections in your brain, which translates into many mental health and wellness benefits.[27]

Fiction reading can also expand your spiritual health by strengthening your inner life and helping you find meaning in your own existence. Fiction engages your imagination in a created world that is separate and different from your own. This can expand your capacity for empathy, your worldview, and your ability to see things from different perspectives. If you are able to focus on the fictional world contained within the book, your attention is by definition off of your own problems and worries. In this way, you are taking a break from your stress and can perhaps look at it differently when you return to your own reality. Additionally, your brain experiences vivid storytelling as if you were actually having the experience.[28]

Key actions: Read to learn new things and expand connections in your brain. Fiction reading, in particular, provides a break from your own reality. Your cognitive health is augmented as you make new connections and engage your imagination.

• Find Your Ikigai

There is a concept called ikigai in Japanese, which does not have a counterpart in the English vocabulary. The direct translation is "life value" but its full meaning carries a deeper significance. It was developed from wellness principles of traditional Japanese medicine that emphasize how physical health is influenced by mental and emotional health, as well as by having a sense of purpose in life.[29] Ikigai is having something that gets you out of bed in the morning and gives you something to look forward to even in challenging times. Many people find ikigai in their work.

The ideology of ikigai can be captured in a Venn diagram of four realms and their point of intersection: what you value, what the world needs, what you are good at, and what you can be paid for. You have found ikigai when you can do something well and find pleasure and satisfaction in it.

Having a reason to get up each morning has been found to prolong life. In one study, people with a strong sense of purpose in life were found to be half as likely to die from cardiovascular diseases.[30] The authors of this study suggest that this relates to purpose-lacking individuals having higher levels of stress hormones and lower levels of chemicals that protect the body from inflammation.

Studies also suggest that ikigai is an important contributor to the fact that Japanese people have some of the longest lifespans in the world. Ikigai has been shown to increase physical and mental health.[31] Researcher Dan Buettner found that in other cultures around the world with high longevity, members also embrace a similar mindset about having a purpose in life.[32]

106 Connecting and Thriving

Key actions: Draw a Venn diagram with four overlapping circles. These are readily available on the internet, if you'd prefer to print one rather than draw it yourself. In each circle, fill in one of the four realms: what you value, what the world needs, what you're good at, and what you can be paid for. Let your search for ikigai serve as a guide to aligning your actions with your passion and purpose.

• Practice Gratitude

Clinical researcher Brené Brown spent over a decade interviewing thousands of people about their experiences of joy, vulnerability, and shame. She was surprised to find in her research that having a joyful life did not lead to gratitude. Instead, she found that it was the regular practice of gratitude which led to the experience of a more joyful life in her research participants.[33] There was variety in the way people practiced gratitude, from keeping gratitude journals to sharing what they are grateful for over dinner each night.

Psychologist Robert Emmons has also studied gratitude practices. He reports impressive results from the practice of writing what you are grateful for in a journal for three weeks. Those who practiced regular gratitude were shown to benefit from stronger immune systems, better sleep, and improved overall physical health. They also experienced more positive emotions, including happiness and joy, and more feelings of social connectedness.[34]

Other studies have shown that people who practice gratitude are more resistant to stress and depression. There are many reasons why this might be so. Practicing gratitude helps your brain attribute positive outcomes to forces partially outside of yourself and believe in a greater good. Gratitude can also deepen your trust in others and promote a positive attitude towards them. It can push out negative emotions, including fear, jealousy, or regret, that you carry in response to external circumstances. Your attention will be increasingly drawn to positive things in your daily life. Over time and with practice, the ability to approach life with a grateful state of mind increases.

Key actions: Spend a few minutes at the end of the day writing down three things that you are grateful for. They can be very significant things, such as recovery from an illness or gratitude for health. But they can also be small things, such as having a nice walk outside that day. You can also cultivate gratitude by thanking someone for doing something nice or for having a positive impact on you, or reflecting on what went well or what you are grateful for. It becomes easier to separate yourself from stressors at the end of the day as your mind becomes more trained at focusing on positive things.

In this chapter, we discussed how to intercept the stress response early. Controlling the stress response improves your health and wellness, making it easier to focus on connecting with others. The next chapter delves into how you can work with a fully engaged brain. Health, wellness, and a fully engaged brain create the conditions for deeper human connection.

Go forward, with this in mind

1 **You can make the remote experience better**:
   - Start at the most basic level with a focus on health and wellness.
   - Learn how to intercept stress early and control it.

2 **Wellness is the presence of health in multiple aspects of your life**
   - Physical health
   - Emotional health
   - Cognitive health
   - Occupational health
   - Social health
   - Spiritual health

3 **The stress response, a physiological reaction to a challenge, requires resolution**
   - The Drive Phase refers to the initial boost of energy that stress provides to help you face a challenge.
   - Stress in the Drive Phase is helpful because it facilitates action or change.
   - The Drain Phase occurs when stress is prolonged and unresolved.
   - Stress in the Drain Phase is no longer helpful and causes fatigue and mental fogginess.

4 **Understand how your body and mind handle stress**
   - People who carry the warrior gene perform best under pressure and deadlines.
   - People who carry the worrier gene think most clearly under low stress.
   - Some stress responses are learned as a child and may need to be unlearned.
   - Stress can manifest physically, mentally, or both.

5 **Consider ways of controlling stress and achieving wellness to create the conditions for human connection**
   - Proven strategies grounded in science
   - Body-based strategies
   - Mind-based strategies

Note: None of the suggested strategies in this book are intended to be a substitute for medical treatment of severe mental health issues. There is a list of mental health resources in the appendix for your reference.

Notes

1 National Center for Chronic Disease Prevention and Health Promotion, Division of Population Health. "Well-being concepts." October 31, 2018, www.cdc.gov/hrqol/wellbeing.htm
2 American Psychological Association. "Building your resilience." February 1, 2020: paragraph 4, www.apa.org/topics/resilience
3 Stein, Dan J., Timothy K. Newman, Jonathan Savitz and Rajkumar Ramesar. "Warriors versus worriers: The role of COMT gene variants." *CNS Spectrums* 11, no. 10 (2006): 745–748, doi:10.1017/S1092852900014863.
4 Klipper, Miriam Z., and Herbert Benson. *The Relaxation Response.* New York: HarperCollins e-books, 2009, xvii.
5 Habib, Navaz. *Activate Your Vagus Nerve: Unleash Your Body's Natural Ability to Heal.* Berkeley, CA: Ulysses Press, 2019, 223.
6 Walker, Matthew. *Why We Sleep: Unlocking the Power of Sleep and Dreams.* New York: Simon and Schuster, 2017, 8.
7 Walker, Matthew. *Why We Sleep: Unlocking the Power of Sleep and Dreams.* New York: Simon and Schuster, 2017.
8 Stilwell, Blake. "Here's what NASA says is the perfect length for a power nap." *Business Insider*, August 26, 2021, www.businessinsider.com/nasa-research-found-the-perfect-length-for-a-power-nap-2019-3
9 Naska, Androniki, Eleni Oikonomou, Antonia Trichopoulou, Theodora Psaltopoulou, and Dimitrios Trichopoulos. "Siesta in healthy adults and coronary mortality in the general population." *Archives of internal medicine* 167, no. 3 (2007): 296–301, doi:10.1001/archinte.167.3.296.
10 Diamond, Madeline. "Why mental health is a top priority for the US Surgeon General." *HuffPost*, July 14, 2016, www.huffpost.com/entry/why-emotional-well-being-is-a-top-priority-for-the-us-surgeon-general_n_57866486e4b08608d3327828
11 Penders, Thomas M., Cornel N. Stanciu, Alexander M. Schoemann, Philip T. Ninan, Richard Bloch, and Sy A. Saeed. "Bright light therapy as augmentation of pharmacotherapy for treatment of depression: A systematic review and meta-analysis." *Primary care companion, CNS disorders* 18, no. 5 (2016), doi:10.4088/PCC.15r01906.
12 Kabat-Zinn, John. *Wherever You Go, There You Are: Mindfulness Meditation in Everyday Life.* New York: Hachette Books, 2009, 28.
13 Kabat-Zinn, John. *Wherever You Go, There You Are: Mindfulness Meditation in Everyday Life.* New York: Hachette Books, 2009, 39.
14 Kabat-Zinn, John. *Wherever You Go, There You Are: Mindfulness Meditation in Everyday Life.* New York: Hachette Books, 2009, 30.
15 For a review see: Hölzel, Britta K., James Carmody, Mark Vangel, Christina Congleton, Sita M. Yerramsetti, Tim Gard, and Sara W. Lazar. "Mindfulness practice leads to increases in regional brain gray matter density." *Psychiatry research: neuroimaging* 191, no. 1 (2011): 36–43, doi:10.1016/j.pscychresns.2010.08.006
16 Wallace, B. Alan, and Shauna L. Shapiro. "Mental balance and well-being: Building bridges between Buddhism and Western psychology." *American Psychologist* 61, no. 7 (2006): 690, doi:10.1037/0003–066X.61.7.690.

17 Luders, Eileen, Nicolas Cherbuin, and Florian Kurth. "Forever young(er): Potential age-defying effects of long-term meditation on gray matter atrophy." *Frontiers in psychology* 5 (2015): 1551, www.frontiersin.org/article/10.3389/fpsyg.2014.01551
18 Kabat-Zinn, John. *Wherever You Go, There You Are: Mindfulness Meditation in Everyday Life.* New York: Hachette Books, 2009, 49.
19 Siegel, Daniel J. *Brainstorm: The Power and Purpose of the Teenage Brain.* New York: Penguin Publishing Group, 2014, 61.
20 Hariri, Ahmad R., Venkata S. Mattay, Alessandro Tessitore, Francesco Fera, and Daniel R. Weinberger. "Neocortical modulation of the amygdala response to fearful stimuli." *Biological psychiatry* 53, no. 6 (2003): 494–501, https://doi.org/10.1016/S0006-3223(02)01786–9
21 Akṣapāda. *PLATO'S DOCTRINE: 909 Relics of Greek Philosophy.* Independently Published, 2019, 61.
22 Steckl, Carrie. "Reframing: Finding solutions through a new lens." Wellness and Personal Development Resources (blog), MentalHelp.net, paragraph 1, www.mentalhelp.net/blogs/reframing-finding-solutions-through-a-new-lens/
23 Brooks, Alison Wood. "Get excited: Reappraising pre-performance anxiety as excitement." *Journal of experimental psychology: general* 143, no. 3 (2014): 1144–1158, doi:10.1037/a0035325.
24 "18 Incredible Benefits of Journaling (and how to start)." Vanilla Papers (blog), August 9, 2020, https://vanillapapers.net/2020/08/09/journaling-benefits/
25 Petrie, Keith J., Iris Fontanilla, Mark G. Thomas, Roger J. Booth, and James W. Pennebaker. "Effect of written emotional expression on immune function in patients with human immunodeficiency virus infection: A randomized trial." *Psychosomatic medicine* 66, no. 2 (2004): 272–275. doi:10.1097/01.psy.0000116782.49850.d3.
26 Smyth, Joshua M., Arthur A. Stone, Adam Hurewitz, and Alan Kaell. "Effects of writing about stressful experiences on symptom reduction in patients with asthma or rheumatoid arthritis: A randomized trial." *JAMA* 281, no. 14 (1999): 1304–1309.
27 Le Cunff, Anne-Laure. "The science-based benefits of reading." Ness Labs, paragraph 3, https://nesslabs.com/reading-benefits
28 For a review see: Paul, Annie. "Your brain on fiction." *New York Times*, March 17, 2012, www.nytimes.com/2012/03/18/opinion/sunday/the-neuroscience-of-your-brain-on-fiction.html
29 Gaines, Jeffrey. "The philosophy of ikigai: 3 examples about finding purpose." Positive Psychology.com, August 24, 2021, https://positivepsychology.com/ikigai/
30 Alimujiang, Aliya, Ashley Wiensch, Jonathan Boss, Nancy L. Fleischer, Alison M. Mondul, Karen McLean, Bhramar Mukherjee, and Celeste Leigh Pearce. "Association between life purpose and mortality among US adults older than 50 years." *JAMA network open* 2, no. 5 (2019): e194270. doi:10.1001/jamanetworkopen.2019.4270.
31 García, Héctor, and Francesc Miralles. *Ikigai: The Japanese Secret to a Long and Happy Life.* United Kingdom: Penguin Publishing Group, 2017.
32 Buettner, Dan. *The Blue Zones: 9 Lessons for Living Longer from the People Who've Lived the Longest.* Washington, DC: National Geographic Books, 2012.
33 Brown, Brené. "Brené Brown on joy and gratitude." Global Leadership Network, November 21, 2018, https://globalleadership.org/articles/leading-yourself/brene-brown-on-joy-and-gratitude/
34 Emmons, Robert. "Why gratitude is good." *Mind and Body*, November 16, 2010, https://greatergood.berkeley.edu/article/item/why_gratitude_is_good

Chapter 5

Energy to Engage

Engagement is a positive state of mind characterized by vigor (energy and resilience), dedication (sense of significance in your pursuits), and absorption (concentration and full involvement in activities).[1]

Health and wellness are essential for engagement. We have discussed ways to achieve wellness by addressing the six areas of health: physical, emotional, cognitive, occupational, social, and spiritual. Wellness provides the energy that is required for everything you do. The more energy you have from the six types of health, the more engaged you can be.

When you are deeply engaged, all of your focus goes to the task at hand. This is true whether you're working on a project, studying for an exam, or actively listening to a conversation. Engagement occurs in a focused brain state. Most of your brain's energy is being devoted to thinking about the current task and minimal energy is being wasted on thinking or worrying about other things.

Energy is your brain's most basic and important resource but there is a limited supply. No matter how enjoyable or productive a task, rewards will diminish over time if you try to stay in a focused brain state continuously. Sometimes you might think that if you just keep trying to focus until all your work is done you will have time to rest and enjoy yourself later. But in fact, your brain will probably be so tired later on that it will be difficult to enjoy leisure activities after work. Instead, the best way to support engagement is to understand the energy it requires, and know how to alternate it with sufficient rest.

Your brain needs a lot of energy to focus during periods of engagement. By letting the brain relax into an unfocused resting state for small amounts of time, energy is recovered. You are ready to engage again. This is the most efficient way to make use of the limited fuel available to the brain. Effective energy management means there will still be enough left to understand each other and connect meaningfully.

In this chapter, we will discuss the engaged brain: what your brain is capable of when it is focused. We will also discuss the resting brain: what your brain does to recover energy during unfocused time. Then, we will

DOI: 10.4324/9781003170488-8

Energy to Engage 111

suggest strategies for effectively managing your energy, avoiding cognitive overload, and preventing burnout when interacting virtually.

Engagement Requires a Focused Brain

Engagement is a beneficial state in all realms of life, whether you are working, learning, or socializing. Engaged employees have more energy and are willing to invest it in work. They are more likely to find meaning in their work, feel dedicated to it, and feel fully immersed in the work environment.[2]

Student engagement can be observed in three separate realms where each builds on the next: First, students are behaviorally engaged when they are paying attention and following directions. Second, students demonstrate emotional engagement when they are invested in the learning process. Third, students have achieved cognitive engagement when their minds are truly on the topic being taught and they are able to think critically to solve problems.[3]

Social engagement has similar elements to employee and student engagement. To be socially engaged means being absorbed in the interactions you are having. It enables you to take actions to keep relationships strong and meaningful.

At its most extreme, a high level of engagement in a task is referred to as a flow state. Flow theory was first proposed by psychologist Mihaly Csikszentmihalyi in 1975, who described a state of optimal experience characterized by complete task immersion. In a state of flow a person will experience high intrinsic reward, increased perception of control, and decreased perception of passing time. As Csikszentmihalyi writes:

> Contrary to what we usually believe, moments like these, the best moments in our lives, are not the passive, receptive, relaxing times— although such experiences can also be enjoyable, if we have worked hard to attain them. The best moments usually occur when a person's body or mind is stretched to its limits in a voluntary effort to accomplish something difficult and worthwhile. Optimal experience is thus something that we *make* happen.[4]

The Brain Requires Time to Rest

Whereas the focused brain state is highly active, the unfocused brain state is at rest. Here you can wander, with no central focus at all. Your thoughts are internally focused and not concerned much with external stimuli. This unfocused state can occur any time you let your thoughts drift, such as when you stare out the window without any particular thought in mind.

Focused brain and unfocused brain are both important states that serve functions necessary for activity and optimal energy use. In the focused,

112 Connecting and Thriving

engaged state, you are productive and able to pay attention to what is happening in the present moment. In the unfocused brain state, you rest and recover. With skillful management of time spent in each state, you can make the best use of the energy available to you.

There are negative consequences if you do not skillfully manage your energy. Trying to push your focused brain past its limits will cause your mental, physical, and emotional energy to drop. You will experience a tug-of-war in which your tired brain is pulling you toward an unfocused state as you keep trying to pull it back into focus. Trying to force the brain into a focused state all day long, for example if you are under a strict deadline, will likely trigger the stress response. This will increase your energy and mental acuity short term, but at a high cost. The initial adrenaline burst from the stress response helps you meet the deadline in the short term but has detrimental long-term effects on your overall health. Instead, skillfully managing your time spent in the focused and unfocused brain states will enable sustained engagement.

Alternate Focused and Unfocused Brain Time for Optimal Engagement

Energy is required to function. The focused brain must periodically rest because sustained attention requires so much energy. By alternating focused brain time with recovery through unfocused brain time, you can keep your physical, emotional, cognitive, and spiritual energy at their optimal levels.

If you want your brain to be engaged, you must also give it time to be unfocused and at rest. Muscular strength is increased by alternating activity with rest and recovery. Research has shown that the brain too benefits from alternating activity with rest. You can engage with your focused brain, and then move into an unfocused brain state when you need a mental break. Over time, alternating activity with rest will train your brain to quickly engage when needed.

In today's fast-paced world, people tend to have a strong desire to get things done and to resist taking breaks until they absolutely must. Yet it is essential to give the focused brain some time off. Rest should not only occur at the point of exhaustion. Instead, regularly alternating the high-energy, engaged focused brain state with the unfocused brain state is critical to achieving periods of sustained engagement throughout the day.

Wellness and an Engaged Brain Create the Conditions for Deeper Human Connection

Controlling the way you engage with the world around you by alternating engagement with rest provides benefits to all facets of health. By using your energy wisely and becoming more engaged as a result, you can positively impact your health and ability to focus on human connections.

Physical health benefits from engagement. The fight-or-flight system is quiet when the brain is in a focused state. This is why blood pressure and heart rate lower during meditative activities. Your stress response is not activated because you feel in control of the current situation and there is no perception of threat. By not using up all your energy in a stress response, you have energy available to be active and stay connected with others. Your strength is greater and your endurance for challenges increases.

Emotional health increases with engagement as well. Your outlook is more positive when you are engaged and using your strengths. When you are engaged, you are aware of your inner state and what's happening around you. Engagement also helps build self-esteem and a sense of well-being that facilitate positive interactions and allow for satisfying relationships.

Cognitive health, a measure of how well you think, learn, and remember, improves with full engagement. When you engage with one task at a time using your focused brain, you avoid overtaxing your working memory. That prevents cognitive overload and fatigue. You build mental endurance and the ability to sustain concentration over time. Being focused, attentive, and present benefits your interactions with others.

Occupational health benefits naturally follow from these other positive health results. If you are healthy and engaged in your work, your productivity increases along with your sense of personal fulfillment. Innovation, collaboration, and enthusiasm towards work also increase. At the end of a workday, you still feel energized enough to engage with the people in your life.

Being engaged in your experiences also has spiritual health benefits. Engagement can make the difference between being a spectator and being a true participant in what gives your life meaning. Your actions are consistent with your values and beliefs, strengthening your worldview.

Finally, engagement augments social health and makes deeper connections possible. Being truly engaged with others means having meaningful and fulfilling social relationships, not mere transactional encounters. As researchers Jim Loehr and Tony Schwartz write, "Without time for recovery, our lives become a blur of *doing* unbalanced by much opportunity for *being*."[5] When all of your energy isn't being used up on getting things done, energy is available for being with others in a satisfying way.

Staying Engaged When Physically Apart

The need for sustaining quality engagement has never been greater as work, learning, and social activities occur remotely more than ever. Even when interactions are virtual, you have the capacity to stay engaged from moment to moment. This will prevent you from becoming distracted, overwhelmed, cognitively overloaded, and fatigued.

We are suggesting three categories of science-based engagement strategies that can stimulate the human brain in the remote experience: alternate activity with rest, decrease cognitive load, and regularly reenergize to prevent burnout.

Science-Based Strategies: Suggestions to Optimize Engagement

Alternate Activity with Rest

Research studies have shown that you can attain about 90 minutes of focused engagement before you begin to fatigue and the quality of your performance declines. Athletes make their muscles stronger by active use followed by rest and recovery. In the same way, the brain will be strongest when you alternate periods of high-energy focused brain activity with periods of unfocused brain rest. Researchers Jim Loehr and Tony Schwartz suggest alternating a schedule of 90 to 120 minutes of focused brain engagement with 15 to 20 minutes of unfocused rest. In their book, *The Power of Full Engagement: Managing Energy, Not Time, Is the Key to High Performance and Personal Renewal*, they write, "Intermittently disengaging is what allows us to passionately reengage."[6]

A workplace survey with nearly 20,000 respondents found that employees who take a break every 90 minutes report a 40% increase in the ability to think creatively, a 30% increase in health, and 28% better focus.[7]

• Rest: Your Brain Needs Downtime to Unfocus

Dedicating time to rest, allowing unfocused brain time, is an essential part of staying engaged. It might surprise you that the most important contributor to being engaged is what you're doing in the times when you're not engaged. This is what Loehr and Schwartz found in their research on high performance in professional athletes.

Loehr and Schwartz explain how they came to this conclusion: "Jim spent hundreds of hours watching top players and studying tapes of their matches. To his growing frustration, he could detect almost no significant differences in their competitive habits during points. It was only when he began to notice what they did between points that he suddenly saw a difference."[8] The researchers found that the rest and recovery between points was what made the difference. Rest and recovery make the biggest contribution to the energy a person has available for engagement.

Author Malcolm Gladwell makes a point in his book *Outliers: The Story of Success* that has often been quoted: it takes 10,000 hours of practice to become an expert at anything.[9] This was based on a study by psychologist Anders Ericsson, world-renowned for his research in the psychology of expertise and human performance.[10] Gladwell's emphasis, like many who have also cited Ericsson's study, is on those 10,000 focused brain hours. Often overlooked is what else was going on for those who were becoming experts with their 10,000 hours of work: their unfocused rest times.

As Alex Soojung-Kim Pang explains in his book *Rest: Why You Get More Done When You Work Less*, "We've come to believe that world-class performance comes after 10,000 hours of practice. But that's wrong. It comes after 10,000 hours of deliberate practice, 12,500 hours of deliberate rest, and 30,000 hours of sleep."[11]

When you are ready for a break, consider going out in nature. Research shows that there are tangible physiological benefits of exposure to nature. This was demonstrated in a 1991 study in which researchers showed that exposure to a natural scene, as compared to an urban scene, physically reduced the stress response in participants.[12] In Japan, this has turned into an entire field of therapy called Shinrin-yoku, translated as "forest bathing." A more recent study confirmed the importance of exposure to nature and showed profound benefits to cognitive performance. Participants in the study were assigned cognitively challenging problems to solve, with a break in between each task. Half of the participants spent their break walking through nature, and the other half walked along a busy city street. The participants exposed to nature had significantly better cognitive performance and focus on the task after their break.[13]

If you are able to go out in nature for a brief break, your brain and body will recover more quickly than if you stay at your desk. You can enjoy the health benefits of nature even if you are not able to go outside. Simply looking out your window or at a photograph of a natural scene has demonstrated health benefits.

Your brain will have the opportunity to think and recover its energy when you let it rest. Idle time may be when inspiration and new ideas are most likely to occur to you.

Key actions: Plan for at least 15 to 20 minutes of rest after every 90 minutes of high-focus activity. Choose something that gives your mind a break and lets you stop thinking about work. Whenever possible, spend your downtime outside in nature or look at a natural scene. Use your downtime to allow the brain to renew its energy and drive for action. This will boost creativity and productivity, and make it possible to achieve high levels of performance.[14]

• Activity: Prepare, Schedule, and Reflect on Focused Brain Activity

Get into your best frame of mind for high-energy, focused brain activity. To achieve this frame of mind, prepare for focused brain activity, decide when to use your focused brain, and reflect afterward on how you used your focused brain.

Prepare for focused brain activity. Researchers in organizational psychology have identified that how you start your day is important to the level of engagement you will go on to experience.[15] Employees who undergo a process called 'reattachment" prior to starting work are more likely to be engaged during the day. Reattachment is defined as "rebuilding a mental connection to one's work after a nonwork period." This brings the attention from nonwork to work and begins the psychological transition between the different roles you play in life. It involves thinking forward to the upcoming day and reflecting on your goals. Effectively going through this reattachment process has been shown to create optimal conditions for effective engagement: higher focus, more positive feelings, increased receipt of social support, and increased feelings of job control.

Even if there is negative content in these preparatory thoughts about the day, reattachment can still be helpful. Thinking in advance about expected negative events and mentally planning ways to overcome them is a productive way to reattach. This process can activate positive emotions and mental resources that will be more readily accessible when the negative event is encountered later.

Schedule focused brain activity. Blocking off time for focused brain activity each day will condition your brain for that kind of thinking. There may be external factors in a workday that you can't control, such as meetings and unscheduled situations. However, you can still think about how you schedule your workday and allot your focused brain time.

There is a wide body of research that supports timed routines on a set schedule as the most effective way of working. In his book *Rest: Why You Get More Done When You Work Less*, Alex Soojung-Kim Pang analyzes many scientific studies that provide evidence of this. He shows how the world's most effective, creative, and productive minds managed their time, including famous scientists, mathematicians, artists, and university professors. The common pattern among all these individuals is that they spent approximately four hours each day on the work that required the deepest thinking. Charles Darwin, for example, followed a set schedule that enabled him to publish 19 books and contribute widely to mankind's understanding of evolution. He worked from 10:30 am to noon each morning, then took a nap and a long walk. He returned to his work from 3:00 pm to 5:30 pm each afternoon, and then joined his family for dinner. The highest levels of productivity and creativity in history seem to flow from regular, focused blocks of time.

Reflect on focused brain activity. When you think back on the progress you made during the day, the positive feelings you experience will fuel future engagement. The importance of recognizing small accomplishments is demonstrated in the work of researchers Teresa Amabile and Steven Kramer. After 15 years of studying the habits and psychology of people doing complex work within organizations, they concluded that "of all the things that can boost emotions, motivation, and perception during a workday, the single most important is making progress in meaningful work. And the more frequently people experience that sense of progress, the more likely they are to be creatively productive in the long run."[16]

Progress fuels engagement when it is acknowledged and recognized. Amabile and Kramer explain that this is "because inner work life has such a potent effect on creativity and productivity, and because small but consistent steps forward, shared by many people, can accumulate into excellent execution, progress events that often go unnoticed are critical to the overall performance of organizations."[17]

On the individual level, recognizing progress involves pausing briefly to give yourself credit for something that you accomplished even if it's a small task. This acknowledgment reinforces the motivation that comes from making incremental progress. You can also motivate others by being attentive to their incremental progress and acknowledging it. Studies show that supporting progress is the number one motivator for employees. As Amabile and Kramer point out, "If a person is motivated and happy at the end of the workday, it's a good bet that he or she made some progress. If the person drags out of the office disengaged and joyless, a setback is most likely to blame."[18]

Key actions: Take time to mentally prepare for work before you begin your day. Complete the important mental work of reattaching, even if the commute to your computer is only a few steps. Set out your goals and plan ahead for potential problems. When you notice sustained focus is becoming more difficult, put down what you are doing rather than trying to push harder. Choose the times of the day when you intend to do focused brain activity. At the end of the day, write down at least three areas where you made progress that gives you a sense of accomplishment. By thinking back on your progress for the day, you create positive feelings that fuel future engagement.

Decrease Cognitive Load

Your brain has a limited processing capacity and can therefore become overloaded. Trying to keep working when you are in a state of cognitive overload causes difficulties in concentration, memory, and the processing of new information. As a result, you feel frustrated, overwhelmed, discouraged, or irritable. These emotional reactions can detract from social connections if you take out your frustrations on those around you. Cognitive overload can even affect you physically if the overwork triggers your stress response. However, cognitive overload is preventable. You can decrease cognitive load and avoid entering a state of overload by effectively using focused brain time.

• Prioritize

Prioritizing means deliberately choosing the order in which tasks will receive your attention, based on their relative importance. Prioritizing decreases your cognitive load, the number of things your working memory has to keep track of

118 Connecting and Thriving

at a given time. By making a decision ahead of time about what matters to you, you avoid squandering brain energy on other things.

The ability to prioritize is critical for staying engaged and cognitively healthy but it can be challenging when you have many commitments and devices competing for your attention. Also, blurring of boundaries between work, home, and play in the digital realm can make it difficult to decide what is important to focus on in a given moment. Despite these obstacles, you can prioritize the areas where you want to be engaged.

"The key is not to prioritize what's on your schedule, but to schedule your priorities." This is the advice laid out by Steven Covey in his book *The 7 Habits of Highly Effective People: Powerful Lessons in Personal Change.*[19] Though written decades ago, his advice on prioritizing is often quoted and has become increasingly relevant in the modern day. More than one thing can seem to be top priority when you have many stimuli competing for your attention. It is helpful to prioritize what you choose to do based on your values, not based on what grabs your attention in the moment.

Covey popularized a helpful system of time management that was inspired by the extremely productive United States President Dwight D. Eisenhower. Eisenhower was known for making decisions about allocating time and attention based on levels of importance and urgency. Covey's system asks users to consider tasks along the same dimensions of importance and urgency. "Important" signifies any task that contributes to your larger goals. "Urgent" describes tasks which are time-sensitive.

Research and experience show that the most effective long-term strategy is to prioritize the tasks that fall in the important category.[20] Using your time to do the things that advance your goals sounds obvious but is actually contrary to human nature. Humans have a natural tendency to prioritize based more on urgency than on importance. Researchers call this the "mere urgency effect."[21] The human brain evolved in more dangerous environments where a tendency to address what was most urgent was a clear survival benefit. Unfortunately, in the remote environment with its ubiquitous pop-ups and notifications, prioritizing urgency has become a liability.

Urgent tasks that are time-sensitive and easy to complete come with a quick and obvious payoff. The brain tends to prefer these over more important but less immediately gratifying or time-sensitive tasks. Your brain leans toward completing urgent tasks because they grab your attention and can be quickly checked off your list. This comes at the expense of tasks that are important for goal achievement yet don't carry the same sense of urgency. These important tasks are more likely to be neglected.

By prioritizing based on importance, you are using your own values and goals to decide what to do next. This is the healthy alternative to using a sense of urgency to decide what to do next. Prioritizing based only on urgency enables you to complete many easy tasks, such as quick email responses, but then your day ends without accomplishing the things that

Energy to Engage 119

mattered. Once you choose the important things, you can spend focused time working your way through these. By using your focused brain to address one important item at a time, you can sustain engagement and accomplish what matters most to you. You will be devoting the most energy to the actions that will best serve you.

Important and urgent tasks are easy to identify. On the other hand, the most difficult tasks to prioritize can be the ones which are important but not urgent. These are tasks that advance your goals but don't necessarily grab your attention. The lack of urgency should not be a reason to neglect these goals. Instead, you can take your time in finding the right place in your schedule to address them. By prioritizing time to give your full attention to these important but not urgent tasks, you will be investing energy in goals that benefit you in the long run. This will require working against the natural tendency toward addressing urgency.

When people devote an extended period of time to prioritizing tasks, they can end up "thrashing." This is a computer science term that Brian Christian and Tom Griffiths describe in their book *Algorithms to Live By: The Computer Science of Human Decisions*:

> When merely remembering everything we need to be doing occupies our full attention—or prioritizing every task consumes all the time we had to do them—or our train of thought is continually interrupted before those thoughts can translate to action—it feels like panic, like paralysis by way of hyperactivity. It's thrashing, and computers know it well.[22]

The more things on your plate, the longer it could take to decide what to do next. Prioritizing tasks is important but it's best to avoid allowing it to become a burdensome or time-intensive activity.

Key actions: Figure out what is most important to you and make it the priority to address during your engaged, focused brain time. List the tasks you would like to accomplish in a given day. Have your short-term and long-term goals clearly in your mind. Create a priority list by circling the items that you consider most important. Make sure you are paying attention to those tasks that matter most to your goals, not just the ones that feel most urgent. You can develop the ability to control your attention by clearly prioritizing where you are going to direct it.

- **Form Habits**

   Habit formation is incredibly useful because the conscious mind is the bottleneck of the brain. It can only pay attention to one problem at a time. As a result, your brain is always working to preserve your conscious attention for whatever task is most essential... Habits reduce cognitive load and free up mental capacity, so you can allocate your attention to other tasks.

This is the advice of James Clear in his book *Atomic Habits: An Easy & Proven Way to Build Good Habits & Break Bad Ones*. Clear recognizes that any strategy that reduces cognitive load will improve cognitive health. Having more cognitive health means that your thought processes will be clear and you will be ready to engage for long periods of time in a meaningful way.[23]

You can avoid cognitive overload by using habits. The more habitual the task, the less mental energy it takes up. The brains of professional athletes playing their sports show surprisingly low activity compared to amateurs going through the same actions. This is because athletes' expert actions have been moved to a part of their brain reserved for automatic actions that don't require conscious thoughts or mental calculations.

Stanford neuroscientist David Eagleman describes this phenomenon in his book *Livewired: The Inside Story of the Ever-Changing Brain*:

> The expert's brain has developed neural circuitry specific to soccer, allowing him to make his moves with surprisingly little brain activity. In a sense, the expert has made himself one with the game. In contrast, the amateur's brain is on fire with activity. He's trying to figure out which movements matter… As a result of burning soccer into the circuitry, the pro's performance is both fast and efficient. He's optimized his internal wiring for that which is important in his outside world.[24]

It is possible to "optimize your internal wiring" by developing habits that decrease cognitive load. Clear describes habits as mental shortcuts that are developed with repetition. He explains four steps for building habits.

The first step is to establish the cue that triggers your behavior. The cue should be something obvious. For example, if you are trying to develop a habit of going to the gym every morning, you can leave your gym shoes by the door. Alternatively, you can use the method known as "habit stacking." This involves associating a new habit with something you already do each day, such as brushing your teeth. This cue serves as a daily reminder to do the activity that you want to develop into a new habit.

The second, third, and fourth steps all relate to making the new habit easy and rewarding. The second step is to couple the habit with a concrete reward, such as treating yourself to your favorite smoothie on the way home from the gym. The third step is to make the habit as easy as possible, by anticipating obstacles that could keep you from doing the activity. If it is a challenge to get to the gym, you could arrange to meet a friend there. That way, it will be harder to avoid going to the gym when your friend is waiting there for you. The fourth step is to associate completion of the habit with a sense of satisfaction. One way to acknowledge completion is with a habit tracker app,

Energy to Engage 121

which shows your progress visually and can make you feel good about how far you have come.

Repeating these four specific steps will eventually make the habit automatic. When behaviors become automatic, it decreases your cognitive load.

Key actions: Decide on habits that you would like to commit to. Repeat them until they have to think about. Use the techniques of habit stacking, setting up rewards, and decreasing obstacles to make sure the habits become routines. You can use the newly freed up time and energy to engage with your most important challenges and pursuits throughout the day.

• Use Available Resources

Working on problems physically decreases cognitive load and increases available space in working memory. Studies have shown that people who are given physical items with which to solve problems perform better than those who are asked to solve them only by mental representation. The same benefits are shown for students who learn about new subject matter using objects that they can manipulate rather than simply concepts to be grasped in their minds. For example, it is easier for students to learn the laws of physics by seeing how they affect real objects than by hearing a lecture about them.

When a problem doesn't lend itself to solving using three-dimensional space, it can help to put it down on paper. Making things concrete, whether written on a piece of paper or typed on a computer, helps you hold onto thoughts and process ideas. In *Thinking Fast and Slow*, Daniel Kahneman encourages thinkers to decrease load "by dividing our tasks into multiple easy steps, committing intermediate results... to paper rather than to an easily overloaded working memory."[25] The more you break up tasks into smaller pieces and use material resources, the more mental space you have available.

As soon as you jot down the thing you are trying to remember, your working memory is no longer responsible for tracking and holding on to it. Instead, your working memory can process something else. You will have more mental space to process things both cognitively and emotionally throughout the day. The value of writing down ideas was deeply espoused by the founder of Amazon, Jeff Bezos. He required that before any new idea or product was introduced, his executives write a narratively structured six-page memo. The team sat down with the prepared memo in meetings and gave everyone time to read it. Bezos found that the higher the quality of the memo writing, the higher the quality of the subsequent discussion.[26] Writing things down is an excellent way to clarify your thinking and explore ideas using the senses.

You can also augment your working memory's capacity by joining it with the working memory of others. Harvard Professor of Psychology David Wegner termed this "transactive memory" in a 1985 paper. He studied the way that groups work collectively to remember things since no one individual can remember everything. Each person in a group holds on to certain pieces of information, and is aware of who knows the information that they don't.[27] Other people are a resource, and our brains are designed to work together to solve problems.

Key Actions: Use resources outside of your brain to decrease your cognitive load and use up less mental energy. Use physical objects to represent a problem you're working on so you can look at it from different angles. Write things down and make lists in order to store less in your own head. Work on problems with other people to use their brains as well. Using all the resources that are available to you prevents cognitive overload.

Prevent Burnout by Keeping Your Fuel Tank Full

In this final category of science-based strategies to optimize engagement, we focus on regular reenergizing to prevent burnout. It is essential to recover the energy that you expended. You can also increase the amount of fuel from all your sources of health: physical, emotional, cognitive, occupational, spiritual, and social. We suggest here some strategies for filling up your fuel tank.

Regular refueling keeps you from experiencing the symptoms of burnout. These symptoms are: exhaustion (depleted energy), detachment (disengagement from your job and negative or cynical feelings about it), and inefficacy (feeling a lack of productivity or competence). The opposite of burnout is sustained quality engagement. Researchers have identified dimensions of engagement that oppose each of the components of burnout: vigor in place of exhaustion, dedication in place of detachment, and absorption in place of inefficacy.[28]

Burnout occurs when your natural capacities are continually exceeded by the demands of your work. Implementing reenergizing strategies builds up a store of fuel and protects you from burning out. As Loehr and Schwartz state, 'Energy is our most important individual and organizational resource."[29]

Keep in mind that prevention is the best cure for burnout. Burnout in the workplace can be averted by taking actions that prevent exhaustion, detachment, and feelings of inefficacy. As the foremost researcher in burnout Christina Maslach writes: "People who are engaged with their work are better able to cope with the challenges they encounter and thus are more likely to recover from stress. So building an engaged workforce, before there are major problems, is a great prevention strategy."[30]

• Prevent Profound Exhaustion: Modify Heavy Workloads

A Gallup survey of 7,500 full-time employees identified unmanageable workload and unreasonable time pressure as two of the top causes of burnout.[31] Experiencing the burnout symptom of profound physical, emotional, and cognitive exhaustion negatively impacts your work and the effectiveness of your teams and organization.

Chronic exhaustion from excessive workloads and tight deadlines can be prevented. You can analyze patterns of work and activity to see how this could be adding to the development of fatigue. Rethink processes that involve too many purposeless check-ins, tasks without clear expectations, or project demands with insufficient resources or time allotments. Also, take a look at technology use. Consider phasing out any digital technology that is adding a new layer of work and demands. If it is bringing more stress than relief, make sure it is only used for essential tasks.

As an example of technology bringing more stress, studies have found that electronic health records have become a major source of burnout for physicians. Data show that physicians spend one to two hours on electronic health records and other desk work for every hour spent with a patient.[32] These are significant findings given that physicians working 60 or more hours a week who reported burnout were also found to make more medical mistakes.[33]

Key actions: Examine work processes and use of technology. Take steps to resolve the issues causing unmanageable workloads and unreasonable deadline pressures. Consider which tasks can be streamlined or eliminated to free up time and energy for other important work. Energy is your greatest resource and that holds true for your organization as well.

• Prevent Profound Exhaustion: Create an End-of-Workday Ritual

In professor Cal Newport's book *Deep Work: Rules for Focused Success in a Distracted World*, he recommends a "shutdown ritual" to close out the day:

> This ritual should ensure that every incomplete task, goal, or project has been reviewed and that for each you have confirmed that either (1) you have a plan you trust for its completion, or (2) it's captured in a place where it will be revisited when the time is right. The process should be an algorithm: a series of steps you always conduct, one after another.[34]

He advocates turning off at the end of a workday and getting rest because downtime gives you the energy to work deeply the next day.

Implementing an end-of-workday ritual sends a clear signal to your brain that you are finished with work for the day and can begin to recharge. By using the same ritual each day, your brain will begin to associate it with the revitalization process. Over time, your brain will respond automatically to the cue provided by the ritual and more easily shift out of work mode. Newport speaks a "termination phrase" aloud at the end of his ritual to send a signal to his brain that it's safe to stop thinking about work. He writes:

124 Connecting and Thriving

If a work-related worry pops to mind, I *always* answer it with the following thought process: I said the termination phrase. I wouldn't have said this phrase if I hadn't checked over all of my tasks, my calendar, and my weekly plan and decided that everything was captured and I was on top of everything. Therefore, there is no need to worry.[35]

You can choose any set of actions and any termination phrase. What matters most is not what you do but that you perform a similar set of actions to close out each workday. It can be as simple as reviewing the day's accomplishments, updating a master task list, and then saying a termination phrase. The brain learns well through repetition and ritual.

Research shows that the more effective your end-of-workday ritual, the better you will sleep. A study compared sleep patterns between two groups of adults who did a five-minute writing task before bed. One group was instructed to write down what they had completed that day, while the other wrote a to-do list and thoughts about what they needed to do the next day. The to-do list group fell asleep significantly faster than the other. The more specific the to-do list and written thoughts about the next day, the faster the group participants fell asleep. This ritual seems to prevent the rumination about incomplete future tasks that can make falling asleep difficult.[36]

Key actions: Decide on a deliberate transition out of activity at the end of the day. Implement your end-of-workday ritual, doing the same set of actions and speaking a set termination phrase, at the same time and place if possible. Consider writing a to-do list before bed to help your brain relax into sleep. Having a consistent set of actions that you do at the end of your workday helps you mentally disengage from work and begin to reenergize.

• Prevent Feelings of Detachment: Practice Small Acts of Kindness

Research suggests that small acts of kindness toward others can decrease feelings of disengagement and detachment, helping people regain a sense of connectedness.[37] An example of this was demonstrated by the experience of a physician we interviewed who was experiencing high stress from the demands of hospital work.

This physician had been feeling detached from his work and his colleagues as more and more of their meetings were being held virtually. He worried that his patients' care would suffer as these feelings of detachment were making it more difficult for him to connect to their experiences. One day, he stopped to talk to the janitor in the hospital and thank him for his work. He found out the janitor had worked there for many decades. The janitor was clearly pleased to be recognized in a way that didn't typically occur in the course of his workday. Through the simple act of thanking the janitor, this physician had a renewed sense of connectedness and belonging in a community. There was a double benefit in that the janitor felt good about himself, and the physician went through the rest of the day feeling better and significantly more connected.

Decades of research have shown that receiving compliments, recognition, and praise triggers positive emotions in the recipients. Both the givers and the receivers benefit from kindness. Sometimes giving others compliments, recognition, and praise can make you even happier than receiving them. As a giver, complimenting increases your optimism and feelings of self-worth. It also makes you feel more engaged and socially connected.

Key actions: Practice kindness by acknowledging others to let them know you appreciate them. Instead of turning inward and focusing on yourself when you feel alienated, turn outwards to focus on others in small but meaningful ways. You can send a gratitude email to a colleague or give praise to team members for doing a great job on a project. These small acts of kindness benefit both the receiver and the giver.

• Prevent Feelings of Detachment: Ensure Fair Treatment

Unfair treatment at work is the number one contributor to burnout. Unfair treatment includes bias, mistreatment by a co-worker, unfair compensation or corporate policies, and favoritism. When employees feel they are being treated unfairly, it harms relationships in the organization and leads to a lack of satisfaction at work. When employees cannot trust their managers, leaders, or team members, it is harder to form the kinds of interpersonal bonds that bring meaning to work. As a result of unfair treatment, absenteeism increases and people even leave their jobs permanently.[38]

Constanze Leineweber, researcher and lecturer of organizational behavior at Norwich Business School, makes it clear that reducing unfair treatment must be a priority for those who lead:

> Perceived fairness at work is a modifiable aspect of the work environment, as is job insecurity. Organizations have significant control over both... Organizations might gain by selection of supervisors for their qualities associated with fair practices, training supervisors in justice principles, and implementing performance management practices for them that consider their use of organizational justice.[39]

It is critically important for fair treatment to be held up as an important value in the organization.

Key actions: Recognize that unfair practices can be modified to improve the work environment. Check whether the people with whom you work feel they are being treated equally and respectfully. Pay attention to the level of satisfaction people feel about their work and be aware of employee absenteeism that is

126 Connecting and Thriving

caused by unfair treatment at work. Most importantly, do whatever you can to make sure every voice has the opportunity to be heard. Take every complaint seriously and act on it in an open, prompt manner. Reducing unfair treatment is the best way to prevent burnout.

• Prevent Feelings of Inefficacy: Learn New Skills

Learning a new skill can be more reenergizing than simple relaxation. This was the finding of researchers at the University of Mannheim in Germany and Portland State University. The study looked specifically at what people did during vacations from work, and correlated activities with how reenergized they felt on returning to work. Those who learned a new skill (e.g., scuba diving) reported more revitalization than those who engaged in simple leisure (e.g., sitting on a beach). The researchers hypothesized that skill learning enabled people to truly engage during vacation, and detach effectively from work long enough to replenish their energy. Some of the beachgoers, on the other hand, did not give themselves the opportunity to mentally detach. By continuing to think about work while on vacation, they had no separation from feelings of ineffectiveness and reduced productivity.[40]

This study and many others like it demonstrate how effective it can be to renew your energy by learning new skills when you are not at work. For example, you can learn a new language, a new style of cooking, or a new type of dance. It can be any skill you are interested in or passionate about learning. Using your time off from work to engage with a new challenge gives you a sense of personal accomplishment and renewed feelings of efficacy. It replenishes your energy. When you bring your attention back to work, you will feel reenergized and ready to engage with the next challenge.

A learning process replete with small, tangible goals that you can check off when completed will give you a sense of accomplishment. Learning a new skill brings your awareness to the present moment. The human brain spends a lot of time thinking about the future and planning ahead. Letting the brain focus on something in the present that can be planned and carried out with real-time results can bring cognitive relief and a renewal of energy.

Key actions: Identify a new skill that you would like to develop. Work on this skill in order to keep your brain engaged with the present moment. Doing this during your time off from work gives you a mental break, reenergizes you, and makes you feel accomplished.

• Prevent Feelings of Inefficacy: Work with Your Hands

In Robert Greene's book *Mastery*, he describes the benefits of revitalizing your energy by doing some kind of work with your hands:

> When we work with our hands and build something, we learn how to sequence our actions and how to organize our thoughts. In taking

anything apart in order to fix it, we learn problem-solving skills that have wider applications. Even if it is only as a side activity, you should find a way to work with your hands, or to learn more about the inner workings of the machines and pieces of technology around you.[41]

For thousands of years, humans used their hands to find food and make tools needed for daily survival. Digital technology has now made many tasks achievable with minimal physical effort. You simply push a button, swipe, or click. Doing away with manual tasks is actually going against human nature.

Actively using your hands for any type of manual task is satisfying because it activates the positive feedback loop hard-wired in the brain. Your efforts produce a tangible result and there's a sense of accomplishment from achieving a goal. The rewarding feeling of working with your hands on a task during unfocused brain time makes it easier to return to focused brain engagement. Reenergized from your unfocused time, you can maintain the high energy of the focused brain state without the threat of burnout.

Using your hands on a task, even a simple one like cleaning a sink, keeps you active without putting much demand on you cognitively. There are many different ways you can work with your hands besides scrubbing your plumbing fixtures. These include painting, drawing, guitar playing, planting, sewing, building with Lego, origami, fixing a car, woodworking, and yard work, among others. Working with your hands can release the feel-good brain chemicals serotonin and endorphins, and reduce your level of the stress hormone cortisol. In addition to relieving stress, manual tasks can provide a sense of accomplishment to counteract feelings of inefficacy at work.

Key actions: If you are starting to feel ineffective at work, take a step back. Select a manual task that you find pleasurable and relaxing. Work with your hands on this task during your rest time or time outside of work to build back a feeling of efficacy. Notice how it relieves stress, lifts your mood, and revitalizes your energy.

Energy is essential for engagement. The more energy you have from all sources of wellness, the more you can be engaged. "The number of hours in a day is fixed, but the quantity and quality of energy available to use is not. It is our most precious resource," write Loehr and Schwartz. "The more we take responsibility for the energy we bring to the world, the more empowered and productive we become."[42]

The science-based strategies we suggest for preventing exhaustion, detachment, and feelings of inefficacy can benefit everyone. Consider how you can share with others your first-hand experiences of implementing engagement strategies and give them the space, resources, and support they need for revitalization.

128 Connecting and Thriving

Go forward, with this in mind:

1 **Health and wellness are essential for engagement**

- Wellness provides the energy that is required for everything you do.
- Energy is the brain's most basic and important resource.
- The more energy you have from the six types of health, the more engaged you can be.

2 **Engagement requires a focused brain**

- Engaged employees are willing to invest their energy in their work.
- Students can demonstrate behavioral, emotional, and cognitive engagement.
- Social engagement enables you to make meaningful connections.

3 **The brain requires time to rest**

- Your engaged, focused brain needs time off to rest and recover.
- The unfocused brain state is when your mind is at rest.

4 **Regularly alternate between the focused and unfocused brain states**

- Skillful management of time spent in each state optimizes energy.
- Alternating focused and unfocused brain time is necessary for sustained engagement.

5 **Wellness and an engaged brain create the conditions for deeper human connection.**

Notes

1 Schaufeli, Wilmar B., and Arnold B. Bakker. "Job demands, job resources, and their relationship with burnout and engagement: A multi-sample study." *Journal of organizational behavior: the international journal of industrial, occupational and organizational psychology and behavior* 25, no. 3 (2004): 293–315, https://doi.org/10.1002/job.248
2 Schaufeli, Wilmar B., and Arnold B. Bakker. "Job demands, job resources, and their relationship with burnout and engagement: A multi-sample study." *Journal of Organizational Behavior: The International Journal of Industrial, Occupational and Organizational Psychology and Behavior* 25, no. 3 (2004): 293–315, https://doi.org/10.1002/job.248
3 Almarode, John, and Ann M. Miller. *Captivate, Activate, and Invigorate the Student Brain in Science and Math, Grades 6–12*. Washington, DC: Corwin Press, 2013.
4 Csikszentmihalyi, Mihaly. *Flow: The Psychology of Optimal Experience*. New York: HarperPerennial, 1990, 3.
5 Loehr, Jim, and Tony Schwartz. *The Power of Full Engagement: Managing Energy, Not Time, Is the Key to High Performance and Personal Renewal*. London: Free Press, 2005, 34
6 Loehr, Jim, and Tony Schwartz. *The Power of Full Engagement: Managing Energy, Not Time, Is the Key to High Performance and Personal Renewal*. London: Free Press, 2005, 39.

7 *What Is Your Quality Of Life @ Work?* HBR.org and The Energy Project, November 2013–June 2014, https://uli.org/wp-content/uploads/ULI-Documents/The-Human-Era-at-Work.pdf

8 Loehr, Jim, and Tony Schwartz. *The Power of Full Engagement: Managing Energy, Not Time, Is the Key to High Performance and Personal Renewal.* London: Free Press, 2005, 32.

9 Gladwell, Malcolm. *Outliers: The Story of Success.* London: Penguin Books Limited, 2008.

10 Ericsson, Anders K., Ralf T. Krampe, and Clemens Tesch-Romer. "The Role of Deliberate Practice in the Acquisition of Expert Performance." *Psychological Review* 100, no. 3 (1993): 363–406, doi:10.1037/0033–295x.100.3.363.

11 Pang, Alex Soojung-Kim. *Rest: Why You Get More Done When You Work Less.* London: Basic Books, 2016, 74.

12 Ulrich, Roger S., Robert F. Simons, Barbara D. Losito, Evelyn Fiorito, Mark A. Miles, and Michael Zelson. "Stress recovery during exposure to natural and urban environments." *Journal of environmental psychology* 11, no. 3 (1991): 201–230.

13 Berman, Marc G., John Jonides, and Stephen Kaplan. "The cognitive benefits of interacting with nature." *Psychological science* 19, no. 12 (2008): 1207–1212.

14 Jabr, Ferris. "Why your brain needs more downtime." *Scientific American,* October 15, 2013, www.scientificamerican.com/article/mental-downtime/

15 For example, see: Sonnentag, Sabine, Kathrin Eck, Charlotte Fritz, and Jana Kühnel. "Morning reattachment to work and work engagement during the day: A look at day-level mediators." *Journal of management* 46, no. 8 (2020): 1408–1435.

16 Amabile, Teresa M., and Steven J. Kramer. "The power of small wins." *Harvard Business Review* 89, no. 5 (2011): 72.

17 Amabile, Teresa M., and Steven J. Kramer. "The power of small wins." *Harvard Business Review* 89, no. 5 (2011): 75.

18 Amabile, Teresa M., and Steven J. Kramer. "The power of small wins." *Harvard Business Review* 89, no. 5 (2011): 74.

19 Covey, Stephen R. *The 7 Habits of Highly Effective People: Powerful Lessons in Personal Change.* London: Simon & Schuster, 2013, 170.

20 Herrera, Tim. "Why your brain tricks you into doing less important tasks." *New York Times,* July 9, 2018, www.nytimes.com/2018/07/09/smarter-living/eisenhower-box-productivity-tips.html

21 Meng Zhu, Yang Yang, and Christopher K. Hsee. "The mere urgency effect." *Journal of consumer research* 45, no. 3 (2018): 673–690, https://doi.org/10.1093/jcr/ucy008

22 Christian, Brian and Tom Griffiths. *Algorithms to Live By: The Computer Science of Human Decisions.* New York: Henry Holt and Company, 2016, 123.

23 Clear, James. *Atomic Habits: An Easy & Proven Way to Build Good Habits & Break Bad Ones.* New York: Penguin Publishing Group, 2018, 46.

24 Eagleman, David. *Livewired: The Inside Story of the Ever-Changing Brain.* New York: Knopf Doubleday Publishing Group, 2020, 42–43.

25 Kahneman, Daniel. *Thinking, Fast and Slow.* New York: Farrar, Straus and Giroux, 2011, 38.

26 Bariso, Justin. "Why intelligent minds like Jeff Bezos embrace the rule of writing." *Inc,* August 29, 2021, www.inc.com/justin-bariso/how-to-write-amazon-jeff-bezos-memos-meetings-clear-writing-clear-thinking-rule-of-writing.html

27 Wegner, Daniel M. "Don't fear the cybermind." *New York Times,* August 4, 2012, www.nytimes.com/2012/08/05/opinion/sunday/memory-and-the-cybermind.html

28 Schaufeli, Wilmar B., and Arnold B. Bakker. "Job demands, job resources, and their relationship with burnout and engagement: A multi-sample study."

Journal of Organizational Behavior: The International Journal of Industrial, Occupational and Organizational Psychology and Behavior 25, no. 3 (2004): 293–315, https://doi.org/10.1002/job.248

29 Loehr, Jim, and Tony Schwartz. *The Power of Full Engagement: Managing Energy, Not Time, Is the Key to High Performance and Personal Renewal.* London: Free Press, 2005, 197.

30 Maslach, Christina. "Burnout and engagement in the workplace: New perspectives." *The European health psychologist* 13, no. 3 (2011): 45.

31 Wigert, Ben and Sangeeta Agrawal. "Employee burnout, part 1: The 5 main causes." Gallup, July 12, 2018, www.gallup.com/workplace/237059/employee-burnout-part-main-causes.aspx

32 Arndt, Brian G., John W. Beasley, Michelle D. Watkinson, Jonathan L. Temte, Wen-Jan Tuan, Christine A. Sinsky, and Valerie J. Gilchrist. "Tethered to the EHR: Primary care physician workload assessment using EHR event log data and time-motion observations." *The Annals of Family Medicine* 15, no. 5 (2017): 419–426, https://doi.org/10.1370/afm.2121

33 Wen, Jin, Yongzhong Cheng, Xiuying Hu, Ping Yuan, Tianyou Hao, and Yingkang Shi. "Workload, burnout, and medical mistakes among physicians in China: A cross-sectional study." *Bioscience trends* 10, no. 1 (2016): 27–33, doi:10.5582/bst.2015.01175.

34 Newport, Cal. *Deep Work: Rules for Focused Success in a Distracted World.* New York: Grand Central Publishing, 2016, 170.

35 Newport, Cal. "Drastically reduce stress with a work shutdown ritual." Study Hacks Blog, Cal Newport, June 8, 2009: paragraph 7, www.calnewport.com/blog/2009/06/08/drastically-reduce-stress-with-a-work-shutdown-ritual/

36 Scullin, Michael K., Madison L. Krueger, Hannah K. Ballard, Natalya Pruett, and Donald L. Bliwise. "The effects of bedtime writing on difficulty falling asleep: A polysomnographic study comparing to-do lists and completed activity lists." *Journal of experimental psychology: general* 147, no. 1 (2018): 139–146, https://doi.org/10.1037/xge0000374

37 Schabram, Kira and Yu Tse Heng. "Educators and students are burned out: These strategies can help." *Harvard business publishing: education*, April 29, 2021, https://hbsp.harvard.edu/inspiring-minds/educators-and-students-are-burned-out-these-strategies-can-help

38 Wigert, Ben and Sangeeta Agrawal. "Employee burnout, part 1: The 5 main causes." Gallup, July 12, 2018, www.gallup.com/workplace/237059/employee-burnout-part-main-causes.aspx

39 Leineweber, Constanze, Claudia Bernhard-Oettel, Paraskevi Peristera, Constanze Eib, Anna Nyberg and Hugo Westerlund. "Interactional justice at work is related to sickness absence: A study using repeated measures in the Swedish working population." *BMC public health* 17, no. 912 (2017): Conclusions, https://doi.org/10.1186/s12889-017-4899-y

40 Sonnentag, Sabine, Kathrin Eck, Charlotte Fritz, and Jana Kühnel. "Morning reattachment to work and work engagement during the day: A look at day-level mediators." *Journal of management* 46, no. 8 (2020): 1408–1435.

41 Greene, Robert. *Mastery.* New York: Penguin Books, 2013, 64.

42 Loehr, Jim, and Tony Schwartz. *The Power of Full Engagement: Managing Energy, Not Time, Is the Key to High Performance and Personal Renewal.* United Kingdom: Free Press, 2005, 5.

Chapter 6

Social Creatures

Humans are social creatures. US Surgeon General Vivek H. Murthy makes this point in his book *Together: The Healing Power of Human Connection in a Sometimes Lonely World:* "We have a universal need to connect with one another."[1] The groundwork was laid about 200,000 years ago when the first Homo sapiens began to work cooperatively, and outlive and outsmart their bigger and brawnier competitors. Our ancestors were not designed to forage alone and would not have survived one winter if they had tried. Instead, they learned to work together. Working cooperatively was favored by natural selection.

The need for a sense of belonging in a community became a deeply wired, instinctual need in the human brain. Psychology and neuroscience have scientifically demonstrated that our brains are wired to fulfill our roles as social creatures. This wiring causes humans to crave a sense of belonging. When our primary human need for belonging is met, our brains allow us to function at our highest levels.

In contrast, when deprived of connection and belonging, humans can suffer severe consequences. Infants left on their own cannot survive. Babies given only minimal food and shelter, without love and attention, develop poorly.[2] Adults lacking social connection can have an increased risk for physical consequences, such as heart disease and infections. They also can have cognitive issues, such as poor memory and slowed processing. Emotionally, adults lacking social connection can suffer from severe and prolonged responses to stress.[3]

These consequences prove that the human brain is hard-wired to promote and maintain social connection. Being disconnected from others is experienced as a threat. There are mechanisms in the brain to recognize this threat and activate people-seeking behavior, just as the brain recognizes hunger and activates food-seeking behavior. Meaningful, fulfilling social interactions are what will satisfy the hunger for human connection.

While our basic need for human connection has not changed throughout evolution, the ways in which we interact have changed dramatically. The rapid advance of digital technology has required humans to alter the ways we work and interact with one another. But, as a species, we evolve

DOI: 10.4324/9781003170488-9

at a much slower pace than technology advances. As Rachel Carson wrote of technology in her landmark book *Silent Spring*, "The rapidity of change and the speed with which new situations are created follow the impetuous and heedless pace of man rather than the deliberate pace of nature."[4]

This brings us back to our paradox: the technology humans created to stay connected can leave us feeling disconnected. Technology serves our desire for efficiency but doesn't necessarily take our needs for safety and comfort, understanding, and belonging into account. The basic need for human connection has not changed although more and more of our interactions take place remotely.

"When human groups encounter new environments they must adapt," according to Daniel Berleant, a pioneer in the field of bioinformatics. He emphasizes that even though some people will have to learn to overcome the challenges that surface during the process of adaption, most will learn to exist in the new environment.[5] It is important to consider how best to adapt to the remote experience and seek a sense of belonging among others.

Science has demonstrated that being social is the brain's resting state. We think about other people in our spare moments. Research has also shown that humans crave belonging when disconnected from others, just as much as they crave food when hungry. This hard-wired need drives us toward others.

Belonging to a group enables a person to feel contented and productive. Group members' brain waves synchronize, promoting trust and cohesion in the group. Brain chemicals surge, making us feel good and reinforcing positive social behavior. Oxytocin causes feelings of being bonded with the group and decreases the stress response. Dopamine creates feelings of pleasure and endorphins cause feelings of happiness and decreased pain. Humans are more creative and innovative when we join our brains together instead of working alone.

Social connection can be achieved on a more regular basis by keeping in mind three aspects of a human-centered approach to improving the remote experience: prioritizing people, communicating to connect, and cultivating a sense of purpose and meaning. These are crucial for addressing the human side of work, learning, and social interactions. We will define these ways to humanize the remote experience and review the research that has confirmed their importance for strengthening connections.

Being Connected on a Human Level: Prioritize People

Prioritizing people means taking a human-centered approach to the remote experience. This approach makes people feel seen, heard, and respected. It involves acknowledging their thoughts, feelings, and opinions.

The more you show you care about others, the more they will feel safe, understood, and included.

There are small but simple ways to add depth to virtual interactions. A professor we interviewed illustrates this: "The camera brings us into people's home offices, kitchens, or even bedrooms, where we can get a glimpse of their world that was previously hidden from our professional encounters. This can add depth to how we see and interact with each other." She acknowledges that "working remotely does flatten human interactions, but if we take time to look and talk, the experience can reveal the depth of one's character and challenge our assumptions."

Simple acts can show people you care about them. Another professor shared with us how she acknowledges each student from the first moment they walk into her classroom. "I have a ritual before the start of each course where I learn every student's name and read their one-sheet biographies. When they walk into class for the first time, they are surprised to learn that I not only know their name, I also know something about them." She comments on the benefits of this practice: "It shows them that I care and that I took the time to get to know them as individuals. My intention is to convey the message, 'I know you. I see you. I acknowledge you.'" Often, the first comment she gets in the students' end-of-course evaluations is, "The professor knew all of our names on the first day of class." This feedback makes it clear that a small act can have a big impact.

Recognizing people and accepting them for who they are strengthens connection. Showing empathy and creating psychological safety are also ways to accomplish this.

Dr. Helen Riess of the Empathy and Relational Science program at Harvard Medical School defines empathy as "a complex capability enabling individuals to understand and feel the emotional states of others, resulting in compassionate behavior." Dr. Riess further clarifies that "compassion cannot exist without empathy, as they are part of the same perception and response continuum that moves human beings from observation to action."[6]

Perceiving the feelings of other people is a complex process. It occurs in two ways: cognitive empathy and emotional empathy. Cognitive empathy refers to the ability to recognize and understand how another person feels and what that person might be thinking. Emotional empathy is an automatic and effortless process that is more commonly referenced. This type of empathy is what a person means when they say, "I feel your pain." You might experience this, for example, when observing a colleague receive difficult feedback in a meeting. When you wince in pain, you are sharing the feelings of the person receiving feedback without any direct emotional stimulation to yourself.

Empathizing involves taking another person's perspective. Cognitive perspective-taking refers to the ability to make inferences about others' thoughts and beliefs, whereas affective perspective-taking is the ability to make inferences about their emotional state.[7] Perspective-taking is an extremely important ability because it allows you to see situations in multiple ways and leads to more effective interactions. Considering an issue or situation from another person's point of view not only expands your own perspective, it also fosters understanding and empathy.

Social sensitivity refers to the ability to perceive the feelings and viewpoints of others by paying attention to their cues, such as facial expressions and tone of voice. The meaning of those cues can be analyzed using cognitive empathy. By using both social sensitivity and cognitive empathy, you can gain a deeper understanding of others' experiences and can figure out how to support and connect with them. More deliberate attention to social sensitivity and cognitive empathy is required in virtual interactions where the usual cues are missing or distorted.

Cognitive and emotional empathy are each important. Emotional empathy tends to play more of a role among individuals who have similar goals, backgrounds, and experiences.[8] It is much easier to share the pain of someone when you closely identify with their experience. You may rely more on cognitive empathy and social sensitivity when you haven't had a similar experience of pain. In that case, you can make an effort to understand what another person is feeling even when you do not share the feeling.

A multitude of research studies have taken place in diverse workplaces to quantify the benefits of empathy. Stanford University psychology professor Jamil Zaki gives an account of this research in his book *The War for Kindness: Building Empathy in a Fractured World*. In a workplace with a culture of empathy, employees are more committed to their work and report lower stress levels. In teams that practice empathy, collaboration is more effective. Individuals who are skilled at using empathy are more likely to assist colleagues and to act in an ethical fashion. People who receive empathic treatment from their managers were shown to have fewer physical ailments, and more positive feelings that correlated with increased progress toward goals.[9]

Additional research has been done on the impact of empathy in leaders. When leaders show empathy, it increases employees' creativity, productivity, morale, loyalty, and willingness to work. When leaders give feedback with empathy, employees are better able to make use of the feedback and not become defensive.[10]

Empathy is an essential component of prioritizing people. Increasing levels of cognitive or emotional empathy is one of the most powerful ways to address the interpersonal challenges of being remote. You can model empathic understanding to encourage others to develop this ability. Sharing and understanding the feelings of others leads to more positive human interactions in a remote work environment.

Consider various ways to prioritize people, such as:

- Create opportunities for people to get to know each other's interests, preferences, skills, and strengths.
- Model and reinforce the interpersonal behaviors you want to see in other people. Set an example by being aware of yourself and others, respecting others, caring about them, and explicitly showing that you are listening.
- Show empathy for others. Make inferences about their emotions and imagine how they feel. Understand their views and be willing to take their perspective. Show social sensitivity.
- Foster empathy by creating situations where people learn about their differences, respect them, and accept them.
- Encourage team members to observe and listen to nonverbal cues, such as eye expressions and tone of voice, to better understand the feelings of the group.
- Openly discuss the importance of establishing psychological safety. Make it an explicit priority to accept others and create a safe space for them to feel included, learn, grow, and contribute. Make sure each team member has the chance to speak.
- Show concern and support for team members by soliciting their input, gathering different perspectives, and considering their views on the issues that affect them.
- Respect people's time. Shorten meetings whenever possible. Add recovery time to schedules.
- Focus on building trust by giving team members the benefit of the doubt when it comes to the team's best interests. Draw on the expertise of team members.
- Encourage participation in leadership development programs. Make sure these programs cultivate leadership behaviors that foster psychological safety.

Being Open and Intentional: Communicate to Connect

In the remote environment, communicating to connect with other human beings requires a willingness to speak openly and honestly about your own thoughts and feelings. This makes it easier for others to do the same. Your choice of words and the ways in which you deliver them are both critically important. As Brené Brown writes, "Clear is kind. Unclear is unkind."[11] It is essential for your communication to be clear, concise, and precise.

Clear communication is especially important in virtual interactions when some of the nonverbal signals are missing or distorted. Pioneer of psychological safety Amy Edmondson writes

Distributed work is making us realize we have to be more deliberately—more proactively—open. We have to be explicit in sharing our ideas, questions, and concerns, because we can't just overhear what's happening in the next cubicle. We now have to work a little harder to share what we're thinking, to ask questions.[12]

In addition to sharing your own thoughts and feelings, communicating to connect involves asking questions and listening to others' perspectives. Brené Brown also writes about this: "A brave leader is someone who says I see you. I hear you. I don't have all the answers, but I'm going to keep listening and asking questions."[13] Understanding what's at stake for your team and what matters to them enables you to respond sensitively and make your messages relevant. Gathering information about others through asking deliberate questions and listening to learn is invaluable for creating meaningful connections with others.

Storytelling, one of the oldest forms of human communication, is an effective way to deliver meaningful messages and engage listeners. Stories are often personal, relatable, emotional, and memorable. According to the Ariel Group, a communication training organization, "Storytelling does not require skill or talent but a willingness to be vulnerable and authentic."[14] Telling concise and vivid stories is a powerful way to connect with the hearts and minds of other human beings.

When you listen to facts, only two areas of your brain are activated: one for language comprehension and the other for language processing. But when you listen to a story, another six areas of the brain are also activated: those responsible for processing touch, movement, balance, sound, smell, and visual information. The fact that so much of the brain is activated in this mode of communication underscores how much listeners become involved in listening to the content of stories.

Stories not only engage our imagination and curiosity, they also increase our understanding of others and build human connections. When we listen to another person's story, we understand that person better and appreciate their view of the world. This deepens compassion and human connection.[15]

Another type of communication that can foster connection when used effectively is feedback. Feedback is a way of communicating helpful information about the impact of an individual's behavior on you or on a shared goal. Evidence shows that both giving and receiving feedback can be stressful, even leading to increases in heart rate.[16] Due to this stress, people try to avoid feedback conversations. Some people become defensive when they receive explicit feedback and can even experience a fight-or-flight response. Receiving feedback can be even more difficult in the remote experience where some people are already feeling hypervigilant, oversensitive, or prone to being in threat mode.

A study conducted by researchers at NYU and the NeuroLeadership Institute found that solicited feedback resulted in a reduced threat response as compared to unsolicited feedback.[17] By asking for feedback, the recipient feels more in control of the situation. The provider of feedback feels less uncertainty about how their words will be received. The threat response is reduced in both the asker (the recipient of the feedback) and the provider (the giver of the feedback). Both feel more psychologically safe and are in a better state for engaging in a feedback conversation.

You can influence the feedback culture in your organization by asking for feedback about your own performance more frequently. Over time, others will start asking for frequent feedback and it can become a new communication norm in virtual interactions. Regularly asking for and then receiving feedback opens communication and can strengthen human connections. The exchange of feedback will no longer be seen as threatening, but welcomed as supportive of positive change.

Explicit messaging and intentionally communicating to connect positively impact our virtual interactions. One professor we spoke with reflected, "Working and communicating remotely is not perfect, but ultimately it is how we use the communication channel/tool that defines the human experience."

Consider various ways of communicating to connect, including:

- Be open and honest about your feelings, goals, motivation, and availability.
- Facilitate discussions. Encourage everyone to express their views.
- Ask others about their motivation, workload, availability, and priorities.
- Use active listening to learn about others. Stay curious and flexible.
- Choose your words carefully when you speak. Be as specific as possible to prevent ambiguity.
- Share personal stories to help build a safe environment for others to share their stories.
- Use concise, vivid stories to deliver insights with impact and make key messages memorable.
- Ask group members to co-create norms for discussion and participation so that the group feels ownership of these guidelines and follows them.
- Communicate clear expectations and timelines. Confirm shared understanding of expectations.
- Support others by providing specific, behavior-focused feedback, given soon after the behavior occurred.
- Explicitly ask for feedback. Receiving and giving feedback are equally important.
- Express recognition and appreciation for others in a meaningful way.

Being Part of Something Bigger: Cultivate a Sense of Purpose and Meaning

Creating and cultivating a shared purpose can strengthen virtual connections. When people are working toward a shared purpose, they are more motivated. They also are better able to adapt to change. As General Stanley McChrystal writes in *Team of Teams: New Rules of Engagement for a Complex World*, "Purpose affirms trust, trust affirms purpose, and together they forge individuals into a working team."[18]

General McChrystal goes on to describe how a team that is unified by a common purpose can be adaptable if their circumstances suddenly change. This might be the case, for example, when a client suddenly throws in a difficult demand under a tight deadline or when the whole team has to collaborate remotely. If the feeling of shared purpose is maintained, the team will be better able to stay focused while adapting to the new circumstances. Shared purpose tends to improve solidarity and productivity in any group that is working together. As challenging new things are thrown into the mix, the direction will be clear if everyone is working toward the same shared purpose.

Purpose-driven organizations provide employees with opportunities to do work that makes a difference in people's lives and contributes to society. Deloitte's HR Trends Report of 2019 states, "We see an opportunity for employers to refresh and expand the concept of 'employee experience' to address the 'human experience' at work—building on an understanding of worker aspirations to connect work back to the impact it has on not only the organization, but society as a whole."[19] People seek a sense of purpose in their lives. It is a growing trend to look to the workplace as a source of purpose.

Studies show that purpose-driven organizations have more engaged and intrinsically motivated employees. A research study found that in organizations with a strong sense of purpose 73% of employees were engaged, compared to 23% in organizations without a strong sense of purpose.[20] *Harvard Business Review* found that 89% of executives identified a sense of shared purpose as a key driver of employee satisfaction.[21]

Many motivation theorists and humanistic psychologists support the idea that human beings have an inherent need for meaningful work. Most people want to feel that they are part of something bigger than themselves, make an impact, and create value from their work. Research shows that the main driver of performance and productivity is the sense of purpose employees have when they belong to a community that shares their values, makes a positive impact on the world, and recognizes the work of its members.[22]

Research presented by the Brookings Institution explored what makes work meaningful. This research was guided by the self-determination theory of motivation, focusing on the social conditions that enhance self-motivation and healthy psychological development. According to this theory, the three psychological needs that foster and sustain meaningfulness are competence, autonomy, and relatedness. These must be satisfied to motivate workers. First, meeting the need to feel competent involves having the skills to face and overcome challenges. Second, individuals have the need to feel autonomous in terms of having control over their own choices and actions. The third psychological need that makes work meaningful for workers is feeling related, which occurs when they care about their supervisors or colleagues and feel cared about in return.[23]

According to the Brookings Institution research, relatedness is the most important of the three motivators. The researchers report, "Relatedness, which reflects supportive relationships with colleagues and superiors, emerges as the most important factor for work meaningfulness. These findings highlight the greater salience of self-efficacy and intrinsic motivation for meaningfulness compared to objective working conditions and monetary rewards."[24] Autonomy, relatedness, and competence contributed 4.6 times more to perceptions of having meaningful work than compensation, benefits, career advancement, job security, or working hours.

There are many benefits of engaging individuals in meaningful work at a purpose-driven organization. The people who experience their work as meaningful make more of an effort on the job, call in sick less frequently, and are more likely to participate in professional development training programs. They also postpone retirement, often for as long as possible, when they think of their work as purposeful and meaningful.[25]

Research findings show that connecting personal values to work and cultivating shared purpose lead to sustained effort and greater satisfaction. Doing work that matters not only creates a more rewarding experience for the individual, it also has a positive impact on others.

Consider various ways to foster purpose and meaning, including:

- Have a conversation about what your organization or department does and why it matters.
- Define your shared purpose in terms of what your organization does for the world, what your team does for the organization, and what you as an individual do for the team.
- Continue the conversation about purpose after it is defined. Communicate the shared purpose to others and demonstrate it on a daily basis.
- Discuss core values. Publish them so they can be referred to and made a part of everyday actions.
- Translate core values into concrete, actionable behaviors. Demonstrate and model valued behaviors.
- Facilitate frequent positive interactions with others and make team members and employees feel cared for and appreciated.
- Provide opportunities for professional growth and development. Offer coaching, mentoring, and leadership development programs.

These ways of being and interacting serve our needs as social creatures. To illustrate these ways of strengthening virtual connections, we examine

Strengthening Virtual Connections: Evidence from the COVID-19 Global Pandemic

In the year 2020, the world was struck with a pandemic. The ability to be physically together was suddenly and severely restricted. The need for connection was still present, yet was put to the test by social distancing guidelines. This was a global experiment in which we were forced to rapidly adapt to new ways of interacting. Students were no longer meeting in the classroom. Workers were not meeting with one another in the office. Socializing and traveling were restricted. In spite of the hardships and stress it induced, the experience provided invaluable information about what happens when massive numbers of people interact virtually.

The silver lining of the pandemic is that we now have a lot of data to guide us in effective ways to be together in a remote environment. It is helpful to see what worked when all activities were required to be remote. The evidence collected from this global experiment can be applied to the remote experience even when interactions are no longer exclusively virtual. What follows is a few examples of that evidence.

Prioritizing People Was Fundamental to Preventing Disconnection

- "Social connection is foundational for a person's health and happiness," according to researchers at the Positive Emotions and Psychophysiology Lab at UNC Chapel Hill. They studied the factors that were able to keep people in a positive mindset despite the fear and restrictions of the pandemic. According to their findings, those who cared for or shared positive feelings with someone else were most able to maintain their cognitive and emotional health throughout the pandemic. The positive effect of sharing and connecting with others was strong for face-to-face, phone, and video interactions. There was no positive effect found for text-based interactions alone (email or text messaging). Additionally, they found that helping others by volunteering time or donating supplies was associated with more positive emotional states.[26] These data confirm the importance of prioritizing people, which can create positive feelings even in the midst of an extreme stressor, such as a pandemic.
- A highly experienced corporate trainer told us about his experience creating a sense of community in his remote workshops during the pandemic: "I have had some very positive reactions to the learning groups that we have created remotely. Participants feel a sense of connection and feel that the learning has personal meaning for them.

Of course, this happens in in-person courses too; however, for participants dealing with the pandemic, feeling this sense of community is especially meaningful."

- People who prioritize human connections despite physical distance are able to thrive. Psychology researchers at the University of British Columbia and the University of California, Riverside studied students and non-students in Canada, the United States, and the United Kingdom who were applying social distancing strategies during the pandemic. Study participants' sense of social connection was found to remain largely intact and sometimes even increased, despite the separation. Researchers attributed this to people finding alternate ways to connect virtually, such as virtual "happy hours" and joining with neighbors to cheer on frontline workers. Overall, the researchers concluded that "human beings will find alternative ways to satisfy their fundamental need to belong when previous sources of connection become unavailable."[27]
- An academic administrator reflected on the way that her team adapted to remote work during the pandemic by prioritizing their human connections: "I am a very hands-on leader and I was terrified that I would not be able to maintain a connection with my team at the start of the remote work experience. Almost immediately, I set up one-on-one meetings to check in with each team member. We discussed how they were doing and what they needed to be able to work in this new environment in the midst of so much challenge. Maintaining strong connections, even virtually, was of primary importance to me."

Communicating to Connect Prevented Disengagement

- People thrived at work despite the pandemic when their companies clearly communicated information about their response to this emergency. Explicit communication provided comfort and psychological safety to employees. A McKinsey survey of over 800 US-based employees looked at companies with a "good response" to the pandemic. A good response was identified as one that provided information, made proactive changes to protect employees, and conveyed to employees a general feeling that the company had responded appropriately. Employees in such companies were found to be four times more likely to be engaged, and six times more likely to feel generally positive. Addressing safety concerns and being open about the challenges instilled a feeling in the employees that they were cared about and understood.
- Clear communication during the pandemic had a significant positive impact on the employee engagement of millennials (those born between the early 1980s and late 1990s). Gallup, an organization that

has been reporting employee engagement data since 2000, found striking results when looking at fully remote workers in this age group. Millennials' engagement rate was 37% in 2019, in keeping with the usual national averages, but it had been steadily decreasing over time. Yet in 2021, this number increased to an unprecedented 75%. A closer look at these 75% of workers revealed that they were millennials working remotely who "strongly agree their managers keep them informed and who feel well-prepared at work."[28] The increase in this demographic's engagement was a direct outcome of their managers communicating to connect with them while they worked remotely.

- Educators at Harvard Business School (HBS) have reflected on how ensuring clear communication facilitated their transition to virtual learning during the pandemic. Professors Luis M. Viceira and Karim R. Lakhani report that HBS leaders did not get overwhelmed by technology for remote learning. Instead, they kept it simple by choosing the platform for student-teacher communication that enabled ease of interaction. They remained focused on what was important to them, which was delivering content and providing learning experiences where students could interact with peers and faculty. They also gave faculty a reliable remote platform to use for communicating and collaborating with each other when they could not have faculty meetings in person. Viceira and Lakhani report that this resulted in encouraging experimentation, innovation, dialogue, and a sense of community.[29]

- In the medical world, communicating to connect became more vital than ever as social distancing required providers to shift to remote care whenever possible. One medical study out of Poland found that patient satisfaction with telemedicine hinged on the effectiveness of the provider's communication. Researchers identified that the most important factors for satisfaction in a telemedicine consultation were being listened to, being treated kindly and attentively, and being given clear and comprehensive answers.[30]

- Another study out of Australia examined how the nonverbal communication cues during a telemedicine consultation can strengthen the doctor-patient connection. Cancer care providers Ursula M. Sansom-Daly and Natalie Bradford reflect on their own experiences and acknowledge what works well: "An entirely new intimacy emerges when connecting with an individual using their smartphone while lying on their bed. In this case, their face can fill the entire screen, magnifying every micro-emotion that flashes across their face. Therapeutically, how often would we otherwise spend so much of a session closely observing the changing emotional engagement on a patient's face when they are in their own bedroom? Such experiences counteract the criticism that human connection is not possible."[31]

Cultivating a Sense of Purpose and Meaning Mobilized Collective Action

- Students and faculty at medical centers across the United States were unified by the shared purpose of fighting the pandemic. At the University of Arizona Health Sciences, Michael M.I. Abecassis, Dean of the College of Medicine, described how the pandemic affected their community: "I think that being part of the health care community, we all felt a sense of shared purpose in serving the tripartite mission of education, research and patient care,"[32] Another faculty member at the university, Iman Hakim, Dean of the College of Public Health, says that "when it became clear that COVID had gripped the globe, students pivoted to become active participants in the response to the pandemic."[33]
- Inspired by a shared sense of purpose, medical students around the world opted to complete their training early to join the frontlines of the fight against the coronavirus pandemic. Data from the United Kingdom shows that 19,500 third-year student nurses and midwives and 3,000 medical students chose to graduate early to join the frontlines. An additional 2,200 medical students volunteered to help fight COVID-19 in other ways.[34] In the United States, the same phenomenon was observed in medical schools across the country, especially major metropolitan centers of high virus prevalence such as New York City.[35] Also, people who were not able to join immediately were inspired by others to join the healthcare field. Across the US, enrollment in nursing programs increased 5.6% in 2020 from the year before, according to the American Association of Colleges of Nursing.[36]
- An IndustryWeek survey examined the qualities of a number of healthcare organizations that adjusted well to the sudden paradigm shifts caused by the coronavirus pandemic. Some of these organizations mobilized their employees to make new products, and others modified their entire supply chain to make needed parts for medical devices or protective equipment. The survey results show that for these organizations having a shared purpose increases their openness to creating new systems and streamlining existing processes.[37]

New Zealand Case Study: "Unite Against COVID-19"

We conclude our look at the global experiment with the story of New Zealand's response to the COVID-19 pandemic. This case study shows how prioritizing people, communicating to connect, and focusing on purpose and meaning can save lives. New Zealand's initial response to the coronavirus pandemic, led by Prime Minister Jacinda Ardern, was extremely effective at controlling the initial community transmission of the virus.

144 Connecting and Thriving

Prioritizing People

The New Zealand government took a humanized approach to advising their people about pandemic safety. Government officials made an effort to appeal to their citizens' positive emotions. Their strategies were based on scientific research findings that a focus on caring about people and encouraging them to care about others is most effective for behavior change. For example, telling people what they can do to stay safe and protect themselves and others is more effective than telling them what they cannot or should not do. The latter approach emphasizes fear or guilt, which can make people withdraw instead of engaging. An approach that prioritized people and focused on simple, safe practices in daily life was highly effective. The New Zealand government told people what they could do to help keep each other safe, rather than scaring or alarming them.[38]

Clear Communication

Public health instructions were conveyed clearly and simply, at times with simple pictograms that were favored for their inclusivity. Pictograms, which don't include human characteristics and prevent alienating ethnic groups by lack of representation, were used instead of photographs or drawings. In addition, New Zealand offered a single, streamlined, accredited online source where people could go to find more information about the pandemic. This prevented the ambiguity that could come from consumers having to sort through multiple conflicting information sources, and misinformation from unaccredited sources.

The pandemic response team of the government, advised by psychologists with expertise in supporting people through disasters, delivered messages that were clear and consistent. Analysis of the messaging in the government's daily news briefings confirmed that its effectiveness had to do with being open and specific. For example, case numbers of how many people had been infected that day were always included. The leaders were transparent about their decision-making process. They were honest when they didn't have answers and readily provided reliable public health resources where current information was published.[39]

Researchers studied New Zealand residents' responses to these daily news briefings. Study participants praised the speakers who gave government briefings for being open about what they didn't know, deferring to others' expertise, and modifying advice when new information became available. Honesty and transparency were highly valued and highly effective. Many participants in the study remarked that their prime minister acted like a human being. They responded warmly to her down-to-earth comments, such as when she referred to herself and her people as a "team of five million."[40]

Fostering a Sense of Purpose and Meaning

The government effectively branded its coronavirus pandemic response using specific colors (yellow and white stripes) and slogans (mainly, "Unite Against COVID-19"). People appreciated having these visual and verbal ways to support the common cause of protecting each other. The yellow and white striped pattern was used for birthday cakes and post-lockdown invitations. New Zealanders took ownership of the effort, rather than feeling like it was imposed on them by government authorities. Research conducted on the pandemic response found that this branding strategy provided citizens of New Zealand with a sense of community and collective experience;[41] 78% of New Zealanders had a greater amount of trust in the government because of the way it responded to the COVID-19 pandemic.[42]

Many lessons can be drawn from New Zealand's highly successful response in containing the pandemic. We can learn about the way that prioritizing people and leading with empathy lead to positive results. We can see that positive and direct communication from leaders shows competence and instills trust in those who are led. When people unite behind a common purpose, they experience strong cohesion that carries them through even the most trying of circumstances. The success of these strategies is confirmed by the data: New Zealand experienced tight control of community spread of the virus and one of the world's lowest death rates from COVID-19. The government's communication strategy brought people together in a profound way, just as other countries were letting the challenges of dealing with COVID-19 divide them. New Zealanders showed how much humans can accomplish and overcome when they prioritize each other's well-being, communicate effectively, and have a common purpose.

Social Connection Humanizes the Remote Experience

In the increasingly remote world in which we live, work, and learn, we need to keep in mind that humans are social creatures who require connection with other human beings. "If we want people to fully show up, to bring their whole selves including their unarmored, whole hearts—so that we can innovate, solve problems, and serve people—we have to be vigilant about creating a culture in which people feel safe, seen, heard, and respected," writes Brené Brown.[43] Our basic needs for safety and comfort, understanding each other, and belonging to a community ensure that the overarching need for human connection is fulfilled.

You can strengthen your virtual connections by prioritizing people, communicating to connect, and fostering a sense of purpose and meaning. You can explicitly discuss and elicit from others their strategies to

146 Connecting and Thriving

strengthen social connection. You can also model specific behaviors. Leaders, coaches, educators, and other professionals are in an ideal position to show others how to strengthen their connections when they work, learn, and socialize in the remote environment.

Prioritizing people is integral to a human-centered approach to the remote experience. Empathy, support, and kindness go a long way in making people feel cared about and valued. This human-centered approach leads to quality connections that have a positive impact on work, learning and social life.

Using explicit communication and acting from a place of empathy also strengthens virtual connections. Being open and honest promotes trust and fosters more meaningful connections with others. Active listening is essential because it provides a better understanding of people's priorities and perspectives. Communicating clear visions for the future and addressing concerns and anxieties demonstrates support and care about others.

Engaging in meaningful work with a shared purpose inspires individuals to be intrinsically motivated. Extensive evidence shows that meaningful work and shared purpose result in an experience of human connection that improves work outcomes and morale.[44]

Prioritizing people, communicating clearly, and fostering purpose and meaning are ways to improve the remote experience. The result is establishing and maintaining more fulfilling human connections. You can also bring ideas to others about how they too can feel more connected, and lead by example. Coaching conversations are an invaluable way to support your clients, students, employees, teams, friends, and family as they adapt to their remote experiences. Self-coaching, the process of asking questions and coming up with ways to accomplish your goals, can also be a way to improve and humanize your remote experiences. As a result of this human-centered approach, you can have connections with others that are satisfying and meaningful instead of merely transactional.

Go forward, with this in mind:

1 **The human brain is hard-wired for social connection and belonging.**

- The basic need for human connection has not changed throughout evolution.
- Being social is the brain's preferred state.
- Humans crave belonging when disconnected from others as much as they crave food when hungry.

2 **Prioritizing people by recognizing and accepting them for who they are strengthens connection.**

- Using empathy and acting with compassion shows people that you care about them.

- The two types of empathy, cognitive and emotional, can be developed and practiced.
- Perceiving and understanding the feelings of others is a powerful way to promote positive interactions when people are physically apart.

3 **Communicating to connect requires the willingness to speak openly and honestly.**

- Asking questions, listening to understand others' perspectives, and using feedback effectively deepen the connection between people.
- Storytelling is a powerful way to connect with the hearts and minds of others.
- Explicit communication is especially crucial in virtual interactions.

4 **Cultivating a sense of shared purpose and meaning drives performance and helps people thrive.**

- Teams unified by shared purpose are more able to adapt to changing circumstances.
- Connecting personal values to work leads to sustained effort and greater satisfaction.
- The three psychological needs that foster and sustain meaningfulness at work are competence, autonomy, and relatedness.

5 **The global experiment of the COVID-19 pandemic provides evidence of ways to effectively meet our needs as social creatures even when physically distanced.**

- Prioritizing people was fundamental to preventing disconnection.
- Communicating to connect prevented disengagement.
- Cultivating a sense of purpose and meaning mobilized collective action.

Notes

1 Murthy, Vivek H. *Together: The Healing Power of Human Connection in a Sometimes Lonely World*. New York: Harper Collins, 2020, 51.
2 Brym, Robert J. *Sociology: Your Compass for a New World*. Belmont, CA: Thomson/Wadsworth, 2007.
3 Murthy, Vivek H. *Together: The Healing Power of Human Connection in a Sometimes Lonely World*. New York: Harper Collins, 2020.
4 Carson, Rachel. *Silent Spring*. Boston, MA: Houghton Mifflin, 2002, 7.
5 Anderson, Janna and Lee Rainie. *The Future of Well-Being in a Tech-Saturated World*. Washington DC: Pew Research Center, 2018: 66.
6 Riess, Helen. "The science of empathy." *Journal of patient experience* 4, no. 2 (2017): 76, https://doi.org/10.1177%2F2374373517699267

7 Healey, Meghan L., and Murray Grossman. "Cognitive and affective perspective-taking: Evidence for shared and dissociable anatomical substrates." *Frontiers in neurology* 9 (2018): 491, https://doi.org/10.3389/fneur.2018.00491

8 Riess, Helen. "The science of empathy." *Journal of patient experience* 4, no. 2 (2017): 74–77, https://doi.org/10.1177%2F2374373517699267

9 Zaki, Jamil. *The War for Kindness: Building Empathy in a Fractured World.* New York: Crown, 2019.

10 Emmert, Amy. "Empathy: The glue we need to fix a fractured world." *Strategy +Business*, October 20, 2020, www.strategy-business.com/article/Empathy-The-glue-we-need-to-fix-a-fractured-world

11 Brown, Brené. *Dare to Lead: Brave Work. Tough Conversations. Whole Hearts.* New York: Random House Publishing Group, 2018, 48.

12 Kosner, Anthony Wing. "Amy Edmondson on the power of psychological safety in distributed work." Work in Progress, March 27, 2020: paragraph 5, https://blog.dropbox.com/topics/work-culture/amy-edmondson-on-the-power-of-psychological-safety-in-distribute

13 Brown, Brené. *Dare to Lead: Brave Work. Tough Conversations. Whole Hearts.* New York: Random House Publishing Group, 2018, 195.

14 Ariel Group. "Stories Connect Us: The Power Inside a Homefront Foundation Event." Presence and Leadership (blog), paragraph 1, www.arielgroup.com/stories-connect-us-the-power-inside-a-homefront-foundation-event/

15 Fivush, Robyn. "Listening to stories: The power of story circles." The Stories of Our Lives (blog). *Psychology Today*, August 13, 2020, www.psychologytoday.com/us/blog/the-stories-our-lives/202008/listening-stories-the-power-story-circles

16 Rock, David, Beth Jones, and Chris Weller. "Using neuroscience to make feedback work and feel better." *Strategy+Business*, August 27, 2018, www.strategy-business.com/article/Using-Neuroscience-to-Make-Feedback-Work-and-Feel-Better

17 West, Tessa V., Katherine Thorson, Heidi Grant, and David Rock. "Asked for vs. unasked for feedback: An experimental study." Neuroleadership Institute, https://membership.neuroleadership.com/material/asked-for-vs-unasked-for-feedback-an-experimental-study/

18 McChrystal, Gen. Stanley, Tantum Collins, David Silverman, Chris Fussell. *Team of Teams: New Rules of Engagement for a Complex World.* London: Penguin Publishing Group, 2015, 100.

19 Volini, Erica, Jeff Schwartz, Indranil Roy, Maren Hauptmann, and Yves Van Durme. "Introduction: Leading the social enterprise—Reinvent with a human focus." *Deloitte Insights*, April 11, 2019: paragraph 15, www2.deloitte.com/us/en/insights/focus/human-capital-trends/2019/leading-social-enterprise.html

20 Deloitte. "Culture of purpose—Building business confidence; driving growth. 2014 core beliefs & culture survey." February 2014, www2.deloitte.com/content/dam/Deloitte/us/Documents/about-deloitte/us-leadership-2014-core-beliefs-culture-survey-040414.pdf

21 Harvard Business Review. "The business case for purpose." 2015, https://assets.ey.com/content/dam/ey-sites/ey-com/en_gl/topics/digital/ey-the-business-case-for-purpose.pdf

22 De Smet, Aaron, Mihir Mysore, Angelika Reich, and Bob Sternfels. "Return as a muscle: How lessons from COVID-19 can shape a robust operating model for hybrid and beyond." McKinsey & Company, July 9, 2021, www.mckinsey.com/business-functions/people-and-organizational-performance/our-insights/return-as-a-muscle-how-lessons-from-covid-19-can-shape-a-robust-operating-model-for-hybrid-and-beyond

23 Nikolova, Milena, and Femke Cnossen. "What makes a job meaningful?" Brookings, April 8, 2020: paragraph 4, www.brookings.edu/blog/up-front/2020/04/08/what-makes-a-job-meaningful/

24 Nikolova, Milena, and Femke Cnossen. "What makes work meaningful and why economists should care about it." IZA Institute of Labor Economics, Discussion Paper Series, April 2020: 2, https://ftp.iza.org/dp13112.pdf

25 Nikolova, Milena, and Femke Cnossen. "What makes a job meaningful?" Brookings, April 8, 2020, www.brookings.edu/blog/up-front/2020/04/08/what-makes-a-job-meaningful/

26 Prinzing, Michael M. and Barbara L. Fredrickson. "How to have a better day during the pandemic." *The Well: The University of North Carolina at Chapel Hill*, June 30, 2020, https://thewell.unc.edu/2020/06/30/how-to-have-a-better-day-during-the-pandemic/

27 Folk, Dunigan, Karynna Okabe-Miyamoto, Elizabeth Dunn, Sonja Lyubomirsky, and Brent Donnellan. "Did social connection decline during the first wave of COVID-19? The role of extraversion." *Collabra: Psychology* 6, no. 1 (2020), https://doi.org/10.1525/collabra.365

28 Robison, Jennifer. "What disruption reveals about engaging millennial employees." Gallup, January 6, 2021, www.gallup.com/workplace/328121/disruption-reveals-engaging-millennial-employees.aspx

29 Lakhani, Karim. R. and Luis M. Viceira. "5 key lessons from HBS's pandemic teaching transformation: And what learnings will stick moving forward." *Harvard Business Publishing Education*, July 1, 2021, https://hbsp.harvard.edu/inspiring-minds/5-key-lessons-from-hbs-pandemic-teaching-transformation

30 Kludacz-Alessandri, Magdalena, Liliana Hawrysz, Piotr Korneta, Grażyna Gierszewska, Wioletta Pomaranik, and Renata Walczak. "The impact of medical teleconsultations on general practitioner-patient communication during COVID-19: A case study from Poland." *PLOS ONE* 16, no. 7 (2021): e0254960, https://doi.org/10.1371/journal.pone.0254960

31 Sansom-Daly, Ursula M., and Natalie Bradford. "Grappling with the 'human' problem hiding behind the technology: Telehealth during and beyond COVID-19." *Psycho-oncology* 29 (2020): 1407, doi:10.1002/pon.5462.

32 The University of Arizona Health Sciences. "How the COVID-19 pandemic forever changed health sciences." August 30, 2021: paragraph 15, https://healthsciences.arizona.edu/connect/features/how-covid-19-pandemic-forever-changed-health-sciences

33 The University of Arizona Health Sciences. "How the COVID-19 pandemic forever changed health sciences." August 30, 2021: paragraph 16, https://healthsciences.arizona.edu/connect/features/how-covid-19-pandemic-forever-changed-health-sciences

34 "Almost 25,000 students in healthcare professions opt to join COVID-19 fight." NHS: Health Education England (blog), April 17, 2020, www.hee.nhs.uk/news-blogs-events/news/more-23000-students-healthcare-professions-opt-join-covid-19-fight

35 Hartle, Terry W. "The courage of medical students." *Inside Higher Ed*, April 20, 2020, www.insidehighered.com/views/2020/04/20/medical-students-are-joining-front-lines-fight-against-covid-19-lets-cheer-them

36 Associated Press, "Applications to US nursing schools rise as students want to 'join the frontline.'" *The Guardian*, October 15, 2021, www.theguardian.com/us-news/2021/oct/15/us-nursing-schools-nurses-pandemic

37 Putre, Laura. "A Shared Purpose: Leadership and Culture at COVID-19 Innovators." *IndustryWeek,* April 24, 2020,

www.industryweek.com/leadership/article/21129706/a-shared-purpose-leadership-and-culture-at-covid19-innovators

38 Hunt, Elle. "Words matter: How New Zealand's clear messaging helped beat Covid." *The Guardian*, February 25, 2021, www.theguardian.com/world/2021/feb/26/words-matter-how-new-zealands-clear-messaging-helped-beat-covid

39 Beattie, Alex and Rebecca Priestley. "Fighting COVID-19 with the team of 5 million: Aotearoa New Zealand government communication during the 2020 lockdown." *Social sciences & humanities open* 4, no. 1 (2021): 100209, https://doi.org/10.1016/j.ssaho.2021.100209

40 Beattie, Alex and Rebecca Priestley. "Fighting COVID-19 with the team of 5 million: Aotearoa New Zealand government communication during the 2020 lockdown." *Social sciences & humanities open* 4, no. 1 (2021): 100209, https://doi.org/10.1016/j.ssaho.2021.100209

41 Hunt, Elle. "Words matter: How New Zealand's clear messaging helped beat Covid." *The Guardian*, February 25, 2021, www.theguardian.com/world/2021/feb/26/words-matter-how-new-zealands-clear-messaging-helped-beat-covid

42 Goldfinch, Shaun, Ross Taplin, and Robin Gauld. "Trust in government increased during the Covid-19 pandemic in Australia and New Zealand." *Australian journal of public administration* 80, no. 1 (2021): 3–11, https://doi.org/10.1111/1467-8500.12459

43 Brown, Brené. *Dare to Lead: Brave Work. Tough Conversations. Whole Hearts.* New York: Random House Publishing Group, 2018, 12.

44 See for example Harvard Business Review. "The business case for purpose." 2015, https://assets.ey.com/content/dam/ey-sites/ey-com/en_gl/topics/digital/ey-the-business-case-for-purpose.pdf

Chapter 7

Together Miles Apart

In the digital age, the use of technology has made it possible to do things faster, more efficiently, and often more conveniently than ever before. We can also have more flexibility in our schedules when working, learning, and socializing take place remotely. But here is the paradox we are living through: the technology we use to connect with others often leaves us feeling less connected. Internet pioneer Brad Templeton acknowledges, "That we need to do a better job mitigating the bad effects does not stop the good effects from being worth it. There are still scores of ways we all find it hard to imagine how we did things in the past without our digital tools."[1]

We increasingly rely on digital technology to engage with others and this can lead to stress, exhaustion, anxiety, and sometimes feelings of disengagement and disconnection. Yet, the remote experience does not have to be stressful, feel exhausting, or cause disconnection.

When you keep your mind and body in a healthy place, you can come to your remote experiences more present and engaged. Then you can be ready to connect with others on a human level even though you are physically apart. How you actually experience social connection in the remote environment is based on the choices you make and the actions you take.

The need for connection is deeply wired and drives our behavior. When that need is met, your interactions will feel fulfilling and satisfying. You can adjust your remote experiences to ensure that they serve this need to connect. You can thrive in your increasingly digital life by focusing not only on the quantity and efficiency of your interactions, but also the quality and depth of your human connections.

In previous chapters, we suggested strategies to help you be your most healthy, engaged self. We also discussed ways of being and acting that humanize the remote experience. In this chapter, we encourage you to consider individual circumstances, then make choices and take actions that strengthen connections with others and improve the remote experience.

DOI: 10.4324/9781003170488-10

Make Choices to Strengthen Human Connections

All the choices you make throughout your day add up to the experience that you have. "Life is a matter of choices," writes John Maxwell, "and every choice you make makes you."[2] To that end, you can decide what type of remote experience you are going to have by making the choices that work best for you. Slow, deliberate choices, not just thinking with your gut, can lead to a humanized remote experience.

There are an increasing number of choices, big and small, that we are faced with making each day. Some are easy and obvious, such as turning on your computer when it is time to work. Some are low stakes, such as deciding what you will eat for lunch. Some are high stakes and long term, such as choosing to leave your job for a new one. When making any choice, your brain acts like a calculator. It weighs your options, factoring in your knowledge and past experiences. It calculates expectations and intentions for the future, influenced by emotions and assumptions. It determines how likely different outcomes are and how important each one is to you. From all of this data comes a decision. Understanding this process will give you more control over it.

Nobel Laureate Daniel Kahneman identified two mental systems that humans use for decision-making. There is a fast system that decides based on instinct and gut reactions. This system evolved to enhance our survival in the wild, causing us to react to a perceived threat as quickly as possible. There is also a slow system that takes more time to come to a decision based on facts and rational, thoughtful deliberation.[3]

There is a role for gut reactions when it is necessary to think fast. However, thoughtful and purposeful decisions are more beneficial in the long run because they consider all the facts and information. If you constantly make quick decisions based on instinct alone, you are bound to run into misunderstandings as a result of not taking all of the data into account. The need for slow decision-making is greater in the remote environment where missing or distorted social cues can make it more difficult for you to gather decision-making data. Making slow and thoughtful decisions will help you to genuinely connect, rather than simply complete quick transactions with other people.

There are various ways to increase deliberate, slow-system thoughts, including:

- *Stay well.* Consider adopting health and wellness suggested strategies (Chapter 4), such as focusing on your breathing, getting sufficient sleep and nutrition, reframing emotions, or journaling. If you are having a stress response, slow-system thoughts will be difficult. Survival mode favors fast, gut reactions, as your brain assumes there is no time for slow deliberate decision-making. Take care of yourself and remember to intercept stress early and control it.

Together Miles Apart 153

- *Give yourself time to make a decision.* Being under time pressure can trigger a stress response. Whenever possible, make decisions well ahead of deadlines and take time to think through all the facts.
- *Decrease your cognitive load.* When your brain's processing capacity is already overwhelmed, there is no capacity for gathering and analyzing additional information. It will be harder to make thoughtful decisions. This situation can be avoided by decreasing cognitive load. You can use the suggested strategies for decreasing cognitive load (Chapter 5), such as prioritizing based on importance and using physical resources outside of your brain. The tendency for fast decision-making can also be decreased by trying not to make any important decisions when you are in cognitive overload.
- *Invite the opinions of others.* This introduces facts and perspectives that differ from the ones you hold internally. Using external information discourages fast, emotion-driven choices. In the remote experience, when no one is spontaneously stopping by your desk to share their thoughts, getting opinions requires actively soliciting them from others.
- *Stay engaged.* When you manage your energy well by alternating high-energy activities with rest (Chapter 6), engagement will come more naturally. If you are fully engaged, you can be more focused for deliberate decision-making.

Snap decisions or gut reactions are fast and easy to make. Quick decisions tend to be ruled by emotion, while making a rational, thoughtful decision takes more time and effort.[4] Thoughtful decisions are more likely to reflect what's important to you. Using the slow decision-making system gives you the opportunity to act with intentionality.

Intentional actions, small or large, are ones which serve the goals you've set for the future. When you make important choices in the remote experience, it's best to avoid being led entirely by your gut, by fear, or by convenience. Instead, with each choice you make, keep in mind your goal. For example, say your goal is to have enough energy when you log off from work to still have fun with friends and family. Every choice you make throughout your entire workday can be chosen with this end goal in mind. You can choose to shorten the remote morning meeting you lead so there is more time to accomplish other tasks early in the day. You can choose to take a walk during lunch to replenish your energy and be able to work more efficiently during the afternoon. Each of these choices can serve your end goal. However, it is not enough just to choose. Once you've made a choice, action is the next step.

Many people have said, "I'm going to exercise more!" at one time or another in their lives. It is particularly pertinent when long parts of the day are spent sedentary at the computer. The decision to exercise more is only meaningful with deliberate action. Thinking about exercising or feeling guilty about not exercising won't improve your health. You can decide to take deliberate action or direct your energy elsewhere.

It's up to you to make choices and take actions that fit your lifestyle. When and how you choose to exercise each day will not necessarily be the same for you as it will be for another person. For example, a parent might choose to take a run outdoors before the children wake up and need help getting ready for school. A team leader who facilitates morning meetings might choose to exercise after work to unwind before going out in the evening to socialize with friends.

We encourage you to consider human-centered actions that will improve your remote experiences. For example, if you're spending all day participating in one Zoom meeting after another, you might consider occasionally making a phone call in place of a video call. Research shows that without having to attend to visual cues, voice-only calls can cause less cognitive load.[5] A phone call might feel better to you and help you focus more on the human connection. There are many choices you can make and actions you can take when working remotely, learning online, and engaging in remote social activities.

Set Boundaries for Yourself

Among the most important choices you can make in the remote experience is the boundaries you set and maintain. Boundaries are physical, mental, and emotional limits humans create to meet their need to feel safe and respected.[6] Setting and maintaining personal boundaries are important ways of taking care of yourself.

Setting boundaries involves defining what is best for you as an individual. "Healthy, robust personal boundaries are the key to living a fulfilled, empowered, and self-directed life," states Terri Cole, a psychotherapist who specializes in boundaries.[7] There are different types of boundaries you can set. These include: physical boundaries to protect your personal space, emotional boundaries to protect your feelings, mental boundaries to protect your thoughts and beliefs, and time boundaries to protect how you spend your time.

Boundaries are set and maintained to make clear what does and does not make you comfortable. The clearer your boundaries, the easier it is to know when they have been crossed and to address the boundary violations early. There are a few ways to indicate to a person that your boundary has been crossed. You can use language and tell them. You can also increase emotional or physical distance from the person as a way of making it clearer where the lines are.[8] Some boundaries are rigid and non-negotiable, while others are more flexible and depend on context. The important thing is to be clear with yourself about where your boundaries are and clear with others if they are crossed.

Together Miles Apart 155

With constant digital connectedness, it is easy to work at any time, from anywhere. Because a person doesn't have to be in the office in order to be reachable, the boundary lines of nine-to-five can easily disappear. Continuing to work at all hours can be a recipe for burnout, as ultimately the demands will become too high and the opportunities for resting and reenergizing will disappear. Maintaining clearly defined boundaries is an excellent way to protect your health and wellness.

In *The Simplicity Principle: Six Steps Towards Clarity in a Complex World*, Julia Hobsbawm recommends controlling what you put into your schedule as thoughtfully as you control what goes into your body.[9] Just as you would consider the nutritional content of food or drink and stop intake when you feel full, so can you think about what you are doing with your time. You can create specific time blocks in your day to control when you answer emails, do work that requires deep thought, or take breaks. It is in your power to schedule a full night of sleep by deciding on a time when you plan to go to bed and wake up each day.

Controlling your time promotes a sense of competence and autonomy. One professor described how she chooses to control her time to avoid being at the mercy of a barrage of incoming emails: "I only check emails during the work week, and then only in the afternoons. I want my fullest attention to be on teaching and connecting with my students in the mornings." Making deliberate choices about how you spend your time and maintaining your time boundaries can increase your effectiveness overall. It also makes it possible to spend more time and energy on prioritizing people and strengthening your virtual connections.

Even when you can't control every aspect of your circumstances, you can choose to set and maintain your own boundaries. You can also choose how you respond to your circumstances.

The Power of Mindset

Ultimately, the quality of your remote experience is determined by your mindset. A mindset is a collection of mental attitudes and beliefs that influence everything you do, feel, think, and experience. It is possible to change a mindset.

According to the research of Stanford psychologist Carol Dweck and her colleagues, there are two types of mindsets: a growth mindset and a fixed mindset. If you have a growth mindset, you believe that your abilities can be developed and improved through effort and persistence. In her book *Mindset: The New Psychology of Success*, Dweck explains that the "growth mindset is based on the belief that your basic qualities are things you can cultivate through your efforts, … strategies, and help from others. Although people may differ in every which way—in their initial talents and aptitudes, interests, or temperaments—everyone can change and grow through application and experience."[10]

The opposite of having a growth mindset is having a fixed mindset. If you have a fixed mindset, you believe that your qualities, including your intelligence and talent, are inborn and unchangeable. You believe that success is predetermined, based on innate traits, and no amount of effort can alter that.

When you have a growth mindset, you are willing to take on challenges, learn from them, and increase your skills. In the modern world where technology is changing at a rapid pace, it is critically important to have a growth mindset. Believing that you can embrace challenges as opportunities and persevere is vital for positively adapting to change.

An organizational development specialist we interviewed described the importance of a growth mindset when adjusting to the remote experience: "I actively adopt a growth mindset in order to successfully embrace the opportunities and challenges presented by working remotely. For instance, to pivot the materials from instructor-led training in a classroom setting to a virtual learning environment took time, patience, and a willingness to adapt." He added, "Just a short few years ago, I couldn't have imagined the scale of training I could facilitate virtually and the level of remote collaboration I have experienced."

Research shows that introducing a growth mindset will have lasting effects only if the environment is a supportive one. In one study, researchers conducted a brief intervention on over 6,000 low-achieving students from a variety of US public schools. The researchers introduced the students to growth mindset ideas through two 25-minute online training sessions. The sessions focused on challenging negative effort beliefs (e.g., trying hard or asking for help means lacking ability); fixed-trait attributions (e.g., failure is due to low ability); and performance avoidance goals (e.g., the goal of school is to avoid looking stupid). In this way, they helped the students develop a growth mindset. After the intervention, the researchers looked for changes in school performance. The data showed widespread improvements in the grade point averages of the 6,000 students after the intervention. It also revealed that the students' improvements were sustained only if their peers generally supported the mindset of facing challenges and being persistent. If these attitudes were looked down on or shamed by their peers, the intervention's effect wore off with time.[11]

When a person believes that things cannot change or are out of their control, it is easy to fall into negative thought patterns. It is human nature to see the negative side more easily and remember it for longer. Psychologists refer to this phenomenon as the "negativity bias": the tendency to remember what went wrong and quickly move past what went right.[12] Negative thoughts can be easy to get stuck on and difficult to question or to move past.

If you are frustrated with some of your remote experiences, you might be getting stuck in negative thinking. A growth mindset is the antidote to this. Instead of accentuating the negative, a growth mindset helps you to keep your focus on areas where things can be changed for the better. Challenges become opportunities rather than something to be avoided. Feedback can inspire you to develop your skills rather than make you feel defensive. Your remote experience will start to feel full of choices rather than predetermined and unchangeable.

Remote experiences present many new challenges that can get in the way of feeling safe and comfortable, understanding one another, and attaining a sense of belonging. But with a growth mindset, you can take on these challenges and learn from them. You can persist when things are challenging and find effective ways to improve your remote experiences.

You can make choices and take actions to improve the remote experience. By reading this book, you are already doing that. We suggest you periodically reflect on your environment, interactions, and virtual connections so you can continue to be proactive in humanizing the remote experience. Through leadership and coaching, you can support the people with whom you work to also take a more human-centered approach to the remote experience.

Go forward, with these ideas in mind:

- The remote experience can be humanized when we focus not only on the quantity and efficiency of our interactions, but also the quality and depth of our human connections.
- Humanizing the remote experience involves meeting the innate human needs for connection: safety and comfort, understanding, and belonging.
- Warning signals that a particular need is not being met points you to problem areas where your remote experience can be improved.
- The physical stress response that manifests as attention difficulties in the remote environment is a warning signal that the human need for safety and comfort is not being met.
- The human brain can move out of a chronic stress response once the need for safety and comfort has been met.
- Issues with cognitive overload and fatigue from interacting in the remote environment can be a warning signal that the human need for understanding others is not being met.
- The human brain works hard to understand others and navigate the social world.
- Creating predictions and then updating the predictions as circumstances demand is a way that the brain makes sense of social interactions.
- Missed and distorted sensory signals in the remote environment trigger prediction errors that the brain needs to fix.

158 Connecting and Thriving

- More work for the brain caused by an increase in prediction errors can lead to mental fatigue and cognitive overload.
- Skillful energy management is necessary to do the difficult work of understanding others and sustaining engagement in the remote environment.
- Alternating between activity and rest, focused and unfocused brain states, optimizes energy.
- Issues with exclusion and isolation can be a warning signal that the human need for belonging is not being met.
- Lacking a feeling of connectedness to a group or community can cause social pain, experienced in a similar way to physical pain.
- The brain chemicals that promote bonding flow less readily in the remote environment without touch and physical interactions.
- Brain-to-brain synchrony is harder to achieve without physical presence and shared attention.
- It is possible to adapt our ways of interacting to meet the human need for belonging.
- A climate of psychological safety where group members trust and respect each other facilitates the sense of connectedness when physically apart.
- Humans are wired for social connection. Humanizing the remote experience requires meeting the innate needs for safety and comfort, understanding, and belonging. This promotes well-being, increases engagement, and strengthens human connections in our increasingly remote lives.

Case Study: Shay, a Team Leader

Shay is an executive and team leader who had a difficult time adapting to working virtually. She had always cared about being a good partner, a good mother, and a good team leader. But by trying to give 100% of herself in each facet of her life, she was losing something. She had the foresight to take a step back before she entered burnout and stopped caring about her work. She asked herself, "What do I have to do differently to continue being who I want to be? What are the steps I can take? What are the needs I am not addressing?" She decided to have conversations with Diane, who had been her coach in the past, and Amy, a long-time friend, to figure out what she might need to change. She didn't want to just cope with her experiences, she wanted to thrive.

In Part One of this book, we previewed some of the difficulties the remote life brought Shay. She had experienced difficulties with attention, alerting, orienting, and sustaining. She had challenges with understanding, missed signals, cognitive load, and fatigue in herself and her team members. There had been struggles with belonging, psychological safety, empathy, and connection among her team members. Conversations with

Diane and Amy helped Shay see where she was not meeting her basic needs for safety and comfort, understanding, and belonging.

Amy showed her the science behind the struggles her brain was having with the remote experience, sometimes outside of her awareness. She helped Shay see the connections between the ways the brain processes experiences, and the ways the mind and body manifest reactions to experiences. Diane had a series of coaching conversations with Shay that started with questions to encourage reflection on her current situation. They worked together to understand needed change, set goals for change, and discover strategies and actions to accomplish the goals.

Buildup to Burnout

Shay held many different roles and felt like she was not doing as good a job as she could at any of them. At night, she put the kids to bed and started working again. She and her partner shared responsibilities around the house and often felt like co-workers or roommates. After finally falling asleep at night, she found herself waking up at any small sound and having difficulty returning back to sleep again. She could barely squeeze in a walk around the block during the workday, let alone a regular exercise program. She could hardly remember the last time she read a novel or had the energy to do something for fun.

After learning about burnout, Shay realized that she was getting dangerously close to it. The typical combination of burnout symptoms—exhaustion, detachment, and feelings of inefficacy at work—was beginning to present itself. Shay had to take a step back and ask herself why these symptoms were starting to appear now. The change to remote work should have resulted in her having more time available instead of less. She worked from home so there was no longer a commute into the city every day. Overall, very little had changed in her job responsibilities, so technically she should have had more time and felt less tired, not the opposite.

Shay was suffering from a condition we refer to as the "Because I Can" syndrome. She ended a remote meeting at 8:59 am and started the next one at 9:00 am because she could. She ended her workday at 6:59 pm and started taking care of her children at 7:00 pm because she could. She stopped work for a lunch break and threw in a load of laundry because she could. She took care of small tasks around the house during the workday that might be shared with her partner later because she could do it herself and get it done now.

Before working remotely, her commute each way was a 90-minute period in which she could transition from thoughts of home to thoughts of work, and the reverse on the way home. Without the commute, she had 180 extra minutes each day. Yet, she did not reclaim that 180 minutes by unwinding and decompressing. She filled the time up trying to complete more items from her long to-do list.

Moving out of Fight-or-Flight

Before she could look at things like cognitive overload or psychological safety, Shay had to face the simple fact that she was stressed out. Stress was a physical reaction that was affecting everything from her mental state to her connections with others. She had to get more comfortable in her new remote environment. Addressing her need for safety and comfort was Shay's first action for change, and she let herself be guided by the warning signals of attention difficulties. Taking a closer look at attention made Shay more aware of the issues that were creating stress.

Seeing the direct effect that stress was having on her attention helped her to finally prove to herself that she needed to make some changes. As she looked closely at the six processes of paying attention, it became clear to her where she was having difficulties and where she could make improvements. Until she felt safe, comfortable, and settled down in her remote environment, her stress levels would remain high. High stress levels meant a decreased ability to focus her attention.

Decreasing her high levels of stress in the remote environment required thinking about her self-care and emotional wellness. For Shay and many of Amy and Diane's high-powered, high-functioning clients, self-care was often a low priority. This tendency emerged when Shay was in college and first started to pull all-nighters. It solidified on the training ground of parenthood, where she put the needs of her children before hers. By the time she was advancing to leadership positions in her career, she was continually putting work first in order to succeed.

As a result of her strong work ethic, Shay did not often stop and listen to her body's signals but instead kept pushing. She had not considered that stopping to address her stress would actually help improve her daily functioning and interactions with her team.

Shay was not listening to her body and was living in fight-or-flight mode. Her stress response was activated all day long without resolution due to the pending deadlines and a long to-do list that was eternally getting longer. She ran on adrenaline and did not allow her brain to sound the all-clear signal that the threat had passed. She was continually problem solving, even as she was falling asleep. She woke up feeling exhausted because her focused brain could not fully turn off to recover. Chronic stress was not helping her get anything done effectively.

The turning point was when Shay came to the realization that chronic stress was causing problems in the way she functioned. Stress was not something she could compartmentalize and think about later, not when it affected the way her brain worked. A brain under chronic stress cannot hold sustained attention and cannot resist switching. It is on a mission to protect the body from the next threat and monitor for that threat at every minute. Shay had been treating stress like it was a separate issue from her daily obligations but it was central to her daily functioning. Stress was affecting her attention and that was creating even more stress.

Guided by her new knowledge of the six processes of attention, Shay came to understand how chronic stress was affecting her brain. The three processes that seemed most relevant to her situation were alerting, sustaining, and switching. She did not have the optimal amount of alertness for calm, focused attention. Instead, being in fight-or-flight mode meant she was often on high alert and sensitive to every distraction in the room around her. This made it difficult to sustain attention for as long as she once could. On top of the difficulty of sustaining attention under stress was the multitude of notifications, devices, and open tabs grabbing her wandering attention throughout the day. Having learned that multitasking is a myth, she started to see the energy cost of these switches of attention from one thing to the next. She became aware that these attention problems were a demonstration of the toll stress was taking on her mental and physical health. She could also see how stress was impeding her ability to meaningfully connect with people in her personal and professional life.

Shay began to implement strategies to prevent the negative impacts of stress. To start, she decided to focus her health efforts on sleep and exercise. She was already a healthy eater. Nutrition had been a priority since early adulthood because she could easily see the tangible benefits to her mood and productivity. On the other hand, she had not made sleep and exercise a high priority. She was not integrating them into her overloaded schedule in the same way as healthy eating.

Learning more about the Drive and Drain Phases of stress helped Shay think differently about her sleep priorities. She realized that there was no benefit to pushing herself into the late hours of the night working harder and harder with diminishing returns. The returns would be higher with a full night's sleep and a fresh outlook to face the world. When she finished putting the kids to bed and cleaning up the house, her habit had been to sit back down at her computer and finish up a few more items related to her team's projects. Now, she experimented with cutting out these late-night work sessions and going to bed instead. Though it was difficult to wind down and let herself sleep, she became more accustomed to it by the fourth night. She ended up adding about two hours of sleep each night. For someone who had only gotten four hours of sleep in a typical night, this 50% increase was a major benefit.

Lessening the Load

Even with more sleep, Shay still had too much to do and not enough energy to do it all. Having begun to address the way that lack of comfort in her environment was contributing to her problems, she started to look at her need for understanding others. Shay was guided in this assessment

162 Connecting and Thriving

by the warning signals of cognitive load and fatigue. It was time to address just how much work her brain was doing on a daily basis. She could no longer just push her brain harder trying to do things the same way she used to do them in person. Her remote experience required adapting to this new way of working.

Shay's cognitive load was extremely high. She had a thousand things going on in her head at one time. There was so much she was keeping track of at any given moment, and so many problems she was working through. She now understood that "Zoom fatigue" was not just a trendy new saying, it was a scientifically proven phenomenon. She was not entirely surprised to learn that video calls are proven to be more work for the brain as they cause a higher cognitive load. Also, she had to consider the new distractions that resulted from the office space being located within her home. She had to acknowledge how much more had been added to her cognitive load. Shay needed to continue finding ways to improve how she managed her time and energy.

Having better sleep habits could not fully restore her energy. A good night's sleep was a start but if she burned up all the gas in her tank by mid-day, she'd be back to square one. It was necessary for Shay to look at her energy use throughout the day and learn how to take breaks to give her brain a rest.

The idea of taking breaks was one of the most difficult for Shay to accept. Her instinct was to power through her to-do list and only stop when she finished. However, Shay never finished because she continually added more items to her to-do list. It did not feel like there was any time to stop. After gaining an understanding of the science behind the brain's need for rest, she committed to taking short breaks. Shay found that setting a timer on her watch was the only way for her to stick to a scheduled break, otherwise she would work non-stop.

Shay began to set a 90-minute timer on her watch and when it went off, she would put down whatever she was doing or do so immediately after a meeting ended. For most of her 15-minute breaks, she would take a walk around the block. She listened to music during these walks. Listening to something other than her own thoughts helped her mind to unfocus. Both the sunlight and the music helped convince her brain that it had left behind the stress of the work environment. After she had gotten used to following this routine, she no longer needed any reminders. She became more able to notice her attention flagging after approximately 90 minutes of focused work. The idea that she could stop was liberating. Her brain had not been failing her. It just needed a break. Stepping away from her desk actually gave her a new vitality. When Shay came back after 15 minutes spent with her brain unfocused, she felt a new type of ease returning to the focused state.

She also decided to take deliberate action to reduce her cognitive load. Shay embraced the simple idea of writing things down. She was already a list-maker but there was still a lot that she held only in her head. It was frustrating when she had to keep switching her attention and would lose her train of thought. Shay also had a habit of trying to do things the moment they occurred to her so she wouldn't have to add them to her list. If she was working on a project, and suddenly remembered she hadn't watered her plants, she would quickly water them so it could be off her mind. If a non-urgent text message came in while she was doing something else, she would reply to the text message immediately. She thought that she was protecting herself by avoiding having to come back to these things later in the day.

To try out a different approach to lessening her cognitive load, she obtained some sticky note pads. If Shay thought of a nonwork item she had to address, she grabbed the nearest pad and wrote down the task instead of switching attention to complete it immediately. When the workday was done, Shay turned to her notes and focused on the nonwork tasks. It gave her a small sense of satisfaction to throw away each note as the task was completed. Managing tasks in this way encouraged her to stop switching from one thing to the next and losing track of the original task. The nonwork items she had to address were clearly delineated on the sticky notes instead of being held in her working memory. She felt her mental clarity increase as a result. She had better focus on her work-related tasks, as well as more mental bandwidth for satisfying connections with others.

One of Shay's biggest challenges was to stop thinking about work when she put it away at the end of the day. Despite stepping away from her computer in the evening, she would ruminate on ways to address the problems she was facing at work. Sometimes she would even sit back down at her desk for a short while to try to resolve a work problem and set her mind at ease.

This mental work was occurring during dinner and bedtime, parts of the evening Shay used to treasure as an opportunity for her family to connect, wind down, and enjoy each other. Lately, instead of enjoying this time, she had half her mind on her work and could sometimes get distracted and short-tempered. She said, "I spend so much of my energy being present and productive. Then, even when I try to mentally switch off and go from the corner of my bedroom down to the kitchen to start our evening routine, I'm not actually switched off." She wanted to be more present and engaged with her family. To be able to switch off, Shay needed to send a clearer message to her brain that work was over and rest and recovery should begin.

Shay needed to develop an end-of-day ritual that could shut the door on her virtual office for the night. She experimented with several different options until she found a few that would give her brain a sense of completion and closure on the workday. Without this sense of completion, she

164   Connecting and Thriving

realized her brain would not let go of the mental loops that pulled her back to unfinished work tasks. She eventually decided on a set of steps she could do every day no matter what. She wrote them down on a note in her workspace so that they would be harder to bypass.

Shay kicked off her end-of-day ritual with a time cue. At 6:05 pm she would start to wrap up her workday and would finish it at 6:35 pm. She stopped scheduling any meetings or obligations after 6:05. By giving herself 30 minutes at the end of the day, she would not have to rush through the ritual.

At 6:05 pm, she began to assess each of the many open tabs on her computer. In the past, she had left everything open and let the computer go to sleep mode so it would be easier to come back to her projects in the morning. The problem with that strategy was that she was mentally coming back to her work all evening. Now instead, she looked at each tab in her browser, resolved what she could in it, bookmarked it as needed, and then closed it. She also shut down and turned off her computer rather than let it sleep or idle. Each click of the "X" on a browser window sent a close down message to her focused work brain. She was beginning to condition her brain to close down its work tasks, rather than keeping them running in the background all night.

As she closed down her computer tabs, she identified some items that needed to be addressed the next day. Rather than keep the tabs open as she had in the past, she wrote each item on a list. This was her to-do list for the next day. She jotted down a priority rank next to each action item so she would be organized and ready to approach them proactively the next day. At the bottom of the to-do list, as another way of closing down actions for the day, she wrote down a single item of gratitude. This practice focused her thoughts on positive emotions and appreciation for people and experiences. It helped her remember the day in a positive light rather than give in to the negativity bias and only remember what went wrong.

The last step in Shay's end-of-day ritual was to put up an out-of-office automated reply on her email. This sustained the work boundaries she had set. A message went out saying that she would not be replying until after 8:00 am the next morning. In the past, she would send "just a few more emails" every night before shutting down for the evening. This usually meant at least 30 minutes spent staring at her phone in bed, getting her brain in work mode right before it was supposed to get into sleep mode. Now instead, those who wrote to Shay at night learned of her boundary and stopped expecting an immediate answer from her.

In a positive turn of events, her team members started to do the same thing. One individual revealed that he had felt obligated to check his emails at night just in case Shay had written to him. Shay had thought she was just doing a casual last-minute check. However, she had actually been conveying an unspoken message that she expected immediate replies from him and other team members. Her new boundary sent a message to her team about their own options. They no longer felt the requirement to be accessible late into the night and that allowed each person to make healthier choices.

The unfinished business that had previously remained buzzing in her brain at the end of the workday was now filed in its proper place. It no longer distracted her throughout the evening.

Reconnecting the Disconnect

Shay looked next at issues related to exclusion, isolation, and a lack of feeling meaningful connections with others. In this assessment, she looked at her own needs and the needs of others. She had learned that feelings of exclusion were warning signals that the human need for belonging was not being met. She ran a small team that she valued and enjoyed spending time with in person. They had all agreed in the past on how pleasurable it made their work lives to enjoy their team interactions. Through coaching and self-examination, Shay realized how much of that feeling was lost in the remote experience. Leading and managing her team felt like something to check off her to-do list, instead of something she enjoyed. She looked at the warning signal that her own feelings of loneliness and isolation were sending. This was an indication that her need for belonging, and likely the same need of her team members, was no longer being met.

The feeling of belonging that everyone on the team had felt inperson was getting lost in virtual interactions. The feeling of camaraderie had decreased and in its place, for all team members, was a drive to just get things done. For the team, the challenge was connecting on a human level. Certain members of Shay's team had never met the other team members in person because they joined after remote work became the norm. The team members had to go out of their way to schedule time to get to know each other better. There were no gatherings at the water coolers or spur-of-the-moment decisions to have coffee or lunches. Even for those who knew each other before then, there were no natural times to connect virtually with their team members.

Every interaction had to be scheduled because the team was physically separate. Shay was not prioritizing the social component of virtual meetings because everyone had so much work to do. The human connection had to be re-established so her team would feel valued, appreciated, and seen. She made a choice to shift her focus to prioritizing people. The work would get done regardless.

Shay had to address the changes that had unwittingly happened to their team bond so that everyone could feel connected once again. Ideas she had learned about brain-to-brain synchrony resonated with her strongly. It sounded like something her team once had but now did not. Shay had

166 Connecting and Thriving

skipped over any type of personal check-ins at the start of remote meetings because she wanted to respect her team members' time. With new thoughts about brain synchrony, Shay tried a different approach.

One day, she experimented with playing a song on her computer as people were entering the remote meeting. She was surprised by the tangible results. Watching her team as each person came on screen in their digital box, she saw facial reactions of surprise and delight. She saw bodies shift slightly, relax, and even move in time with the music. People made off-handed comments about the old song. From their separate digital spaces, they were having a synchronized experience despite being physically apart. Shay observed the demeanor of her team members as they transitioned into the meeting topic. The song and its synchronizing effect added a sense of connection with one another and got them on the same wavelength.

Seeing the positive response of this small change, Shay thought about other ways she could increase social cohesion for her team. She began to schedule a team social hour. Every other week, different team members could sign up to host and choose the way they wanted to spend the time together. By giving them ownership over the social activities, the engagement of team members increased. She also brought a more human-centered approach to her one-on-one meetings, focusing on building stronger bonds with each team member. Her team seemed more motivated and less stressed. Clearly, team morale was improving.

In addition to social cohesion, Shay knew the team required a climate of psychological safety in remote meetings. She had learned that this was part of her role as team leader. Her team worked well together in person, taking turns speaking and being sensitive to one another. She had assumed this would automatically transfer into working remotely but it had not. The interactions were different now that they were fully remote, and Shay had to help her team adapt.

She started by soliciting input from her team members. In addition to the few people who indicated trouble contributing in the remote environment, there was also a common complaint about team cohesion. In the absence of a physical conference table and whiteboard they could gather around together, something different was needed to make the remote team meetings as valuable as possible.

Shay found a variety of ways to start team meetings that helped set the tone of exchange she wanted. In addition, she wanted to structure the meetings in a way that supported discussing, debating, and disagreeing about ideas, then committing to decisions. She decided to use the "open-to-closed cone" structure to improve the team meetings. Shay had learned to ask open questions initially and then "cone" down to elicit more information quickly, and thought this narrowing approach would also work for meetings.

Together Miles Apart 167

She tried out this new meeting structure and her team responded positively to it. Shay facilitated an open discussion in the beginning of the meeting and started narrowing the focus of the meeting about halfway through the allotted time. Shay made sure that everyone was heard and let her team know when it was time to make decisions. At the end of the meeting, she summarized the decisions and made sure there was a shared commitment to implement the next steps. Shay left the last five minutes for her team to discuss what worked well in the meeting and what could make it more effective. The newly structured meeting enabled team members to end the remote meeting on a positive, unified note with a clear direction moving forward. The structural changes helped to keep people engaged and psychologically safe, preventing anyone from getting lost in the group.

To keep her team motivated, Shay also wanted to acknowledge incremental progress in their work. The words of Teresa Amabile stuck with her: "Of all the things that can boost emotions, motivation, and perception during a workday, the single most important is making progress in meaningful work. And the more frequently people experience that sense of progress, the more likely they are to be creatively productive in the long run."[13] Shay found new ways to show progress since they no longer had a bustling office with a whiteboard covered with ideas and progress. With the input of her team, Shay devised a new method where they could share elements of their progress virtually in a visual display. It made their efforts more tangible at the end of the day.

Getting everyone unified and reconnected with their shared purpose revitalized the team. Shay and her team members stopped feeling like work was just something to get through. They ended their workdays feeling less exhausted and having more energy for friends, family, and other pursuits.

Shay was learning to recognize the warning signals that her needs for safety and comfort, understanding, and belonging were not being met. She was increasing her awareness of what her body and brain were trying to tell her as she reflected more on her remote experiences. She was figuring out the actions she could take to meet those needs and face the challenges of remote work. This pairing of awareness and action would be an ongoing process for Shay and she felt capable, competent, and prepared for it. Shay encouraged her team members to also reflect on their remote experiences. She strove to guide them toward making choices and taking deliberate actions to meet their human needs so they could thrive.

In the end, Shay told us:

> I've changed my routine in major ways. Before, I'd been passively checking my email and Slack right up until the second I got in bed. I knew it was bad. But now I see how bad! My morning routine also

used to involve being near my phone at all times, checking email and Slack. Now, no more phone at the table. I talk to my kids at breakfast. After that, I sit down at my desk. Only then do I let myself check emails. And it's 9 am, so no one is complaining that I haven't responded yet! I realized that the pressure to be constantly accessible was self-imposed.

The bigger thing I realized was that the lack of human connection during remote work was staying with me like a deep ache and other people were experiencing the same thing. I used to think there was nothing I could do to change it. Remote is remote. But now I understand that feelings of disconnection are trying to tell me something. They are showing me what I'm missing, and now I know there are ways I can address it. Deepening connections with others is possible even when we're physically apart.

Notes

1 Anderson, Janna and Lee Rainie. *The Future of Well-Being in a Tech-Saturated World*. Washington DC: Pew Research Center, 2018, 18.
2 Maxwell, John C. *Beyond Talent: Become Someone Who Gets Extraordinary Results*. Nashville, TN: HarperCollins, 2011, 10. .
3 Kahneman, Daniel. *Thinking, Fast and Slow*. United States: Farrar, Straus and Giroux, 2011, 38.
4 Liljenström, Hans. "Consciousness, decision making, and volition: Freedom beyond chance and necessity." *Theory in biosciences* (2021): 1–16. doi:10.1007/s12064-021-00346-6.
5 Estes, Adam Clark. "What comes after Zoom fatigue." *Vox*, July 17, 2020, www.vox.com/recode/21314793/zoom-fatigue-video-chat-facebook-google-meet-microsoft-teams
6 Yuko, Elizabeth. "This is what it looks like to set personal and emotional boundaries." *Real Simple*, July 21, 2021, www.realsimple.com/health/mind-mood/emotional-health/how-to-set-boundaries
7 Cole, Terri. *Boundary Boss: The Essential Guide to Talk True, Be Seen, and (Finally) Live Free*. Louisville, CO: Sounds True, 2021, 1.
8 Cloud, Henry, and John Townsend. *Boundaries in Marriage*. Grand Rapids, MI: Zondervan, 2009.
9 Hobsbawm, Julia. *The Simplicity Principle: Six Steps towards Clarity in a Complex World*. London: Kogan Page, 2020.
10 Dweck, Carol S. *Mindset: The New Psychology of Success*. New York: Ballantine Books, 2016, 7.
11 Yeager, David S., Paul Hanselman, Gregory M. Walton, Jared S. Murray, Robert Crosnoe, Chandra Muller, Elizabeth Tipton, Barbara Schneider, Chris S. Hulleman, Cintia P. Hinojosa, David Paunesku, Carissa Romero, Kate Flint, Alice Roberts, Jill Trott, Ronaldo Iachan, Jenny Buontempo, Sophia Man Yang, Carlos M. Carvalho, P. Richard Hahn, Maithreyi Gopalan, Pratik Mhatre, Ronald Ferguson, Angela L. Duckworth, and Carol S. Dweck. "A national experiment reveals where a growth mindset improves

achievement." *Nature 573*, no. *7774* (2019): 364–369, https://doi.org/10.1038/s41586-019-1466-y

12 Cherry, Kendra. "What is the negativity bias?" *Very Well Mind*, April 29, 2020, www.verywellmind.com/negative-bias-4589618

13 Amabile, Teresa M., and Steven J. Kramer. "The power of small wins." *Harvard Business Review* 89, no. 5 (2011): 72.

Afterword

The more we (Diane and Amy) lived the remote life, the more we wanted to know.

After spending a year of our lives thinking about what's missing from virtual interactions and ways to mitigate the challenges, we know there is still a lot more to learn. While that learning continues, one thing is clear: it's in our best interest to be patient with ourselves. Figuring out what strategies, practices, and techniques work best for each of us and each of our lifestyles is an ongoing learning process.

One surprising thing we discovered during our remote work sessions this year is that when we stop for lunch, we can actually get more work done. Amy recognizes that she is becoming more committed to maintaining her work-life boundaries by avoiding phone and computer use during family time. She is managing her energy carefully by scheduling breaks for herself after focused brain time. Diane is continuing to find new ways to create a sense of community in her remote classes, which is extremely important to her. She spends most of her unfocused brain time taking her puppy for long walks in beautiful surroundings. We continue to pay attention to what works in our lives and do our best to change what is not working (e.g., insufficient sleep).

Despite being miles apart and never in the same room throughout the entire writing process, we feel more connected than ever. We intimately know each other's stress responses, health concerns, daily routines, punctuation preferences, and dog walking schedules. We learned what edits needed to be prefaced with "I know you'll hate this but…" and what author's technique could be cited to settle any dispute (e.g., Vivek Murthy). Many months in to our writing process, we finally accepted our own suggestion to take short breaks. We know firsthand that people can stay connected and strengthen that connection, even when apart. A strong connection is what made the creation of this book possible.

Now we turn the book over to you. Our sincere wish is that you can mitigate some of the challenges of virtual interactions, increase human connection, and think and act in ways that lead to greater well-being. Here's to making choices and taking actions that promote well-being in your increasingly remote lives.

Appendix
Where to Find Additional Mental Health Support

Psychology Today

www.psychologytoday.com
This website features location-based directories to find therapists and other health professionals. It also has hundreds of health and wellness blogs written by a wide variety of psychologists, psychiatrists, social workers, medical doctors, anthropologists, sociologists, and science journalists.

7 Cups

www.7cups.com
7 Cups is an on-demand emotional health service and online therapy provider. They anonymously and securely connect real people to real listeners in one-on-one chats. Anyone who wants to talk about whatever is on their mind can quickly reach out to a trained, compassionate listener through their diverse network. Affordable online therapy is also available.

Warmlines

https://screening.mhanational.org/content/need-talk-someone-warmlines
Warmlines were created to give people support when they just need to talk to someone. Speaking to someone on these calls is typically free, confidential, and run by people who understand what it's like to struggle with mental health problems. It's best to call a warmline in your own state. See the website above for a complete listing. If one doesn't exist or it is busy, you can try a warmline in another state that is close to you and provides national service.

172 Appendix

SAMHSA Treatment Referral Helpline

1-877-SAMHSA7 (1-877-726-4727)
https://findtreatment.samhsa.gov
The Substance Abuse and Mental Health Services Administration, part of the US Department of Health and Human Services, provides general information on mental health and can help locate treatment services in your area. Speak to a live person, Monday through Friday from 8 am to 8 pm EST.

National Alliance on Mental Illness (NAMI)

www.nami.org
NAMI is the nation's largest grassroots mental health organization dedicated to building better lives for the millions of Americans affected by mental illness. NAMI identifies its mission as "providing advocacy, education, support and public awareness so that all individuals and families affected by mental illness can build better lives" and its vision as "a world where all people affected by mental illness live healthy, fulfilling lives supported by a community that cares." NAMI offers classes and training for people living with mental illness and their families, as well as community members and professionals.

Mental Health America (MHA)

www.mhanational.org
MHA's programs and initiatives fulfill its mission of promoting mental health and preventing mental illness through advocacy, education, research, and services. MHA's national office and its 200+ affiliates and associates around the country work every day to protect the rights and dignity of individuals with lived experience and ensure that peers and their voices are integrated into all areas of the organization.

Veteran Mental Health

www.mentalhealth.va.gov/get-help/local-care.asp
https://nrd.gov
Visit these websites to find a list of local providers and other resources for help. The National Resource Directory (NRD) is a database of validated resources that supports recovery, rehabilitation, and reintegration for service members, veterans, family members, and caregivers.

References

"18 Incredible Benefits of Journaling (and how to start)." Vanilla Papers (blog), August 9, 2020, https://vanillapapers.net/2020/08/09/journaling-benefits/.

Akṣapāda. *PLATO'S DOCTRINE: 909 Relics of Greek Philosophy*. Independently Published, 2019.

Alimujiang, Aliya, Ashley Wiensch, Jonathan Boss, Nancy L. Fleischer, Alison M. Mondul, Karen McLean, Bhramar Mukherjee, and Celeste Leigh Pearce. "Association between life purpose and mortality among US adults older than 50 years." *JAMA network open* 2, no. 5 (2019): e194270. doi:10.1001/jamanetworkopen.2019.4270.

Almarode, John, and Ann M. Miller. *Captivate, Activate, and Invigorate the Student Brain in Science and Math, Grades 6–12*. Washington, DC: Corwin Press, 2013.

"Almost 25,000 students in healthcare professions opt to join COVID-19 fight." NHS: Health Education England (blog), April 17, 2020, www.hee.nhs.uk/news-blogs-events/news/more-23000-students-healthcare-professions-op t-join-covid-19-fight.

Amabile, Teresa M., and Steven J. Kramer. "The power of small wins." *Harvard Business Review* 89, no. 5 (2011): 70–80.

American Psychological Association. "Building your resilience." February 1, 2020, www.apa.org/topics/resilience.

Anderson, Janna and Lee Rainie. *Stories from Experts about the Impact of Digital Life*. Washington, DC: Pew Research Center, 2018.

Anderson, Janna and Lee Rainie. *The Future of Well-Being in a Tech-Saturated World*. Washington, DC: Pew Research Center, 2018.

Anderson, Monica, Emily A. Vogels, and Erica Turner. "The Virtues and Downsides of Online Dating." Pew Research Center, February 6, 2020, www.pewresearch.org/internet/2020/02/06/the-virtues-and-downsides-of-online-dating/.

Ariel Group. "Stories Connect Us: The Power Inside a Homefront Foundation Event." Presence and Leadership (blog), www.arielgroup.com/stories-connect-us-the-power-inside-a-homefront-foundation-event/.

Armon, Galit, Samuel Melamed, Arie Shirom, and Itzhak Shapira. "Elevated burnout predicts the onset of musculoskeletal pain among apparently healthy employees." *Journal of occupational health psychology* 15, no. 4 (2010): 399.

Arndt, Brian G., John W. Beasley, Michelle D. Watkinson, Jonathan L. Temte, Wen-Jan Tuan, Christine A. Sinsky, and Valerie J. Gilchrist. "Tethered to the

EHR: Primary care physician workload assessment using EHR event log data and time-motion observations." *The Annals of Family Medicine* 15, no. 5 (2017): 419–426, https://doi.org/10.1370/afm.2121.

Associated Press. "Applications to US nursing schools rise as students want to 'join the frontline.'" *The Guardian*, October 15, 2021, www.theguardian.com/us-news/2021/oct/15/us-nursing-schools-nurses-pandemic.

Bariso, Justin. "Why intelligent minds like Jeff Bezos embrace the rule of writing." *Inc*, August 29, 2021, www.inc.com/justin-bariso/how-to-write-amazon-jeff-bezos-memos-meetings-clear-writing-clear-thinking-rule-of-writing.html.

Beattie, Alex and Rebecca Priestley. "Fighting COVID-19 with the team of 5 million: Aotearoa New Zealand government communication during the 2020 lockdown." *Social sciences & humanities open* 4, no. 1 (2021): 100209, https://doi.org/10.1016/j.ssaho.2021.100209.

Berman, Marc G., John Jonides, and Stephen Kaplan. "The cognitive benefits of interacting with nature." *Psychological science* 19, no. 12 (2008): 1207–1212.

Blank, Steve. "What's missing from Zoom reminds us what it means to be human." Steve Blank (blog). April 27, 2020, https://steveblank.com/2020/04/27/whats-missing-from-zoom-reminds-us-what-it-means-to-be-human.

Boksem, Maarten A.S., and Mattie Tops. "Mental fatigue: Costs and benefits." *Brain research reviews* 59, no. 1 (2008): 125–139.

Bradford, Deborah, Jane Goodman-Delahunty, and Kevin R. Brooks. "The impact of presentation modality on perceptions of truthful and deceptive confessions." *Journal of criminology* (2013), http://dx.doi.org/10.1155/2013/164546.

Breuer, Christina, Joachim Hüffmeier, and Guido Hertel. "Does trust matter more in virtual teams? A meta-analysis of trust and team effectiveness considering virtuality and documentation as moderators." *The Journal of applied psychology* 101, no. 8 (2016): 1151–1177, doi:10.1037/apl0000113.

Brooks, Alison Wood. "Get excited: Reappraising pre-performance anxiety as excitement." *Journal of experimental psychology: general* 143, no. 3 (2014): 1144–1158, doi:10.1037/a0035325.

Brown, Brené. "Brené Brown on joy and gratitude." Global Leadership Network, November 21, 2018, https://globalleadership.org/articles/leading-yourself/brene-brown-on-joy-and-gratitude/.

Brown, Brené. *Dare to Lead: Brave Work. Tough Conversations. Whole Hearts.* New York: Random House Publishing Group, 2018.

Brym, Robert J. *Sociology: Your Compass for a New World.* Belmont, CA: Thomson/Wadsworth, 2007.

Buettner, Dan. *The Blue Zones: 9 Lessons for Living Longer from the People Who've Lived the Longest.* Washington, DC: National Geographic Books, 2012.

Carson, Rachel. *Silent Spring.* Boston, MA: Houghton Mifflin, 2002.

Cascio, Christopher N., Christin Scholz, and Emily B. Falk. "Social influence and the brain: Persuasion, susceptibility to influence and retransmission." *Current opinion in behavioral sciences* 3 (2015): 51–57, https://doi.org/10.1016/j.cobeha.2015.01.007.

Chen, Zhansheng, Kipling D. Williams, Julie Fitness, and Nicola C. Newton. "When hurt will not heal: Exploring the capacity to relive social and physical pain." *Psychological science* 19, no. 8 (2008): 789–795, https://doi.org/10.1111/j.1467-9280.2008.02158.x.

Cherry, Kendra. "What is the negativity bias?" *VeryWell Mind*, April 29, 2020, www.verywellmind.com/negative-bias-4589618.

Christian, Brian and Tom Griffiths. *Algorithms to Live By: The Computer Science of Human Decisions*. New York: Henry Holt and Company, 2016.

Clear, James. *Atomic Habits: An Easy & Proven Way to Build Good Habits & Break Bad Ones*. New York: Penguin Publishing Group, 2018.

Coan, James A., and David A. Sbarra. "Social Baseline Theory: the social regulation of risk and effort." *Current opinion in psychology* 1 (2015): 87–91, https://doi.org/10.1016/j.copsyc.2014.12.021.

Cole, Terri. *Boundary Boss: The Essential Guide to Talk True, Be Seen, and (Finally) Live Free*. Louisville, CO: Sounds True, 2021.

Covey, Stephen R. *The 7 Habits of Highly Effective People: Powerful Lessons in Personal Change*. London: Simon & Schuster, 2013.

Croes, Emmelyn A.J., Marjolijn L. Antheunis, and Alexander P. Schouten. "Social attraction in video-mediated communication: The role of nonverbal affiliative behavior." *Journal of social and personal relationships* 36, no. 4 (2019): 1210–1232, https://doi.org/10.1177/0265407518757382.

Csikszentmihalyi, Mihaly. *Flow: The Psychology of Optimal Experience*. New York: HarperPerennial, 1990.

Cutter, Chip. "Companies start to think remote work isn't so great after all." *Wall Street Journal*, July 24, 2020, www.wsj.com/articles/companies-start-to-think-remote-work-isnt-so-great-after-all-11595603397.

De Jong, Bart A., Kurt T. Dirks, and Nicole Gillespie. "Trust and team performance: A meta-analysis of main effects, moderators, and covariates." *Journal of applied psychology* 101, no. 8 (2016): 1134, doi:10.1037/apl0000110.

De Smet, Aaron, Mihir Mysore, Angelika Reich, and Bob Sternfels. "Return as a muscle: How lessons from COVID-19 can shape a robust operating model for hybrid and beyond." McKinsey & Company, July 9, 2021, www.mckinsey.com/business-functions/people-and-organizational-performance/our-insights/return-as-a-muscle-how-lessons-from-covid-19-can-shape-a-robust-operating-model-for-hybrid-and-beyond.

Deloitte. "Analysis: Workplace burnout survey." March 2018, www2.deloitte.com/us/en/pages/about-deloitte/articles/burnout-survey.html.

Deloitte. "Culture of purpose—Building business confidence; driving growth. 2014 core beliefs & culture survey." February 2014, www2.deloitte.com/content/dam/Deloitte/us/Documents/about-deloitte/us-leadership-2014-core-beliefs-culture-survey-040414.pdf.

Denworth, Lydia. "'Hyperscans' show how brains sync as people interact." *Scientific American*, April 10, 2019, www.scientificamerican.com/article/hyperscans-show-how-brains-sync-as-people-interact/.

Diamond, Madeline. "Why mental health is a top priority for the US Surgeon General." *HuffPost*, July 14, 2016, www.huffpost.com/entry/why-emotional-well-being-is-a-top-priority-for-the-us-surgeon-general_n_57866486e4b08608d3327828.

Dikker, Suzanne, Lu Wan, Ido Davidesco, Lisa Kaggen, Matthias Oostrik, James McClintock, Jess Rowland, Georgios Michalareas, Jay J. Van Bavel, Mingzhou Ding, and David Poeppell. "Brain-to-brain synchrony tracks real-world dynamic group interactions in the classroom." *Current biology* 27, no. 9 (2017): 1375–1380, http://dx.doi.org/10.1016/j.cub.2017.04.002.

176 References

Ducheneaut, Nicolas, Nicholas Yee, Eric Nickell, and Robert J. Moore. "'Alone together?' Exploring the social dynamics of massively multiplayer online games." *Proceedings of the SIGCHI Conference on Human Factors in Computing Systems* (April 2006): 407–416, https://doi.org/10.1145/1124772.1124834.

Duhigg, Charles. "What Google Learned From Its Quest to Build the Perfect Team." *The New York Times Magazine*, February 25, 2016, www.nytimes.com/2016/02/28/magazine/what-google-learned-from-its-quest-to-build-the-perfect-team.html?smid=pl-share.

Dweck, Carol S. *Mindset: The New Psychology of Success*. New York: Ballantine Books, 2016.

Eagleman, David. *Livewired: The Inside Story of the Ever-Changing Brain*. New York: Knopf Doubleday Publishing Group, 2020.

Edmondson, Amy C. "How fearless organizations succeed." *Strategy+Business*, November 14, 2018, www.strategy-business.com/article/How-Fearless-Organizations-Succeed.

Eisenberger, Naomi I., and Matthew D. Lieberman. "Why rejection hurts: a common neural alarm system for physical and social pain." *Trends in cognitive sciences* 8, no. 7 (2004): 294–300, https://doi.org/10.1016/j.tics.2004.05.010.

Emmert, Amy. "Empathy: The glue we need to fix a fractured world." *Strategy+Business*, October 20, 2020, www.strategy-business.com/article/Empathy-The-glue-we-need-to-fix-a-fractured-world.

Emmons, Robert. "Why gratitude is good." *Mind and Body*, November 16, 2010, https://greatergood.berkeley.edu/article/item/why_gratitude_is_good.

Entis, Laura. "How COVID-19 and technology that connects us may be making us lonelier." *Vox*, May 26, 2020, www.vox.com/the-highlight/2020/5/26/21256190/zoom-facetime-skype-coronavirus-loneliness.

Ericsson, Anders K., Ralf T. Krampe, and Clemens Tesch-Romer. "The role of deliberate practice in the acquisition of expert performance." *Psychological review* 100, no. 3 (1993): 363–406, doi:10.1037/0033-295x.100.3.363.

Estes, Adam Clark. "What comes after Zoom fatigue." *Vox*, July 17, 2020, www.vox.com/recode/21314793/zoom-fatigue-video-chat-facebook-google-meet-microsoft-teams.

Ferran, Carlos and Stephanie Watts. "Videoconferencing in the field: A heuristic processing model." *Management science* 54, no. 9 (2008): 1565–1578, doi:10.1287/mnsc.1080.0879.

Filkowski, Megan M., R. Nick Cochran, and Brian W. Haas. "Altruistic behavior: mapping responses in the brain." *Neuroscience and neuroeconomics* 5 (2016): 65, https://doi.org/10.2147/NAN.S87718.

Fivush, Robyn. "Listening to stories: The power of story circles." The Stories of Our Lives (blog). *Psychology Today*, August 13, 2020www.psychologytoday.com/us/blog/the-stories-our-lives/202008/listening-stories-the-power-story-circles.

Folk, Dunigan, Karynna Okabe-Miyamoto, Elizabeth Dunn, Sonja Lyubomirsky, and Brent Donnellan. "Did social connection decline during the first wave of COVID-19? The role of extraversion." *Collabra: Psychology* 6, no. 1 (2020), https://doi.org/10.1525/collabra.365.

Gaines, Jeffrey. "The philosophy of ikigai: 3 examples about finding purpose." Positive Psychology.com, August 24, 2021, https://positivepsychology.com/ikigai/

References 177

Gale, Anthony, Graham Spratt, Antony J. Chapman, and Adrian Smallbone. "EEG correlates of eye contact and interpersonal distance." *Biological Psychology* 3, no. 4 (1975): 237–245, https://doi.org/10.1016/0301-0511(75)90023-X.

Gandour, J.T. "Tone: Neurophonetics." In *Encyclopedia of Language & Linguistics* (second edition), edited by Keith Brown. Amsterdam: Elsevier, 2006, https://doi.org/10.1016/B0-08-044854-2/04796-9.

García, Héctor, and Francesc Miralles. *Ikigai: The Japanese Secret to a Long and Happy Life*. London: Penguin Publishing Group, 2017.

Gladwell, Malcolm. *Outliers: The Story of Success*. London: Penguin Books Limited, 2008.

Goh, Joel, Jeffrey Pfeffer, and Stefanos A. Zenios. "The relationship between workplace stressors and mortality and health costs in the United States." *Management science* 62, no. 2 (2015): 608–628, https://doi.org/10.1287/mnsc.2014.2115.

Goldfinch, Shaun, Ross Taplin, and Robin Gauld. "Trust in government increased during the Covid-19 pandemic in Australia and New Zealand." *Australian journal of public administration* 80, no. 1 (2021): 3–11, https://doi.org/10.1111/1467-8500.12459.

Goleman, Daniel. *Focus: The Hidden Driver of Excellence*. New York: Harper, 2013.

Grant, Adam. "Building a culture of learning at work." *Strategy+Business*, February 3, 2021, www.strategy-business.com/article/Building-a-culture-of-learning-at-work.

Greene, Robert. *Mastery*. New York: Penguin Books, 2013.

Habay, Jelle, Jeroen Van Cutsem, Jo Verschueren, Sander De Bock, Matthias Proost, Jonas De Wachter, Bruno Tassignon, Romain Meeusen, and Bart Roelands. "Mental fatigue and sport-specific psychomotor performance: A systematic review." *Sports medicine* 51 (2021): 1527–1548, https://doi.org/10.1007/s40279-021-01429-6.

Habib, Navaz. *Activate Your Vagus Nerve: Unleash Your Body's Natural Ability to Heal*. Berkeley, CA: Ulysses Press, 2019.

Hall, Edward Twitchell. *The Silent Language*. India: Doubleday, 1990.

Hall, Edward Twitchell and Edmund T. Hall. *The Hidden Dimension*. London: Doubleday, 1966.

Hariri, Ahmad R., Venkata S. Mattay, Alessandro Tessitore, Francesco Fera, and Daniel R. Weinberger. "Neocortical modulation of the amygdala response to fearful stimuli." *Biological psychiatry* 53, no. 6 (2003): 494–501, https://doi.org/10.1016/S0006-3223(02)01786–01789.

Hartle, Terry W. "The courage of medical students." *Inside Higher Ed*, April 20, 2020, www.insidehighered.com/views/2020/04/20/medical-students-are-joining-front-lines-fight-against-covid-19-lets-cheer-them.

Harvard Business Review. "The business case for purpose." 2015, https://assets.ey.com/content/dam/ey-sites/ey-com/en_gl/topics/digital/ey-the-business-case-for-purpose.pdf.

Healey, Meghan L., and Murray Grossman. "Cognitive and affective perspective-taking: Evidence for shared and dissociable anatomical substrates." *Frontiers in neurology* 9 (2018): 491, https://doi.org/10.3389/fneur.2018.00491.

Heath, Sara. "Patient satisfaction with telehealth high following COVID-19," Patient Engagement HIT, October 7, 2020, https://patientengagementhit.com/news/patient-satisfaction-with-telehealth-high-following-covid-19.

178 References

Herrera, Tim. "Why your brain tricks you into doing less important tasks." *New York Times*, July 9, 2018, www.nytimes.com/2018/07/09/smarter-living/eisenhower-box-productivity-tips.html.

Hill, Amelia. "Why teenagers can't concentrate: Too much grey matter." *The Guardian*, May 31, 2010, www.theguardian.com/science/2010/may/31/why-teenagers-cant-concentrate-brains.

Hinds, Pamela J. "The cognitive and interpersonal costs of video." *Media psychology* 1, no. 4 (1999): 283–311, https://doi.org/10.1207/s1532785xmep0104_1.

Hobsbawm, Julia. *The Simplicity Principle: Six Steps towards Clarity in a Complex World*. London: Kogan Page, 2020.

Hölzel, Britta K., James Carmody, Mark Vangel, Christina Congleton, Sita M. Yerramsetti, Tim Gard, and Sara W. Lazar. "Mindfulness practice leads to increases in regional brain gray matter density." *Psychiatry research: neuroimaging* 191, no. 1 (2011): 36–43, doi:10.1016/j.pscychresns.2010.08.006.

Howard, Jane. *Families*. New York: Simon and Schuster, 1998.

Hunt, Elle. "Words matter: How New Zealand's clear messaging helped beat Covid." *The Guardian*, February 25, 2021, www.theguardian.com/world/2021/feb/26/words-matter-how-new-zealands-clear-messaging-helped-beat-covid.

Hutchinson, J. Benjamin, and Lisa Feldman Barrett. "The power of predictions: An emerging paradigm for psychological research." *Current directions in psychological science* 28, no. 3 (2019): 280–291.

Jabr, Ferris. "Why your brain needs more downtime." *Scientific American*, October 15, 2013, www.scientificamerican.com/article/mental-downtime/.

James, William. *Principles of Psychology*. New York: Dover Publications, Inc., 1950.

Kabat-Zinn, John. *Wherever You Go, There You Are: Mindfulness Meditation in Everyday Life*. New York: Hachette Books, 2009.

Kahneman, Daniel. *Thinking, Fast and Slow*. New York: Farrar, Straus and Giroux, 2011.

Khan Academy. "What is the history of Khan Academy?" September 2021, https://support.khanacademy.org/hc/en-us/articles/202483180-What-is-the-history-of-Khan-Academy-.

Klipper, Miriam Z., and Herbert Benson. *The Relaxation Response*. New York: HarperCollins e-books, 2009.

Kludacz-Alessandri, Magdalena, Liliana Hawrysz, Piotr Korneta, Grażyna Gierszewska, Wioletta Pomaranik, and Renata Walczak. "The impact of medical teleconsultations on general practitioner-patient communication during COVID-19: A case study from Poland." *PLOS ONE* 16, no. 7 (2021): e0254960, https://doi.org/10.1371/journal.pone.0254960.

Knudsen, Eric I. "Fundamental components of attention." *Annual Review of Neuroscience* 30 (2007): 57–78, https://doi.org/10.1146/annurev.neuro.30.051606.094256.

Kosfeld, Michael, Markus Heinrichs, Paul J. Zak, Urs Fischbacher, and Ernst Fehr. "Oxytocin increases trust in humans." *Nature* 435, no. 7042 (2005): 673–676, https://doi.org/10.1038/nature03701.

Kosner, Anthony Wing. "Amy Edmondson on the power of psychological safety in distributed work." Work in Progress, March 27, 2020, https://blog.dropbox.com/topics/work-culture/amy-edmondson-on-the-power-of-psychological-safety-in-distribute.

References 179

Kret, M.E., A.H. Fischer, and C.K.W. De Dreu. "Pupil mimicry correlates with trust in in-group partners with dilating pupils." *Psychological science* 26, no. 9 (2015): 1401–1410, https://doi.org/10.1177/0956797615588306.

Kubu, Cynthia and Andre Machado. "Why multitasking is bad for you." *Time*, April 20, 2017, https://time.com/4737286/multitasking-mental-health-stress-texting-depression/.

Lagasse, Jeff. "Telehealth claim lines increased more than 4,000% in the past year." *Healthcare Finance*, June 3, 2020, www.healthcarefinancenews.com/news/telehealth-claim-lines-increased-more-4000-past-year.

Lakhani, Karim R., and Luis M. Viceira. "5 key lessons from HBS's pandemic teaching transformation: And what learnings will stick moving forward." *Harvard Business Publishing Education*, July 1, 2021, https://hbsp.harvard.edu/inspiring-minds/5-key-lessons-from-hbs-pandemic-teaching-transformation.

Le Cunff, Anne-Laure. "The science-based benefits of reading." Ness Labs, https://nesslabs.com/reading-benefits.

Leineweber, Constanze, Claudia Bernhard-Oettel, Paraskevi Peristera, Constanze Eib, Anna Nyberg and Hugo Westerlund. "Interactional justice at work is related to sickness absence: A study using repeated measures in the Swedish working population." *BMC public health* 17, no. 912 (2017), https://doi.org/10.1186/s12889-017-4899-y.

Lencioni, Patrick M. *The Five Dysfunctions of a Team: A Leadership Fable*. Berlin: Wiley, 2010.

Levitin, Daniel. *The Organized Mind: Thinking Straight in the Age of Information Overload*. London: Dutton, 2014.

Lick, David J., Clarissa I. Cortland, and Kerri L. Johnson. "The pupils are the windows to sexuality: Pupil dilation as a visual cue to others' sexual interest." *Evolution and Human Behavior* 37, no. 2 (2016): 117–124, https://doi.org/10.1016/j.evolhumbehav.2015.09.004.

Lieberman, Matthew D. *Social: Why Our Brains Are Wired to Connect*. Oxford: Oxford University Press, 2013.

Liljenström, Hans. "Consciousness, decision making, and volition: freedom beyond chance and necessity." *Theory in biosciences* (2021): 1–16. doi:10.1007/s12064-12021-00346-00346.

Loehr, Jim and Tony Schwartz. *The Power of Full Engagement: Managing Energy, Not Time, Is the Key to High Performance and Personal Renewal*. London: Free Press, 2005.

Luders, Eileen, Nicolas Cherbuin, and Florian Kurth. "Forever Young(er): Potential age-defying effects of long-term meditation on gray matter atrophy." *Frontiers in psychology* 5 (2015): 1551, www.frontiersin.org/article/10.3389/fpsyg.2014.01551.

Lund, Susan, Anu Madgavkar, James Manyika, and Sven Smit. "What's next for remote work: An analysis of 2,000 tasks, 800 jobs, and nine countries." McKinsey & Company, November 23, 2020, www.mckinsey.com/featured-insights/future-of-work/whats-next-for-remote-work-an-analysis-of-2000-tasks-800-jobs-and-nine-countries.

Marcora, Samuele M., Walter Staiano, and Victoria Manning. "Mental fatigue impairs physical performance in humans." *Journal of applied physiology* 106, no. 3 (2009): 857–864.

180 References

Maslach, Christina. "Burnout and engagement in the workplace: new perspectives." *The European health psychologist* 13, no. 3 (2011): 44–47.

Maslach, Christina, and Michael P. Leiter. "Understanding the burnout experience: Recent research and its implications for psychiatry." *World psychiatry* 15, no. 2 (2016): 103–111, https://doi.org/10.1002/wps.20311.

Mason, Malia, Bruce Hood, and C. Neil Macrae. "Look into my eyes: Gaze direction and person memory." *Memory* 12, no. 5 (2004): 637–643, doi:10.1080/09658210344000152.

Maxwell, John C. *Beyond Talent: Become Someone Who Gets Extraordinary Results.* Nashville, TN: HarperCollins, 2011.

McChrystal, Gen. Stanley, Tantum Collins, David Silverman, Chris Fussell. *Team of Teams: New Rules of Engagement for a Complex World.* London: Penguin Publishing Group, 2015.

McGill Association of University Teachers. "A brief history of MOOCs." www.mcgill.ca/maut/news-current-affairs/moocs/history.

McGregor, Jena. "Hot new job title in a pandemic: 'Head of remote work.'" *Washington Post*, September 9, 2020, www.washingtonpost.com/business/2020/09/09/head-of-remote-work-jobs/.

Mehrabian, Albert. *Silent Messages.* Belmont, CA: Wadsworth Publishing Company, 1971.

Meng Zhu, Yang Yang, and Christopher K. Hsee. "The mere urgency effect." *Journal of Consumer Research* 45, no. 3 (2018): 673–690, https://doi.org/10.1093/jcr/ucy008.

Moray, N. "Attention in dichotic listening: Affective cues and the influence of instructions." *Quarterly Journal of Experimental Psychology* 11 (1959): 56–60, doi:10.1080/17470215908416289.

Morris, Betsy. "Why does Zoom exhaust you? Science has an answer." *The Wall Street Journal*, May 27, 2020, www.wsj.com/articles/why-does-zoom-exhaust-you-science-has-an-answer-11590600269.

Mu, Yan, Chunyan Guo, and Shihui Han. "Oxytocin enhances inter-brain synchrony during social coordination in male adults." *Social cognitive and affective neuroscience* 11, no. 12 (2016): 1882–1893, doi:10.1093/scan/nsw106.

Murthy, Vivek H. *Together: The Healing Power of Human Connection in a Sometimes Lonely World.* New York: Harper Collins, 2020.

Nadler, Robby. "Understanding 'Zoom fatigue': Theorizing spatial dynamics as third skins in computer-mediated communication." *Computers and composition* 58 (2020), https://doi.org/10.1016/j.compcom.2020.102613.

Naska, Androniki, Eleni Oikonomou, Antonia Trichopoulou, Theodora Psaltopoulou, and Dimitrios Trichopoulos. "Siesta in healthy adults and coronary mortality in the general population." *Archives of internal medicine* 167, no. 3 (2007): 296–301, doi:10.1001/archinte.167.3.296.

National Center for Chronic Disease Prevention and Health Promotion, Division of Population Health. "Well-being concepts." October 31, 2018, www.cdc.gov/hrqol/wellbeing.htm.

Nesbitt, Thomas S., and Jana Katz-Bell. "History of telehealth." In *Understanding Telehealth*, edited by Karen Schulder Rheuban and Elizabeth A. Krupinski. New York: McGraw-Hill, 2018, https://accessmedicine.mhmedical.com/content.aspx?bookid=2217&sectionid=187794434.

References 181

Neville, Helen. *Is This a Phase? Child Development & Parent Strategies from Birth to 6 Years*. Seattle, WA: Parenting Press, 2007.

Newport, Cal. "Drastically reduce stress with a work shutdown ritual." Study Hacks Blog, Cal Newport, June 8, 2009, www.calnewport.com/blog/2009/06/08/drastically-reduce-stress-with-a-work-shutdown-ritual/.

Newport, Cal. *Deep Work: Rules for Focused Success in a Distracted World*. New York: Grand Central Publishing, 2016.

Nielson, Stevan Lars, and Irwin G. Sarason. "Emotion, personality, and selective attention." *Journal of personality and social psychology* 41, no. 5 (1981): 945–960, doi:10.1037/0022-3514.41.5.945.

Nikolova, Milena, and Femke Cnossen. "What makes a job meaningful?" *Brookings*, April 8, 2020, www.brookings.edu/blog/up-front/2020/04/08/what-makes-a-job-meaningful/.

Nikolova, Milena, and Femke Cnossen. "What makes work meaningful and why economists should care about it." IZA Institute of Labor Economics, Discussion Paper Series, April 2020: 2, https://ftp.iza.org/dp13112.pdf.

Ophir, Eyal, Clifford Nass, and Anthony D. Wagner. "Cognitive control in media multitaskers." *Proceedings of the National Academy of Sciences* 106, no. 37 (2009): 15583–15587, https://doi.org/10.1073/pnas.0903620106.

Ormrod, Jeanne Ellis. *Human Learning*. Harlow: Pearson Education Limited, 2016.

Oxford University Press. "Altruism." *Oxford Learners Dictionaries*, 2021, www.oxfordlearnersdictionaries.com/definition/english/altruism?q=altruism.

Pang, Alex Soojung-Kim. *Rest: Why You Get More Done When You Work Less*. London: Basic Books, 2016.

Paul, Annie Murphy. "Your brain on fiction." *New York Times*, March 17, 2012, www.nytimes.com/2012/03/18/opinion/sunday/the-neuroscience-of-your-brain-on-fiction.html.

Penders, Thomas M., Cornel N. Stanciu, Alexander M. Schoemann, Philip T. Ninan, Richard Bloch, and Sy A. Saeed. "Bright light therapy as augmentation of pharmacotherapy for treatment of depression: A systematic review and meta-analysis." *Primary care companion, CNS disorders* 18, no. 5 (2016), doi:10.4088/PCC.15r01906.

Perez, Sarah. "Meditation and mindfulness apps continue their surge amid pandemic." *TechCrunch+*, May 28, 2020, https://techcrunch.com/2020/05/28/meditation-and-mindfulness-apps-continue-their-surge-amid-pandemic/.

Perrone, Matthew. "Virus drives new demand for Talkspace's online therapy." *ABCnews.com*, May 10, 2020, https://abcnews.go.com/US/wireStory/virus-drives-demand-talkspaces-online-therapy-70603681.

Petersen, Steven E., and Michael I. Posner. "The attention system of the human brain: 20 years after." *Annual review of neuroscience* 35 (2012): 73–89, https://doi.org/10.1146/annurev-neuro-062111-150525.

Petrie, Keith J., Iris Fontanilla, Mark G. Thomas, Roger J. Booth, and James W. Pennebaker. "Effect of written emotional expression on immune function in patients with human immunodeficiency virus infection: a randomized trial." *Psychosomatic medicine* 66, no. 2 (2004): 272–275. doi:10.1097/01.psy.0000116782.49850.d3.

Prinzing, Michael M., and Barbara L. Fredrickson. "How to have a better day during the pandemic." *The Well: The University of North Carolina at Chapel*

Hill, June 30, 2020, https://thewell.unc.edu/2020/06/30/how-to-have-a-better-day-during-the-pandemic/.

Putre, Laura. "A shared purpose: Leadership and culture at COVID-19 innovators." *Industry Week*, April 24, 2020, www.industryweek.com/leadership/article/21129706/a-shared-purpose-leadership-and-culture-at-covid19-innovators.

Raz, Amir. "Anatomy of attentional networks." *The anatomical record Part B: The new anatomist* 281, no. 1 (2004): 21–36, https://doi.org/10.1002/ar.b.20035.

Reinero, Diego A., Suzanne Dikker, and Jay J. Van Bavel. "Inter-brain synchrony in teams predicts collective performance." *Social cognitive and affective neuroscience* 16, no. 1–2 (2021): 43–57, https://doi.org/10.1093/scan/nsaa135.

Riess, Helen. "The science of empathy." *Journal of patient experience* 4, no. 2 (2017): 74–77, https://doi.org/10.1177%2F2374373517699267.

Robison, Jennifer. "What disruption reveals about engaging millennial employees." Gallup, January 6, 2021, www.gallup.com/workplace/328121/disruption-reveals-engaging-millennial-employees.aspx.

Rock, David, Beth Jones, and Chris Weller. "Using neuroscience to make feedback work and feel better." *Strategy+Business*, August 27, 2018, www.strategy-business.com/article/Using-Neuroscience-to-Make-Feedback-Work-and-Feel-Better.

Sansom-Daly, Ursula M., and Natalie Bradford. "Grappling with the 'human' problem hiding behind the technology: Telehealth during and beyond COVID-19." *Psycho-oncology* 29 (2020): 1404–1408, doi:10.1002/pon.5462.

Schabram, Kira, and Yu Tse Heng. "Educators and students are burned out: These strategies can help." *Harvard business publishing: education*, April 29, 2021, https://hbsp.harvard.edu/inspiring-minds/educators-and-students-are-burned-out-these-strategies-can-help.

Schaufeli, Wilmar B., and Arnold B. Bakker. "Job demands, job resources, and their relationship with burnout and engagement: A multi-sample study." *Journal of organizational behavior: the international journal of industrial, occupational and organizational psychology and behavior* 25, no. 3 (2004): 293–315, https://doi.org/10.1002/job.248.

Schoenenberg, Katrin, Alexander Raake, and Judith Koeppe. "Why are you so slow? Misattribution of transmission delay to attributes of the conversation partner at the far-end." *International journal of human-computer studies* 72, no. 5 (2014): 477–487, https://doi.org/10.1016/j.ijhcs.2014.02.004.

Scullin, Michael K., Madison L. Krueger, Hannah K. Ballard, Natalya Pruett, and Donald L. Bliwise. "The effects of bedtime writing on difficulty falling asleep: A polysomnographic study comparing to-do lists and completed activity lists." *Journal of experimental psychology: general* 147, no. 1 (2018): 139–146, https://doi.org/10.1037/xge0000374.

Shockley, Kristen M., Allison S. Gabriel, Daron Robertson, Christopher C. Rosen, Nitya Chawla, Mahira L. Ganster, and Maira E. Ezerins. "The fatiguing effects of camera use in virtual meetings: A within-person field experiment." *Journal of applied psychology* 106, no. 8 (2021): 1137.

Siegel, Daniel J. *Brainstorm: The Power and Purpose of the Teenage Brain.* New York: Penguin Publishing Group, 2014.

Simons, Daniel J. "Inattentional blindness." *Scholarpedia* 2, no. 5 (2007): 3244, www.scholarpedia.org/article/Inattentional_blindness.

Simons, Daniel J., and Christopher F. Chabris. "Gorillas in our midst: Sustained inattentional blindness for dynamic events." *Perception* 28, no. 9 (1999): 1059–1074. doi:10.1068/p281059.

Sklar, Julia. "'Zoom fatigue' is taxing the brain. Here's why that happens," *National Geographic*, April 24, 2020, www.nationalgeographic.com/science/a rticle/coronavirus-zoom-fatigue-is-taxing-the-brain-here-is-why-that-happens.

Smyth, Joshua M., Arthur A. Stone, Adam Hurewitz, and Alan Kaell. "Effects of writing about stressful experiences on symptom reduction in patients with asthma or rheumatoid arthritis: A randomized trial." *JAMA* 281, no. 14 (1999): 1304–1309.

Sonnentag, Sabine, Kathrin Eck, Charlotte Fritz, and Jana Kühnel. "Morning reattachment to work and work engagement during the day: A look at day-level mediators." *Journal of management* 46, no. 8 (2020): 1408–1435.

Steckl, Carrie. "Reframing: Finding solutions through a new lens." Wellness and Personal Development Resources (blog), MentalHelp.net, www.mentalhelp.net/ blogs/reframing-finding-solutions-through-a-new-lens/.

Stein, Dan J., Timothy K. Newman, Jonathan Savitz, and Rajkumar Ramesar. "Warriors versus worriers: The role of COMT gene variants." *CNS spectrums* 11, no. 10 (2006): 745–748, doi:10.1017/S1092852900014863.

Stilwell, Blake. "Here's what NASA says is the perfect length for a power nap." *Business Insider*, Aug 26, 2021, www.businessinsider.com/nasa-research-found-the-perfect-length-for-a-power-nap-2019-3.

Sukel, Kayt. "In sync: How humans are hard-wired for social relationships." Dana Foundation, November 13, 2019, https://dana.org/article/in-sync-how-humans-a re-hard-wired-for-social-relationships/.

The University of Arizona Health Sciences. "How the COVID-19 pandemic for-ever changed health sciences." August 30, 2021, https://healthsciences.arizona. edu/connect/features/how-covid-19-pandemic-forever-changed-health-sciences.

Thornton, Mark A., Miriam E. Weaverdyck, and Diana I. Tamir. "The social brain automatically predicts others' future mental states." *Journal of Neu-roscience* 39, no. 1 (2019): 140–148, https://doi.org/10.1523/JNEUROSCI. 1431-18.2018.

Tomova, Livia, Kimberly L. Wang, Todd Thompson, Gillian A. Matthews, Atsushi Takahashi, Kay M. Tye, and Rebecca Saxe. "Acute social isolation evokes midbrain craving responses similar to hunger." *Nature Neuroscience* 23, no. 12 (2020): 1597–1605, https://doi.org/10.1038/s41593-020-00742-z.

Cloud, Henry, and John Townsend. *Boundaries in Marriage*. Grand Rapids, MI: Zondervan, 2009.

Ulrich, Roger S., Robert F. Simons, Barbara D. Losito, Evelyn Fiorito, Mark A. Miles, and Michael Zelson. "Stress recovery during exposure to natural and urban environments." *Journal of environmental psychology* 11, no. 3 (1991): 201–230.

Valcour, Monique. "Beating Burnout." *Harvard Business Review*, November 2016, https://hbr.org/2016/11/beating-burnout.

Van der Kolk, Bessel A. *The Body Keeps the Score: Brain, Mind, and Body in the Healing of Trauma*. London: Penguin Publishing Group, 2015.

Villwock, Jennifer A., Lindsay B. Sobin, Lindsey A. Koester, and Tucker M. Harris. "Impostor syndrome and burnout among American medical students: A pilot study." *International Journal of Medical Education* 7 (2016): 364–369, doi:10.5116/ijme.5801.eac4.

Volini, Erica, Jeff Schwartz, Indranil Roy, Maren Hauptmann, and Yves Van Durme. "Introduction: Leading the social enterprise—Reinvent with a human focus." *Deloitte Insights*, April 11, 2019, www2.deloitte.com/us/en/insights/focus/human-capital-trends/2019/leading-social-enterprise.html.

Walker, Matthew. *Why We Sleep: Unlocking the Power of Sleep and Dreams.* New York: Simon and Schuster, 2017.

Wallace, B. Alan, and Shauna L. Shapiro. "Mental balance and well-being: Building bridges between Buddhism and Western psychology." *American Psychologist* 61, no. 7 (2006): 690, doi:10.1037/0003-066X.61.7.690.

Wallis, Claudia. "The Multitasking Generation." *Time Magazine*, March 19, 2006, http://content.time.com/time/magazine/article/0,9171,1174696,00.html.

Wang, Yilu, Jianqiao Ge, Hanqi Zhang, Haixia Wang, and Xiaofei Xie. "Altruistic behaviors relieve physical pain." *Proceedings of the National Academy of Sciences* 117, no. 2 (2020): 950–958, https://doi.org/10.1073/pnas.1911861117.

Wegner, Daniel M. "Don't fear the cybermind." *New York Times*, August 4, 2012, www.nytimes.com/2012/08/05/opinion/sunday/memory-and-the-cybermind.html.

Wen, Jin, Yongzhong Cheng, Xiuying Hu, Ping Yuan, Tianyou Hao, and Yingkang Shi. "Workload, burnout, and medical mistakes among physicians in China: A cross-sectional study." *Bioscience trends* 10, no. 1 (2016): 27–33, doi:10.5582/bst.2015.01175.

West, Tessa V., Katherine Thorson, Heidi Grant, and David Rock. "Asked for vs. unasked for feedback: An experimental study." Neuroleadership Institute, https://membership.neuroleadership.com/material/asked-for-vs-unasked-for-feedback-an-experimental-study/.

What Is Your Quality Of Life @ Work? HBR.org and The Energy Project, November 2013–June 2014, https://uli.org/wp-content/uploads/ULI-Documents/The-Human-Era-at-Work.pdf.

Wiederhold, Brenda K. "Connecting through technology during the coronavirus disease 2019 pandemic: Avoiding 'Zoom fatigue.'" *Cyberpsychology, Behavior, and Social Networking* 23, no. 7 (2020): 437–438, https://doi.org/10.1089/cyber.2020.29188.bkw.

Wigert, Ben, and Sangeeta Agrawal. "Employee burnout, part 1: The 5 main causes." Gallup, July 12, 2018, www.gallup.com/workplace/237059/employee-burnout-part-main-causes.aspx.

Woolley, Anita Williams, Christopher F. Chabris, Alex Pentland, Nada Hashmi, and Thomas W. Malone. "Evidence for a collective intelligence factor in the performance of human groups." *Science* 330, no. 6004 (2010): 686–688.

World Health Organization. "Burn-out an 'occupational phenomenon': International Classification of Diseases." May 28, 2019, www.who.int/news/item/28-05-2019-burn-out-an-occupational-phenomenon-international-classification-of-diseases.

Yeager, David S., Paul Hanselman, Gregory M. Walton, Jared S. Murray, Robert Crosnoe, Chandra Muller, Elizabeth Tipton, Barbara Schneider, Chris S. Hulleman, Cintia P. Hinojosa, David Paunesku, Carissa Romero, Kate Flint, Alice Roberts, Jill Trott, Ronaldo Iachan, Jenny Buontempo, Sophia Man Yang, Carlos M. Carvalho, P. Richard Hahn, Maithreyi Gopalan, Pratik Mhatre,

Ronald Ferguson, Angela L. Duckworth, and Carol S. Dweck. "A national experiment reveals where a growth mindset improves achievement." *Nature* 573, no. 7774 (2019): 364–369, https://doi.org/10.1038/s41586-019-1466-y.

Yuko, Elizabeth. "This is what it looks like to set personal and emotional boundaries." *Real Simple*, July 21, 2021, www.realsimple.com/health/mind-mood/emotional-health/how-to-set-boundaries.

Zaki, Jamil. *The War for Kindness: Building Empathy in a Fractured World*. New York: Crown, 2019.

Index

Page numbers in italics refer to figures. Page numbers followed by 'n' refer to notes.

7 Cups 171

Abecassis, Michael M.I. 143
access 9, 13; human costs of 16–17; instant 14–16; remote 13–17; to wellness resources 16
actions 91, 92, 95, 139, 151, 153–154, 157, 167
active listening 136, 137, 146
activity, alternating with rest 114–117, 153
adrenaline 28, 60, 89, 90, 92, 97, 112, 160
affective perspective-taking 133–134
alerting 27–29, 42
altruism 7
AltumView Systems 15
Amabile, Teresa 116–117, 167
amygdala 67, 102
Anderson, Janna 9
Apple watch 15
Ardern, Jacinda 143
attention 25, 59, 160, 161; alerting 27–29, 42; and brain 26–27, 31–32; definition of 26; ignoring 35–37, 38, 43; joint 69–70; orienting 29–31, 42; prioritizing 32–35, 37, 42, 117–119; in remote environments 41–44; selective 31–41; sustaining 38–41, 43; switching 37–38, 41, 43
attention-deficit/hyperactivity disorder (ADHD) 32, 39
audio cues 53
autonomy 139, 155

Babyscripts 15
Because I Can syndrome 159

behavior(s) 73–74; imitation of 4, 5; nonverbal 49–50; overcompensating 57; people-seeking 131; and social influence 8
belonging 65–66, 131, 132, 145, 165; and brain 66–67; group acceptance 7; preserving 8; psychological safety 72–75; rejection 6–7; social bonds 67–68; social disconnection 75–76; social influence 7–8; synchrony 68–70; trust 70–72
benefits: of alternating engagement with rest 112–113; of digital life 9–12, 13–16, 17–19; of empathy 134; health benefits of nature 115; of kindness 124–125; of meaningful work 139; of working with hands 126–127
Benjamin, Ivor 15
Benson, Herbert 96
Berleant, Daniel 132
Bezos, Jeff 121
bibliophiles 18
biomedical informatics 16
Black, Ed 15
Blank, Steve 39–40, 52, 54, 61
blue light, and sleep 99, 100
body 151; -based strategies, for stress control 95–100; effects of stress on 93, 95; and pain 7; see also energy; stress
book clubs 19
boundaries 17, 118, 154–155, 164–165
Bradford, Natalie 142
brain 2, 25, 46, 54; and alertness 27, 28; and altruism 7; and attention 26–27,

31–32; and belonging 66, 131; and choices 152; and cognitive load 56–57, 58–59, 77; and distress system 3; energy supply of 59, 110; and eye contact 50–51; and fatigue 60–61; filters 34; focused 110, 111–112, 113, 114–117, 119, 127; and ignoring 35, 36, 43; and imitation 4–5; and multitasking 38; and orienting 29, 30, 31, 42; and prediction errors 55–56; and predictions 5, 47, 48, 49; and prioritizing 32–34, 118; and reading 104–105; and rejection 6–7; response to social influence 7–8; rest for 111–112, 114–117; and safety/comfort 2–3, 4, 6, 25, 41; social 5–6, 67, 76, 132; and social bonds 67–68; and social connection 131; and social disconnection 75–76; and social thinking 3–4, 66–67; and sound 54; and spatial signals 53; and storytelling 136; and stress response 93, 94; and sustaining 39; and switching 37; synchrony 68–70, 158, 165–166; and understanding 4–6, 47, 48, 77; unfocused 111, 112, 114–115, 127; and verbal/nonverbal signals 47; *see also* engagement
brain cells 4–5, 47, 99, 104
breathing 90, 93, 96–97
Brooks, Alison Wood 103
Brown, Brené 106, 135, 136, 145
Buettner, Dan 105
burnout 76–78, 81–82, 155, 159; detachment 78–80; exhaustion 78; inefficacy 80; prevention of 122–127

Calm (app) 16
carbohydrates 48
Carson, Rachel 132
Cascio, Christopher 7–8
Chabris, Christopher 35
challenges: and growth mindset 156, 157; to prediction 54–55; to prioritizing 34–35; to remote work 71–72; and stress response 89, 90, 91, 95
choices 139, 151, 152–154, 155, 157, 165, 167
Christian, Brian 119
chronic stress 79, 90–91, 92, 95, 160, 161
Clear, James 120

clients 89–90, 138
coaching 10, 12, 16, 139, 157, 158, 159, 165
coaching conversations 146
Coan, James 66
cognitive empathy 133, 134
cognitive engagement 111
cognitive health 88, 95, 101, 104, 105, 113, 118, 120
cognitive load 56–58, 71, 72, 117–122, 153, 154, 161–163
cognitive overload 56, 58–59, 77, 78, 113, 117
cognitive perspective-taking 133
Cole, Terri 154
communicating to connect 135–137, 141–142, 147
communication 135–137, 141–142, 144, 146; *see also* nonverbal signals; verbal signals competence 138–139, 155
COMT gene 93
contextual cues 52
convenience 9; entertainment 17–18, 19; human costs of 19–20; and preference 18–19
cortisol 89, 97
Coursera 12
Covey, Steven 118
COVID-19 pandemic 14, 16, 61; New Zealand's response to 143–145; strengthening virtual connections during 140–143
Csikszentmihalyi, Mihaly 111

Dankasa, Jacob 9
Darwin, Charles 116
dating sites and apps 19
decision-making 33, 34, 118, 152–153
default mode network (DMN) 66
detachment 77, 78–80, 124–125
diaphragmatic breathing 96, 97
dichotic listening task 36
digital technology 1–2, 9, 87, 127, 131, 151; access 13–17; convenience 17–20; and efficiency 9–13; and sustaining attention 41
Dikker, Suzanne 69
directness of eye contact 50–51
disengagement 74, 75, 76, 81, 124–125
distance of eye contact 50–51
distance zones in human interactions 52

188 Index

distorted signals 46–47, 49, 56, 157;
and exhaustion 78; eye contact
50–51; sound and silence 53–54;
spatial signals 51–53
distractions 39–41, 43, 162
distress system 3
dopamine 32, 67, 68, 76, 77, 132
drain phase 90–91, 92, 95, 161
drive phase 90, 91–92, 93, 97, 161
Ducheneaut, Nicolas 19
Dweck, Carol 155

Eagleman, David 120
Edmondson, Amy 72, 135–136
edX 12
efficiency 9–10, 132; human costs of 13;
remote learning 11–12; remote work
9, 10–11
Eisenberger, Naomi 7
Eisenhower, Dwight D. 118
electronic devices, and sleep 99
electronic medical records 15,
17, 123
email 125, 155, 164–165
Emmons, Robert 106
emotional distance 76, 77, 79
emotional empathy 133, 134
emotional engagement 111
emotional fatigue 78
emotional health 87–88, 95, 101, 103,
105, 113
emotions 73; and amygdala 67; naming
101–102; reframing 103
empathy 68, 133–134, 135, 145, 146
employees: engagement of 111,
115–116, 141–142; experience 138;
fair treatment of 125; remote,
well-being of 11; rest for 114;
workloads of 122
end-of-workday rituals 123–124,
163–164
endorphins 67, 68, 76, 77, 127
energy 48, 110–111, 122, 158, 161, 162;
and engagement 111, 113, 127; and
focused brain 112; and habits 120;
learning new skills 126; requirements,
for understanding 47–48, 56; and
stress 89, 90, 91–92, 95; supply, of
brain 59; and unfocused brain 112;
working with hands 126–127; see also
burnout
energy management 110, 112, 113, 153

engagement 110; alternating activity
with rest 114–117, 153; alternating
focused and unfocused brain time
112; decreasing cognitive load
117–122; employee, and
communication 141–142; flow state
111; and focused brain 111; and
human connection 112–113;
prevention of burnout 122–127; in
remote environment 113–114; rest
for brain 111–112
entertainment 17–18, 19
epinephrine 28
equal conversational turn-taking 73–74
Ericsson, Anders 114
evolution 36, 41, 49, 118; and belonging 65; and human connection 2, 3;
and social thinking 4
exercise 97, 161
exhaustion 26, 43, 58, 61, 77, 78,
122–124; see also fatigue
external correction strategy 55
extrinsic cognitive load 56–57
extroverts 25, 26, 29, 74
eye contact 50–51, 67, 79

facial expressions 5, 40, 51
fairness 125
false conclusions, and cognitive load 58
family see friends and family
fast decision-making 152, 153
fatigue 55, 57, 58, 59–61, 77, 78, 92,
113, 114, 162
fear 102
feedback 136–137
feelings 5, 49, 75, 124–127, 132, 133,
134, 135, 140
fiction reading 104–105
fight-or-flight system 28, 76, 93, 94,
96–97, 160–161; and eye contact 51;
and feedback 136; and focused brain
113; and oxytocin 67–68
filters, brain 34
fixed mindset 155, 156
flow state 111
flow theory 111
focused brain 110, 111–112, 113,
114–117, 119, 127
focusing 96–97, 100–101
food choices, and stress response 97–98
friends and family 17, 18, 19, 20, 99, 153
fuel 38, 48, 89, 110, 122; see also energy

Index

gaming communities 17–18
genes, and stress response 93
Gitlab 11
Gladwell, Malcolm 114
glucose 48
Goleman, Daniel 59
Goodreads 19
Google 73–75
gratitude 106, 125, 164
Greene, Robert 126
Griffiths, Tom 119
group(s) 6, 65–66, 67, 132; acceptance 7; members, synchrony among 68–69; psychological safety in 72–75; social bonds 67–68; social disconnection 75–76; and social influence 8; transactive memory 121–122; trust in 70–72
growth mindset 155, 156–157

Habib, Navaz 97
habits 119–121
habit stacking 120
Hakim, Iman 143
Hall, Edward T. 52, 63n11
hands, working with 126–127
haptics 49, 53
Harvard University 12
Hasson, Uri 69
Headspace (app) 16
health 152; and belonging 65; benefits, of nature 115; and boundaries 155; and engagement 110, 112–113; facets of 87–88; impact of stress on 95; mental health support 171–172; remote monitoring of 15; and wellness 87–89; *see also* stress
high context cultures 63n11
Hobsbawm, Julia 155
Howard, Jane 65
human-centered approach 132–135, 140–141, 144, 146, 154, 157, 166
human connections 1–2, 13, 81, 131–132, 151, 165; choices to strengthen 152–154; and communication 136, 137, 142; conditions, and wellness/engaged brain 112–113; essentialness of 2–3; prioritizing 141; and safety and comfort 2–3, 4; social thinking 3–4; *see also* social connections

human costs 1, 9, 10; of access 16–17; of convenience 19–20; of efficiency 13
hybrid work 10
hypervigilance 25, 26, 42, 68

ignoring 35–37, 38, 43
ikigai 105
imitation 4–5
impostor syndrome 80
inattentional blindness 35
inefficacy 77, 80, 126–127
in-person interactions 35, 40, 49, 51, 53, 54, 71, 75
internal correction strategy 55
interpersonal sensitivity 74
interpersonal space 49, 51–52
intrinsic cognitive load 56, 57
introverts 25–26, 29
invisible gorilla experiment 35–36

James, William 26
joint attention 69–70
journaling 103–104, 106

Kabat-Zinn, John 100, 101
Kahneman, Daniel 121, 152
Khan, Sal 11
Khan Academy 11–12
kindness 124–125, 146
kinesics 49
Kramer, Steven 116–117

Lakhani, Karim R. 142
leaders 73, 125, 134, 136, 142, 144, 145, 146, 157, 158–168
leadership development programs 135, 139
learning: and cognitive health 88, 104; and engagement 111; groups 140; from imitation 4–5; new skills 126; and psychological safety 73; students 111, 121; *see also* remote learning
Le Cunff, Anne-Laure 104
Leineweber, Constanze 125
Leiter, Michael P. 79
Lencioni, Patrick 70–71
Levitin, Daniel J. 38
Lieberman, Matthew 3–4, 7, 8, 66
lifestyle 87, 88, 97
light: and orienting 31; and stress control 99–100, 162
listening 136, 137, 146

190 Index

Loehr, Jim 113, 114, 122, 127
loneliness 28–29, 66, 72, 76, 165
low context cultures 63n11

McChrystal, Stanley 138
magnetic resonance imaging (MRI) 5
Marcora, Samuele 60
Maslach, Christina 79, 122
massive open online courses (MOOCs) 12
Maxwell, John 152
meaning, sense of 116, 137–138, 140–141, 143, 145, 146, 167
medical access, remote 13–17
medical data, access to 15–16
meditation mobile apps 16
Meditopia (app) 16
Mehrabian, Albert 49
melatonin 99
memo writing 121
Mental Health America (MHA) 172
mere urgency effect 118
millennials 141–142
mind 115, 151; -based strategies, for stress control 100–106; effects of stress on 94, 95; theory of mind 5–6
mindfulness 100–101
mindset 155–157
missing signals 46, 47, 49, 56, 78, 79, 157; eye contact 50–51; sound and silence 53–54; spatial signals 51–53
MIT 12
multitasking 37–38, 161
Murph, Darren 11
Murthy, Vivek H. 131
music 162

Nadler, Robby 52
naming emotions 101–102
napping 98–99
NASA 13
National Alliance on Mental Illness (NAMI) 172
National Resource Directory (NRD) 172
natural selection 2–3, 131
nature: health benefits of 115; and stress response 92, 93
negativity bias 156
neural see-saw 3–4
Newport, Cal 123–124
New Zealand 143–145
non-social thinking 4

nonverbal signals 46, 47, 49–50, 58, 142; eye contact 50–51, 67, 79; sound and silence 53–54; spatial signals 51–53
norepinephrine 27, 28, 67
nurture 92, 93
nutrition 97–98, 161

occupational health 88, 89, 95, 113
Office for the Advancement of Telemedicine 13
olfactory cues 53
orienting 29–31, 42
overcompensation, and cognitive load 57
oxytocin 67–69, 71, 72, 76, 77, 132

pain 7, 68, 77; rejection and 6–7; social 7; and social disconnection 75–76; and synchrony 69
pandemic 14, 16, 61, 140–145
Pang, Alex Soojung-Kim 115, 116
paradox 1–2, 1, 4, 6, 8, 9, 81, 132, 151
paralanguage 49, 53
parasympathetic nervous system 28, 89, 90, 96, 97
people, prioritizing 132–135, 140–141, 144, 146
perspective-taking 133–134
Peterson, Steven 26–27
phones 16, 99, 142, 154
physical health 87, 95, 97, 98, 105, 113
pictograms 144
Plato 102
Posner, Michael 26–27
prediction 56, 157; and brain 5, 47–48; challenges, in remote environment 54–55; errors 49, 50, 51, 52, 53, 54, 55–56, 57, 81, 157–158; and eye contact 50–51; generation 56, 77, 81; and sound 53; and spatial signals 52–53; and verbal/nonverbal signals 46, 47
predictive processing theory 48
predictive trust 71
prefrontal cortex (PFC) 26, 28
prioritizing 32–35, 37, 42, 117–119
productivity 9, 10, 95, 99, 113, 115, 116, 138
progress, and engagement 116–117, 167
Project Aristotle 73–75
proxemics 49, 52

Index 191

psychological safety 72–75, 133, 135, 137, 141, 158, 166
Psychology Today 171
psychotherapy, remote 16
pupils 50
purpose, sense of 137–140, 143, 145, 146, 167

Rainie, Lee 9
reading 18, 104–105
reappraisal 102–103
reattachment 116
reflecting on focused brain activity 116–117
reframing 102–103
rejection 6–7
relatedness 139
relationships 66, 67, 68, 71, 79, 139
relaxation response 96–97
remote learning 9, 156; and cognitive load 58; and communication 142; global classrooms 11–12; human costs of 13; and sense of community 140
remote monitoring 14, 15, 16
remote psychotherapy 16
remote socializing 146, 151
remote work 9, 10, 18, 25; and belonging 165; and boundaries 155, 164–165; and burnout 77–78; and cognitive load 57–58; and communication 141–142; and distractions 39–40, 162; human costs of 13; lack of informal interactions in 71–72; and loneliness 28; new approaches to 10–11; and orienting 30, 42; psychological safety 166; social bonds 166; and social connections 141; and stress 29; Zoom fatigue 61
resilience 89
resources 16, 121–122
rest 66–67, 110, 111–112, 114–117, 162
rewards 59–60, 120
Riess, Helen 133
rituals 123–124, 163–164
routines 116, 121

safety and comfort 4, 6, 41, 81, 87, 145, 160; and alertness 28, 29, 42; and attention 25; and communication 141; and human connection 2–3;

and loneliness 28–29; and stress 76; *see also* psychological safety
Sansom-Daly, Ursula M. 142
Saxon, Leslie A. 15
scheduling of focused brain activity 116
Schoolhouse.world 12
Schwartz, Tony 113, 114, 122, 127
science 54–55, 132
science-based strategies: for optimizing engagement 114–127; for wellness and stress control 95–106
selective attention 31–32; ignoring 35–37, 38, 43; prioritizing 32–35, 37, 42; sustaining 38–41, 43; switching 37–38, 41, 43
selective inattention 36
self-care 160
self-coaching 146
self-concept, and social influence 8
self-control 7
self-monitoring 57
self-view 40, 43
serotonin 99, 127
Shamay-Tsoory, Simone 69
Shinrin-yoku 115
shutdown ritual 123
Siegel, Daniel J. 101
silence 53–54, 56
Simons, Daniel 35, 36
skills 6, 80, 126
sleep 98–99, 161, 162
slow decision-making 152–153
smell, sense of 53
social baseline theory 66
social bonds 53, 67–68, 71, 166
social brain 5–6, 67, 76, 132
social connections 1, 2, 25–26, 29, 81, 131, 132, 151; communication 135–137, 141–142, 144, 146; New Zealand's response to COVID-19 pandemic 143–145; prioritizing people 132–135, 140–141, 144, 146; and remote experience 145–146; sense of purpose/meaning 137–140, 143, 145, 146, 167; strengthening virtual connections during COVID-19 pandemic 140–143; *see also* human connections
social engagement 111
social health 88, 113
social influence, response of brain to 7–8

192 Index

social interactions 19, 26, 52, 68, 79, 104, 131
socializing 3, 146, 151
social pain 7
social sensitivity 73, 74–75, 134
social thinking 3–4, 66
solicited feedback 136–137
sound 53–54; delay 54; and orienting 30–31
spatial cues 30, 39, 43, 51–53
spiritual health 88, 95, 104–105, 113
Stanford University 12
Steckl, Carrie 103
sticky notes 163
storytelling 69, 136, 137
stress 28, 43, 76, 81, 87, 89–90, 152, 160–161; chronic 79, 90–91, 92, 95, 160, 161; and distress system 3, 41–42; and loneliness 28–29; negative impacts in remote experience 95; stimulation of action/change 91–92, 95; strategies to control 95–106; subtypes of 92–94; *see also* burnout
stress hormones 28, 43, 67, 89, 91, 92, 97, 105
stress response 76, 89–91, 92, 93–94, 113, 157, 160; and alertness 28, 42; and cognitive overload 117; and focused brain 112; and food choices 97–98; and rest 115; *see also* fight-or-flight system
students 133, 141; engagement 69, 111; growth mindset 156; learning using resources 121; sense of purpose/meaning 143; student-teacher communication 142
Substance Abuse and Mental Health Services Administration (SAMHSA) 172
sunlight 99, 100, 162
survival 28, 36, 118, 131; and belonging 65, 66; and decision-making 152; and human connection 2, 4, 43; and prioritizing 118; relaxation response 96; and safety/comfort 3
sustaining 38–41, 43
switch cost 37–38
switching 37–38, 41, 43
sympathetic nervous system 28, 89, 90, 96
synchrony 68–70, 158, 165–166

Talkspace 16
tasks: and cognitive load 56–57; flow state 111; manual 127; multitasking 37–38, 161; prioritizing 117–119; sustaining attention on 38, 43; and working memory 33
team(s): cohesion 166; dynamics 8; empathy in 134; meetings 166–167; members, trust among 70–71, 72; prioritizing people 141; psychological safety in 72–75; sense of belonging 165; sense of purpose and meaning 138
tele-ICUs 14
telemedicine 13–14, 16, 142
Teleparty 19
Templeton, Brad 151
theory of mind 5–6
thrashing 119
time boundaries 155
time management 118
touch 53
transactive memory 121–122
transitional periods, and orienting 30
trust 70–72, 135, 145, 146; among team members 70–71, 72; and nonverbal signals 49, 50; and oxytocin 67, 68, 71, 72; predictive 71; and psychological safety 72; and purpose 138; vulnerability-based 71

understanding 47–48, 77, 134, 145; energy requirements for 47–48; enhancing 6; imitation 4–5; prediction 5, 47, 48–49; social brain 5–6; and verbal/nonverbal signals 49; *see also* prediction
unfocused brain 111, 112, 114–115, 127
updates, technology 57–58

vagus nerve 96, 97
Van der Kolk, Bessel A. 4
verbal signals 46, 47, 49, 55
Veteran Mental Health 172
Viceira, Luis M. 142
video: information, judgments based on 54; platforms, switching in 43; Teleparty 19
videoconference 14; and cognitive load 57; and distractions 39–40; and errors in judgment 54; and eye contact 51; lack of informal

interactions in 71–72; spatial signals in 52; *see also* telemedicine
video games 17–18, 19
virtual connections during COVID-19 pandemic 140–143
vulnerability-based trust 71

Walker, Matthew 98
Warmlines 171
warning signals 157, 158, 160, 162, 165, 167
warrior 93, 94
Wegner, David 121
wellness 2, 11, 13, 87, 152; and boundaries 155; and engagement 110; and health 87–89; and human connection 112–113; prevention of negative impacts of stress in remote experience 95; resources, access to 16; and stress 89–94; stress control strategies 95–106
wellness apps 16
Wiederhold, Brenda 61–62

Woolley, Anita Williams 73
work: boundaries 164; burnout 77–80; detachment from 124; end-of-work-day rituals 123–124, 163–164; and engagement 111, 113; fair treatment at 125; groups, psychological safety in 72–75; hybrid model 10; learning new skills 126; meaningful 116, 138–139, 146, 167; productivity 9, 10, 95, 99, 113, 115, 116, 138; reattachment 116; rewards at 60; working with hands 126–127; *see also* remote work
working memory 32–34, 35, 36, 37, 42, 56, 121
work-life balance 17
workloads 122–123
worrier 93, 94

yoga 97

Zaki, Jamil 134
Zoom fatigue 58, 61, 162

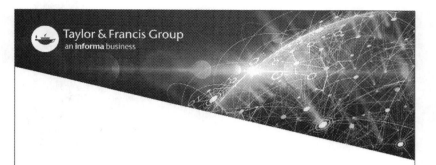

Printed in the United States
by Baker & Taylor Publisher Services